Varieties of Cultural History

Varieties of Cultural History

PETER BURKE

Cornell University Press
Ithaca, New York

Copyright © 1997 this collection by Peter Burke

All rights reserved. Except for brief quotations in a review, this book, or parts thereof, must not be reproduced in any form without permission in writing from the publisher. For information, address Cornell University Press, Sage House, 512 East State Street, Ithaca, New York 14850.

First published in 1997 by Cornell University Press in association with Polity Press (UK), the originating publisher.

A CIP catalogue record is available from the Library of Congress.

ISBN 0–8014–3491–2 (cloth)
ISBN 0–8014–8492–8 (paperback)

This book is printed on acid-free paper.

Printed in Great Britain.

Contents

Preface

꧁꧂

The aim of this collection of twelve essays is to discuss and illustrate some of the main varieties of cultural history which have emerged since the questioning of what might be called its 'classic' form, exemplified in the work of Jacob Burckhardt and Johan Huizinga. This classic model has not been replaced by any new orthodoxy, despite the importance of approaches inspired by social and cultural anthropology.

The collection opens with a chapter on the origins of cultural history which raises general questions about the identity of the subject. The chapters on dreams and memory are substantive but they are also comparative and they too attempt to engage with general problems in the practice of cultural history.

There follow five case-studies of early modern Italy, which was the main area of my research from the mid-1960s to the mid-1980s. All these studies are located on the frontiers of cultural history (in the sense of areas only recently explored) and also on cultural frontiers – between learned and popular culture, between the public and the private spheres, between the serious and the comic.

Then come two essays on the New World, especially Brazil (a new world I discovered only a decade ago). They focus on romances of chivalry and on carnival but their essential concern is with cultural 'translation' in the etymological, literal and metaphorical senses of that term. Particular emphasis is placed on the consequences of cultural encounters, whether they should be described in terms of mixing, syncretism or synthesis.

The volume ends with two theoretical pieces, an essay on mentalities which offers both a criticism of that concept and a
defence of the approach associated with it against recent critics,
and a general discussion of varieties of cultural history, compar-
ing and contrasting the classic style with the 'new' or 'anthropological' one and attempting to answer the question whether the
so-called 'new' cultural history is condemned to fragmentation.

The ideas presented here have developed out of a kind of dialogue between sixteenth- and seventeenth-century sources, earlier
historians (Jacob Burckhardt, Aby Warburg, Marc Bloch, Johan
Huizinga), and modern cultural theorists, from Sigmund Freud,
Norbert Elias and Mikhail Bakhtin to Michel Foucault, Michel
de Certeau, and Pierre Bourdieu. In the essays which follow, I
shall be trying to avoid the opposite dangers of new-fangled 'constructivism' (the idea of the cultural or discursive construction of
reality), and old-fashioned 'positivism' (in the sense of an empiri-
cism confident that 'the documents' will reveal 'the facts').

I dedicate this book to my beloved wife and fellow-historian,
Maria Lúcia Garcia Pallares-Burke.

Acknowledgements

In the course of elaborating these essays I have learned much from dialogues over the years with Jim Amelang, Anton Blok, Jan Bremmer, Maria Lúcia Pallares-Burke, Roger Chartier, Bob Darnton, Natalie Davis, Rudolf Dekker, Florike Egmond, Carlo Ginzburg, Eric Hobsbawm, Gábor Klaniczay, Reinhart Koselleck, Giovanni Levi, Eva Österberg, Krzysztof Pomian, Jacques Revel, Peter Rietbergen, Herman Roodenburg, Joan Pau Rubies i Mirabet, Bob Scribner, and Keith Thomas. In the study of dreams I was helped by Alan Macfarlane, Norman Mackenzie, Anthony Ryle, and Riccardo Steiner. Gwyn Prins and Vincent Viaene eased my way into African history. For the title of chapter 6 I am grateful to Aldo da Maddalena.

Chapter 1 is a revised version of 'Reflections on the Origins of Cultural History', in *Interpretation in Cultural History*, ed. Joan Pittock and Andrew Wear (1991), pp. 5–24, by permission of Macmillan Press.

Chapter 2 has been revised from the original English version of 'L'histoire sociale des rêves', *Annales: Économies, Sociétés, Civilisations* 28 (1973) pp. 329–42. It is published in English for the first time.

Chapter 3 is a revised version of 'History as Social Memory', in *Memory*, ed. Thomas Butler (1989); pp. 97–113 by permission of Blackwell Publishers.

Chapter 4 is a revised version of 'The Language of Gesture in Early Modern Italy', in *A Cultural History of Gesture*, ed. Jan

Bremmer and Herman Roodenburg (1991), pp. 71–83. Copyright © Peter Burke 1991, by permission of Polity Press and Cornell University Press.

Chapter 5 is a revised version of 'Frontiers of the Comic in Early Modern Italy', in *A Cultural History of Humour*, ed. Jan Bremmer and Herman Roodenburg (1997) pp. 61–75, by permission of Polity Press.

Chapter 9 is a revised version of 'Chivalry in the New World', in *Chivalry in the Renaissance*, ed. Sydney Anglo (1990), pp. 253–62, by permission of Boydell and Brewer Ltd.

Chapter 11 is a revised version of 'Strengths and Weaknesses of the History of Mentalities', *History of European Ideas* 7 (1986), 439–51, by permission of Elsevier Science Ltd.

I

Origins of Cultural History

❦

There is no agreement over what constitutes cultural history, any more than agreement over what constitutes culture. Over forty years ago, two American scholars set out to chart the variations in the use of the term in English, and collected more than two hundred rival definitions.[1] Taking other languages and the last four decades into account, it would be easy to collect many more. In the search for our subject it may therefore be appropriate to adapt the existentialists' definition of man and to say that cultural history has no essence. It can only be defined in terms of its own history.

How can anyone write a history of something which lacks a fixed identity? It is rather like trying to catch a cloud in a butterfly net. However, in their very different ways, Herbert Butterfield and Michel Foucault both demonstrated that all historians face this problem. Butterfield criticized what he called the 'Whig interpretation of history', in other words the use of the past to justify the present, while Foucault emphasized epistemological 'ruptures'. If we wish to avoid the anachronistic attribution of our own intentions, interests and values to the dead, we cannot write the continuous history of anything.[2] On one side we face the danger of 'present-mindedness', but on the other the risk of being unable to write at all.

---

[1] Kroeber and Kluckhohn (1952).
[2] Butterfield (1931); Foucault (1966).

Perhaps there is a middle way, an approach to the past which asks present-minded questions but refuses to give present-minded answers; which concerns itself with traditions but allows for their continual reinterpretation; and which notes the importance of unintended consequences in the history of historical writing as well as in the history of political events. To follow such a route is the aim of this chapter, which is concerned with the history of culture before the 'classic' period discussed in the concluding chapter, in other words before the term 'culture' came into general use.[3]

In this case the present-minded questions are the following: how old is cultural history, and how have conceptions of cultural history changed over time? The difficulty to be avoided is that of giving these questions equally present-minded answers. The problem is a slippery one. We are not the first people in the world to realize that culture, as we now call it, has a history. The term 'cultural history' goes back to the late eighteenth century, at least in German. Johan Christoph Adelung published an 'Essay in a history of the culture of the human race', *Versuch einer Geschichte der Kultur des menschlichen Geschlechts* (1782), while Johan Gottfried Eichhorn published a 'General history of culture', *Allgemeine Geschichte der Kultur* (1796–9), presented as an introduction to the 'special histories' (*Spezialgeschichte*) of the different arts and sciences.

The idea that literature and philosophy and the arts have histories is much older. This tradition deserves to be remembered. The difficulty is to do this without falling into the error of imagining that what we have defined (and indeed in some places, institutionalized), as a 'subject' or 'subdiscipline' existed in the past in this form.

In some respects the most historically minded manner of approaching the problem would be to tell the story backwards from today, showing how Huizinga's conception of cultural history differs from that of the 1990s, how Burckhardt's differed from Huizinga's, and so on. In liberating us from assumptions of continuity, however, this backward narrative would obscure the ways in which practical, partial and short-term aims and motives (such as civic pride and the search for precedent) contributed to the development over the long term of a more general study often

[3] Bruford (1962), ch. 4.

pursued for its own sake. The best thing to do is perhaps for the author to share the difficulties with the reader in the course of the narrative. In other words, like some contemporary novelists and critics, I shall try to tell a story and at the same time to reflect on it and even, perhaps, to undermine it.

Whenever one begins the story, it can be argued that it would have been better to have started earlier. This chapter begins with the humanists of Renaissance Italy, from Petrarch onwards, whose attempts to undo the work of what they were the first to call the 'Middle Ages' and to revive the literature and learning of classical antiquity implied a view of three ages of culture: ancient, medieval and modern. In fact, as the humanists well knew, some ancient Greeks and Romans had already claimed that language has a history, that philosophy has a history, that literary genres have a history, and that human life has been changed by a succession of inventions. Ideas of this kind can be found in Aristotle's *Poetics*, for example, in Varro's treatise on language, in Cicero's discussion of the rise and fall of oratory, and in the account of the early history of man given in the poem of Lucretius on the nature of things (so important for Vico, and others in the seventeenth and eighteenth centuries).[4]

History of Language and Literature

However, the humanists had a more dramatic story to tell about language and literature than their ancient models. A story of barbarian invasions and of the consequent decline and destruction of classical Latin, followed by an account of revival, the work (of course) of the humanists themselves. In other words, an age of light was followed by the 'Dark Ages', followed in turn by the dawn of another age of light. This is the story which emerges from some Italian texts of the early fifteenth century, Leonardo Bruni's lives of Dante and Petrarch, for example, the history of Latin literature written by Sicco Polenton, or the historical introduction to Lorenzo Valla's Latin grammar, the *Elegantiae*.[5] This interpretation of the history of literature formed part of the justification of the humanist movement.

[4] Edelstein (1967).
[5] Ferguson (1948), 20ff.; McLaughlin (1988).

In the fifteenth and sixteenth centuries, debates about the relative merits of Latin and Italian as a literary language and the best form of Italian to use generated research into the history of language by Leonardo Bruni, Flavio Biondo, and others. They discussed, for example, what language the ancient Romans had actually spoken, Latin or Italian.[6] In the early sixteenth century, the humanist cardinal Adriano Castellesi produced a history of Latin, *De sermone latino* (1516), divided into four periods – 'very old', 'old', 'perfect' (the age of Cicero), and 'imperfect' (ever since). Another humanist and critic, Pietro Bembo, who did as much as anyone to freeze Italian at a particular point in its development, allowed one of the characters in his famous dialogue on the vernacular, the *Prose della volgar lingua* (1525), to point out that language changes 'like fashions in clothes, modes of warfare, and all other manners and customs' (book 1, chapter 17).

Northern humanists, at once imitators and rivals of their Italian predecessors, amplified the story by drawing attention to literary and linguistic developments in their own countries. In France, for instance, two humanist lawyers, Étienne Pasquier in his *Recherches de la France* (1566) and Claude Fauchet in his *Origine de la langue et poésie françoises* (1581), chronicled and celebrated the achievements of French writers from the thirteenth century to the age of François I and the Pléiade.[7] In England, a discussion of English poetry from Chaucer onwards can be found in the treatise called *The Arte of English Poesie* published in 1589 and attributed to George Puttenham. A history of Spanish, *Del origen y principio de la lengua castellana*, was published by Bernardo Aldrete in 1606, in the same year as a similar study of Portuguese, *Origem da língua portuguesa*, by the lawyer Duarte Nunes de Leão. The Germans had to wait until the later seventeenth century for an equivalent history, just as they had to wait until the seventeenth century for an equivalent of the poets of the Pléiade, but the history, when it arrived, was more elaborate and comparative. The polymath Daniel Morhof placed the history of the German language and German poetry in a comparative European framework in his *Unterricht von der Teutschen Sprache und Poesie* (1682).[8]

Building on these foundations, a number of eighteenth-century

[6] Grayson (1959).
[7] Huppert (1970).
[8] Batts (1987).

scholars produced multivolume histories of national literatures, notably those of France (by a research team of Benedictine monks headed by Rivet de la Grange), and of Italy (compiled single-handed by Girolamo Tiraboschi). The breadth of Tiraboschi's notion of 'literature' is worth noting.[9] In Britain there were similar plans afoot. Alexander Pope put forward a 'scheme of the history of English poetry'; Thomas Gray amended it. Meanwhile, the history had been undertaken by Thomas Warton. Warton never went beyond the early seventeenth century, but his unfinished *History of English Poetry* (4 vols, 1774–8) remains impressive.[10]

Monographs were also written on the history of particular literary genres. The French Protestant scholar Isaac Casaubon published a study of Greek satire in 1605, and John Dryden, following his example, wrote a *Discourse concerning the Original and Progress of Satire* (1693) discussing its development from what he called the 'rough-cast, unhewn' extempore satire of ancient Rome to the polished productions of a period when the Romans 'began to be somewhat better bred, and were entering, as I may say, into the rudiments of civil conversation'. Again, the rise of the novel in the seventeenth and eighteenth centuries was accompanied by investigations of its oriental and medieval origins by the polymath bishop Pierre-Daniel Huet, in his *Lettre sur l'origine des romans* (1669), and following him by Thomas Warton, who inserted into his history of poetry a digression 'On the Origin of Romantic Fiction in Europe'.

History of Artists, Art and Music

It is hardly surprising to find men of letters devoting attention to the history of literature. Art was a less obvious object for a historian's attention, even in the Renaissance. Learned men did not always take artists seriously, while artists generally lacked the kind of preparation necessary for historical research. When, in fifteenth-century Florence, the sculptor Lorenzo Ghiberti produced a literary sketch of the history of art in his autobiographical *Commentaries*, he was doing something rather unusual.[11]

[9] Escarpit (1958); Goulemot (1986); Sapegno (1993).
[10] Wellek (1941); Lipking (1970), 352f.; Pittock (1973), ch. 5.
[11] Grinten (1952); Tanturli (1976).

We ought not to take Vasari for granted either. He was remarkable in his own day because he had a double education, not only a training in an artist's workshop but a humanist education sponsored by Cardinal Passerini.[12] His *Lives of the Painters, Sculptors and Architects*, first published in 1550, was written, so the author tells us, in order that young artists might learn from the example of their great predecessors, and also (one may reasonably suspect) for the greater glory of his adopted city Florence, and his patrons the Medici (it was in fact published by the Grand Duke's press).[13]

However, Vasari's book is much more than a work of propaganda. It is also, of course, a good deal more than a biographical collection. The prefaces to the three parts into which the work is divided include an account of the rise of art in antiquity, its decline in the Middle Ages, and its revival in Italy in three stages, culminating in Vasari's master Michelangelo. It has been shown by Ernst Gombrich that Vasari's developmental scheme was adapted from Cicero's account of the history of rhetoric. Without Vasari's double education, such an adaptation would have been virtually inconceivable, even if we allow for the fact that Vasari was helped by a circle of scholars including Gianbattista Adriani, Cosimo Bartoli, Vincenzo Borghini, and Paolo Giovio.[14] Vasari's concern with art rather than artists was given still more emphasis in the second edition (1568).

Vasari's book was treated as a challenge. Artists and scholars from other parts of Italy compiled lives of local artists in order to show that Rome, Venice, Genoa, and Bologna were worthy rivals to Florence. However, they paid much less attention than Vasari had done to general trends in art. The same goes for responses to Vasari outside Italy, in the Netherlands, by Karel van Mander in *Het Schilderboek* (1604), and in Germany, by Joachim von Sandrart in his *Deutsche Akademie* (1675–9), who argued that the age of Albrecht Dürer marked the shift of cultural leadership from southern Europe to the north. It was only in the mid-eighteenth century that Horace Walpole's *Anecdotes of Painting*, intended as a Vasari for England (Walpole joked about his 'Vasarihood'), found room not only for biographies but also for chapters on the 'state of painting' at different periods, the equiva-

---

[12] Rubin (1995).
[13] Cf. Chastel (1961), 21ff.
[14] Gombrich (1960a).

lent of the chapters on economic, social and literary history to be found in the contemporary *History of England* by David Hume.[15]

The rise of what it is retrospectively convenient to call the history of art as opposed to the biographies of artists took place earlier in studies of classical antiquity, for a sufficiently obvious reason. Despite the famous anecdotes of Greek artists told by Pliny (and adapted by Vasari), little was known about Apelles, Phidias and the rest, making it difficult to organize a study of ancient art as a series of biographies. The Florentine scholar Gianbattista Adriani, who composed a brief history of ancient art in the form of a letter to Vasari (1567), to help him in his second edition of the *Lives*, chose to arrange it around the idea of artistic progress. Other studies of ancient art were made by the Dutch humanist Franciscus Junius in his *De pictura veterum* (1637), and by André Félibien (historian of buildings to Louis XIV, apparently the first post in art history ever to be created), in his *Origine de la peinture* (1660).[16]

Félibien's essay on the origin of painting and Huet's on the origin of romances were written in France in the same decade, the 1660s, as if expressing a more general change in historiographical taste. In the tradition of Félibien was the work of the court painter Monier, *Histoire des arts* (1698), originally lectures for students of the Royal Academy of Painting. Monier's cyclical interpretation began with the rise of art in antiquity and proceeded to its decline in the Dark Ages and its revival between 1000 and 1600. The relatively early dating of the revival allowed Monier to give an important role to the French, like Pasquier and Fauchet in the domain of literature.

The outstanding achievement in this area, Johan Joachim Winckelmann's great *History of Ancient Art* (1764), should be considered not as a radically new departure but as the culmination of a trend, a trend which was encouraged not only by the example of histories of literature but also by several new cultural practices, among them the rise of art collecting, the art market and connoisseurship.[17]

The history of music, on the other hand, was virtually an eighteenth-century invention. Some sixteenth- and seventeenth-century scholars, such as Vincenzo Galilei (father of the scientist)

[15] Lipking (1970), 127f.
[16] Lipking (1970), 23ff.; Grinten (1952).
[17] Grinten (1952); Alsop (1982).

and Girolamo Mei, had been well aware of changes in style over the long term and indeed discussed them in their comparisons of ancient and modern music published in 1581 and 1602 respectively, but their aim was simply to attack or defend particular styles. In the eighteenth century, on the other hand, there was an explosion of interest in music history. In France, one major study, *Histoire de la musique*, was published in 1715 by the Bonnet-Bourdelot family, and another was written, but not published, by P. J. Caffiaux, a learned Benedictine who was, appropriately, doing for music something like what his colleague Rivet was doing for literature. In Italy, Gianbattista Martini published an important study of the music of antiquity, *Storia della musica* (1757). In Switzerland another Benedictine, Martin Gerbert, made an important contribution to the history of church music in his *De cantu et musica sacra* (1774). In England, Charles Burney and John Hawkins were contemporaries and rivals, Hawkins with his *General History of the Science and Practice of Music* (1766) and Burney with *A General History of Music* (1776–89). In Germany, J. N. Forkel of the University of Göttingen summed up the work of the century in his *Allgemeine Geschichte der Musik* (1788–1801).[18]

The History of Doctrine

The histories of language, literature and the arts seem to have begun as side-effects of the Renaissance. The Reformation also had its historical by-products. As the humanists defined their place in history by dividing the past into ancient, medieval and modern, so did the reformers, who saw themselves as going back behind the Middle Ages and reviving Christian antiquity or the 'primitive church', as they called it. Histories of the Reformation begin with the Reformation itself. Among the most famous were the *Commentaries* of Johann Sleidan (1555) and the *Acts and Monuments* of John Foxe (1563). They tended to be histories of events or histories of institutions, but some of them – like their

---

[18] *Grove's* (1980), article 'Caffiaux'; Heger (1932); Lipking (1970), 229ff., 269ff.

model the *Ecclesiastical History* by the early Christian, Eusebius of Caesarea – found a place for the history of doctrines.[19]

The concern with changes in doctrine can be seen with still greater clarity in the seventeenth century. On the Protestant side, Heinrich Alting's *Theologia historica* (1664) argued for a 'historical theology' on the grounds that church history was not only the story of events but also of dogmas (*dogmatum narratio*), their corruption (*depravatio*) and their reform (*reparatio, restitutio, reformatio*). On the Catholic side, the idea of change in the doctrines of the church was more difficult to accept, despite the example of the Spanish Jesuit Rodriguez de Arriaga (d. 1667), who presented what has been called 'one of the most extreme theories of development ever put forward by a reputable Catholic thinker'. Arriaga, a professor in Prague, taught that the proclamation of doctrine by the church 'is the making explicit what was not explicit, and need not have been implicit, earlier'.[20]

It was easier to accept change in the history of heresy, as some seventeenth-century Catholic histories of the Reformation did: Florimond de Raemond, for example, in his *Histoire de la naissance, progrès et décadence de l'hérésie de ce siècle* (1623); Louis Maimbourg, in his *Histoire du Calvinisme* (1682); and, most famous of all, Jacques-Bénigne Bossuet in his *Histoire des variations des églises protestantes* (1688).[21]

These three works were not exactly examples of the study of the past for its own sake; they were highly polemical. The books of Maimbourg and Bossuet were written for a political purpose, to support Louis XIV's anti-Protestant policies at the time of the Revocation of the Edict of Nantes. However, their central idea that doctrines (at least false doctrines) have a history, an idea expounded most fully, brilliantly and destructively by Bossuet, was to have a considerable appeal outside the polemical context in which it was originally developed. It was deployed, for instance, by an apologist for unorthodoxy, Gottfried Arnold, in his *Unpartheyische Kirche- und Ketzer-Historie* (1699–1700). For Arnold, church history was little more than the history of

---

[19] Headley (1963); Dickens and Tonkin (1985). On Eusebius, Momigliano (1963).
[20] Chadwick (1957), 20, 45–7.
[21] Chadwick (1957), 6–10.

heresies, some of which hardened into official doctrine (as Luther's had done), only to be challenged by later generations.[22]

From the history of religious doctrine it seems no great step to its secular equivalents. Yet in this area (unlike art history or the history of literature and language), there seem to have been few significant developments before the year 1600. Perhaps the need to assess past achievements was a by-product of the scientific revolution of the seventeenth century, in which the 'new' mechanical philosophy, as it was often called, became a matter for debate. In any case, the seventeenth century saw a number of histories of philosophy, including Georg Horn's *Historia philosophiae* (1655) and Thomas Stanley's *History of Philosophy* (1655). In the eighteenth century the trend continued with A. F. Boureau-Deslande's *Histoire critique de la philosophie* (1735), and Jacob Brucker's *Historia critica philosophiae* (1767).[23] A certain Johannes Jonsonius even produced a history of the history of philosophy, published in 1716.

The classical exemplar for the history of philosophy was the *Lives of the Philosophers* written in the third century AD by Diogenes Laertius, a model which Eusebius adapted in the following century for his account of early Christian sects and which Vasari reshaped still more radically for his lives of artists.[24] This biographical model remained a tempting one. However, attempts were also made to tell a story as well as to collect biographies, to practise what Thomas Burnet (nearly three centuries before Foucault) called 'philosophical archaeology', and to write the intellectual history not only of the Greeks and Romans but also of the 'barbarians', as in the case of Otto Heurn's *Barbarica philosophia* (1600) and Christian Kortholt's *Philosophia barbarica* (1660). Scholars studied the ideas of the Chaldeans, the Egyptians, the Persians, the Carthaginians, the Scythians, the Indians, the Japanese and the Chinese (Jacob Friedrich Reimann's history of Chinese philosophy was published in 1727).

Some of these histories were written for their own sake, others with polemical intent, for example to encourage scepticism by emphasizing the contradictions between one philosopher and another. They modified the traditional biographical framework by discussing the development of philosophical schools or 'sects', as in the *De philosophorum sectis* (1657) of the Dutch scholar

---

[22] Seeberg (1923); Meinhold (1967).
[23] Rak (1971); Braun (1973); Del Torre (1976).
[24] Momigliano (1963).

Gerard Voss, or by distinguishing periods, as Horn did, contrasting the 'heroic', 'theological or mythical' and the 'philosophical' ages of Greek thought.

The phrase 'history of ideas' is generally believed to have been launched by the American philosopher Arthur Lovejoy when he founded the History of Ideas Club at Johns Hopkins University in the 1920s. It had actually been employed two hundred years earlier, by Jacob Brucker, who referred to the *historia de ideis*, and by Gianbattista Vico, who called in his *New Science* for 'una storia dell'umane idee'.

The History of Disciplines

Out of the history-of-philosophy tradition branched a number of studies of specific disciplines.[25]

On the arts side, the history of rhetoric and the history of history itself deserve to be mentioned. A French Jesuit, Louis de Cresolles, produced a remarkable history of the rhetoric of the ancient sophists, the *Theatrum veterum rhetorum* (1620), in which he discussed, among other topics, the training of the sophists, the competition between them, their income, and the honours they received.[26] The first history of historical writing was produced by the seigneur de La Popelinière in his *L'Histoire des histoires* (1599), arguing that historiography went through four stages – poetry, myth, annals and finally a 'perfect history' (*histoire accomplie*), which was philosophical as well as accurate.[27]

The history of the graduate discipline of law also attracted considerable interest. Fifteenth-century humanists such as Lorenzo Valla and Angelo Poliziano concerned themselves with the history of Roman law as part of the ancient Roman world which they were trying to revive, criticizing the professional lawyers of their own day for misinterpreting the texts. Valla and Poliziano were amateurs in this field but they were followed in the sixteenth century by scholars such as Andrea Alciato and Guillaume Budé who were trained in both law and the humanities. One of these humanist lawyers, François Baudouin, went so far as to suggest that 'historians would do better to study the

---

[25] Graham et al. (1983); Kelley and Popkin (1991).
[26] Fumaroli (1980), 299–326.
[27] Butterfield (1955), 205–6; Kelley (1970), 140–1; Huppert (1970), 137–8.

development of laws and institutions than devote themselves to the investigation of armies, the description of camps of war, the tale of battles and the counting of dead bodies', a critique of 'drum-and-trumpet history' of a kind which would become commonplace by the eighteenth century.[28]

In the case of medicine, some sixteenth-century physicians (notably Vesalius and Fernel), took sufficient interest in history to place their own work in the context of the intellectual revival or Renaissance through which they were living. The first substantial study of medical history, however, was published considerably later, at the end of the seventeenth century. This history of medicine by Daniel Leclerc (the brother of the critic Jean Leclerc) begins by surveying earlier studies and dismisses them for concentrating on biography. 'There is a big difference between writing the history or biographies of physicians', he remarks in his preface, '. . . and writing the history of medicine, studying the origin of that art, and looking at its progress from century to century and the changes in its systems and methods . . . which is what I have undertaken.' Leclerc's title page also emphasizes his concern with medical 'sects' along the lines of the interest in sects of the history of philosophy, which he seems to have taken as his model.

Unfortunately, Leclerc's account (like Martini's history of music) never got beyond classical antiquity. For the modern part of the story it was necessary to wait until 1725 and the second volume of Freind's *History of Physick*, which took the story from the Arabs to Linacre (deliberately stopping short of Paracelsus). As his title page boasted, Freind differed from Leclerc in concentrating on 'practice'. His second volume is as much a history of illness (notably the sweating sickness, venereal disease, and scurvy) as it is a history of medicine. It is almost a history of the body.

In the historiography of most other disciplines, the eighteenth century marks a turning point. For example, although a short account of the development of astronomy was given by Johan Kepler, this history was much amplified by Johann Friedrich Weidler (1740) and by Pierre Estève (1755).[29] Estève criticized his predecessors for being too narrow and tried to produce what

---

[28] Kelley (1970).
[29] Jardine (1984).

he called a 'general history' of astronomy, linked to other intellectual changes, as well as a 'particular' history focused on detail. In Voltairean style he declared that 'the history of the sciences is much more useful than that of the revolutions of empires.'

In the history of mathematics, studies of the lives of mathematicians on the model of Diogenes Laertius were followed in the eighteenth century by more ambitious enterprises. Pierre Rémond de Montmort intended to write a history of geometry on the model of the existing histories of painting, music and so on, but died in 1719 before he could carry out his plans. The *Histoire des mathématiques* (1758) by Jean Étienne Montucla, a member of Diderot's circle, criticized the biographical approach, just as Leclerc (discussed below) had already done for medicine. Montucla aimed instead at making a contribution to the history of the development of the human mind.

So did the author of *Geschichte der Chemie* (1797–9), a history of chemistry which made a considerable effort to place the development of the subject in its social, political and cultural context. This monograph was presented by its author, J. F. Gmelin, a Göttingen man, as a contribution to a series of histories of arts and sciences from the time of their 'Renaissance' (*Wiederherstellung*) onwards, a project on which a society of learned men was currently at work. The milieu of the new University of Göttingen seems to have been particularly favourable to cultural history. Forkel was writing his history of music there at much the same time as Gmelin was working on the history of chemistry.[30]

With the history of disciplines we may group the history of inventions, which goes back to the Italian humanist Polydore Vergil at the beginning of the sixteenth century and his *De inventoribus* (1500). Polydore's concept of 'invention' was a wide one by modern standards. For instance, according to him, the English parliament was invented by King Henry III.[31] Two inventions dear to scholars, writing and printing, had monographs devoted to them in the seventeenth and eighteenth centuries. Writing was studied by Herman Hugo (1617) and Bernard Malinckrott (1638), and their works were used by Vico for his now famous

---

[30] Butterfield (1955), 39–50; Iggers (1982).
[31] Hay (1952); Copenhaver (1978).

reflections on orality and literacy. Samuel Palmer's *General History of Printing* (1732) was the work of a scholar-printer.

The History of Modes of Thought

Another development from the history of disciplines was the history of modes of thought.[32] This development bears a striking and not altogether illusory resemblance to some of the 'new directions' preached and practised today. It is necessary to walk an intellectual tightrope at this point in order to give the eighteenth-century historians of mentalities the credit that is due to them without turning them into clones of the French historians associated with the journal *Annales*.

In the seventeenth century, John Selden had already recommended to the listeners to his Table-Talk the study of 'what was generally believed in all ages', adding that in order to discover this, 'the way is to consult the liturgies, not any private man's writings.' In other words, rituals reveal mentalities. John Locke was acutely aware of differences between modes of thought in different parts of the world. 'Had you or I' (he wrote in *Concerning Human Understanding*), 'been born at the Bay of Saldanha, possibly our thoughts and notions had not exceeded those brutish ones of the Hottentots that inhabit there.' This relativist argument, nourished by recent accounts of Africa, gives obvious support to Locke's polemic against innate ideas.

It is not such a long step from a concern with variations in thinking in different places to a concern with different periods. It may well have been the revolution in thought associated with the rise of the 'mechanical philosophy' which made some Europeans aware of the intellectual 'world they had lost'. Curiously enough, the eighteenth-century scholar Richard Hurd employs a similar phrase when discussing the rise of reason since Spenser's day. 'What we have gotten by this revolution, you will say, is a great deal of good sense. What we have lost is a world of fine fabling.'[33] At all events, one finds this awareness in Fontenelle, in Vico, in Montesquieu and elsewhere in the eighteenth century, especially in the context of attempts to understand alien features of early literature and law.

[32] Crombie (1994), 1587–633.
[33] Quoted in Pittock (1973), 85.

Fontenelle's essay *De l'origine des fables* (or, as we would say, the origin of 'myths'), published in 1724 but written in the 1690s, argued that in less polished ages (*siècles grossiers*), systems of philosophy were necessarily anthropomorphic and magical. Vico arrived independently at similar conclusions, expressed with rather more sympathy for what he called the 'poetic logic' of early man. A Danish scholar called Jens Kraft published in 1760 a general description of the 'savage mind', or more exactly of savage peoples (*de Vilde Folk*) and their 'mode of thought' (*Taenke-Maade*). A similar phrase had been used by Montesquieu in his *De l'esprit des lois* (1744), when he was trying to reconstruct the logic of the medieval ordeal, in other words establishing one's innocence by carrying a hot iron without being burned, and so on (book 28, chapter 17). Montesquieu explained this custom by what he called 'the mode of thought of our ancestors' ('la manière de penser de nos pères').

The same kind of concern with an exotic mentality underlay the increasing interest in the history of chivalry, studied by the French scholar Jean-Baptiste de La Curne de Sainte-Palaye on the basis of medieval romances and other sources.[34] Sainte-Palaye's *Mémoires sur l'ancienne chevalerie* (1746–50) was studied by a number of the thinkers cited in this essay, including Voltaire, Herder, Horace Walpole and William Robertson. In the famous 'view of the progress of society' prefixed to his *History of Charles V* (1769), Robertson argued that 'chivalry ... though considered commonly as a wild institution, the effect of caprice, and the source of extravagance, arose naturally from the state of society at that period, and had a very serious influence in refining the manners of the European nations.' In his *Letters on Chivalry* (1762), Richard Hurd had already discussed medieval romances (and even the *Faerie Queene*) as expressions of what he called the 'Gothic system' of 'heroic manners'.

Hurd's friend Thomas Warton had similar interests. He too read Sainte-Palaye. His essay on the rise of 'romantic fiction' argued that it originated 'at a time when a new and unnatural mode of thinking took place in Europe, introduced by our communication with the East', in other words the Crusades. His *Observations on the Faerie Queene* (1754) showed rather more sympathy for alien mentalities,

[34] Gossman (1968).

indeed empathy with them, and his observations on method have lost none of their relevance today.

> In reading the works of an author, who lived in a remote age, it is necessary that ... we should place ourselves in his situation and circumstances; that we may be the better enabled to judge and discern how his turn of thinking, and manner of composing, were biass'd, influenc'd and as it were tinctur'd, by very familiar and reigning appearances, which were utterly different from those with which we are at present surrounded.

The history of unspoken assumptions and of representations remains central to the enterprise of cultural history, as the following chapter will argue.

Some men of letters took an interest in the history of what J. C. Adelung and J. G. Herder, both writing at the end of the eighteenth century, seem to have been the first to call 'popular culture' (*Kultur des Volkes*). A group of learned Jesuits writing the lives of the saints had already (in 1757) coined the phrase 'little traditions of the people' (*populares traditiunculae*), much like the 'Little Tradition' to which the American anthropologist Robert Redfield drew attention in the 1930s. By the year 1800 there was so much interest in folksongs and folktales that it seems reasonable to speak of the 'discovery' of popular culture on the part of European intellectuals.[35]

The History of Culture

Given the increasing number of histories of arts and sciences in the early modern period, it is scarcely surprising to find that some people attempted to fit them together. For example, in his polemical treatise *On the Causes of the Corruption of the Arts* (1531), the Spanish humanist Juan Luis Vives pressed the history of learning, conceived more or less along the lines of Valla's history of language, into the service of a campaign for the reform of universities. Among the causes of corruption listed by this disciple of Erasmus were 'arrogance' and 'wars'.

However, the principal model of general cultural history in the early modern period might be described as that of the *translatio*

[35] Burke (1978), ch. 1.

studii, in other words the successive dominance either of different regions of the world or of different disciplines. In his remarkable essay in comparative history, the *Vicissitudes* (1575), the French humanist Louis Le Roy argued that that 'all liberal and mechanical arts have flourished and declined together' ('tous arts liberaux et mecaniques ont fleuri ensemble, puis decheu'), so that different civilizations, Greek, Arab, Chinese and so on, have their different peaks and troughs. A minor German humanist, Rainer Reineck, in his *Method for Reading History* (1583), modelled on Jean Bodin's famous study of the same name, discussed what he called *historia scholastica*, in other words the history of literature, the arts and intellectual disciplines.

Francis Bacon was acquainted with the work of Le Roy, as he was with the treatise by Vives, but he went further, at least in intention, in his famous call in the second book of his *Advancement of Learning* (1605) for 'a just story of learning, containing the antiquities and original of knowledge and their sects, their inventions, their traditions, their diverse administrations and managings, their flourishings, their oppositions, decays, depressions, oblivions, removes, with the causes and occasions of them'. The reference, unusual for its time, to the 'administrations and managings' of learning surely betrays the man of affairs. These affairs prevented Bacon from producing such a history of learning but his programme inspired some writers of the following century.

Voltaire's *Essay on Manners* (1751) and his *Age of Louis XIV* (1756) were manifestos for a new kind of history which would give less space to war and politics and more to 'the progress of the human mind'. In practice, Voltaire gave more space to the wars of Louis XIV than to his patronage of the arts and sciences, but his histories do have a good deal to say on the revival of letters and the refinement of manners. D'Alembert gave a similar account of intellectual progress in his preliminary discourse to the *Encyclopédie* (1751), drawing on some of the histories of disciplines (such as Montucla on mathematics), and arguing that history should be concerned with culture as well as with politics, with 'great geniuses' as well as 'great nations', with men of letters as well as kings, with philosophers as well as conquerors.

Decline attracted attention as well as progress and there was considerable debate about the reasons for cultural peaks and troughs. Some scholars suggested that despotism leads to cultural decline – this was the opinion of the humanist Leonardo Bruni in the early fifteenth century, as it was the view of the Earl of Shaftesbury three hundred years later. Others searched for physical rather than moral causes, notably the climate, which Vasari had invoked as an explanation for Florentine artistic achievements, and which was discussed in a more systematic manner – together with patronage, wealth, manners, and other factors – in the *Réflexions critiques sur la poésie et la peinture* (1719) of the Abbé Jean-Baptiste Dubos. Winckelmann too was interested in the influence of climate on art.

In short, there was an interest in the links between what we call 'culture' and 'society'. Voltaire's famous *Essay on Manners* was far from alone in this respect. It was commonly assumed by eighteenth-century intellectuals that differences between 'rough' and 'polished' manners were associated with different modes of thought. More precise studies of the topic were also produced at this time.

In Germany, for instance, Adelung's essay, discussed at the beginning of this chapter, attempted to relate 'spiritual culture' to 'social life' and the 'refinement of manners', and suggested that every state had the level of culture it deserved.[36] In Britain, Horace Walpole's *Anecdotes of Painting* (1761) suggested various connections between the 'state of English painting' at particular moments and the state of society. In the second chapter on the late Middle Ages, for instance, the dominance of 'a proud, a warlike and ignorant nobility' was responsible for work which was 'magnificent without luxury and pompous without elegance'. David Hume's essay 'of refinement in the arts' discussed the relation between art, liberty, and luxury. It is likely that the history of literature and philosophy planned by Adam Smith at the end of his life would have adopted a similar approach.

A concern for the relation between what he calls *le cose d'ingegno* (matters of intelligence) and *umani costumi* (human customs) can also be found in a remarkable essay published in 1775 by the Italian Jesuit Saverio Bettinelli, dealing with the *risorgimento* or 'revival' of Italy after the year 1000. Bettinelli ranged from art, literature and music to chivalry, commerce, luxury and festivals. Robert Henry's six-volume *History of Great Britain* (1771–93) was still more ambitious, attempting what

[36] Garber (1983), 76–97.

would later be called a 'total' history of Britain from the arrival of the Romans to the death of Henry VIII, drawing on the work of Warton, Brucker and Sainte-Palaye (among others) and paying attention to religion, learning and the arts as well as to politics, commerce and 'manners'. Connections between changes in society and changes in the arts were also emphasized in the *Life of Lorenzo de' Medici* (1795) by the Liverpool banker William Roscoe, and in the Swiss historian J. C. L. S. de Sismondi's *Histoire des républiques italiennes* (1807–18), in which the central theme was the rise and fall of liberty.[37]

The idea that a culture is a totality, or at least that the connections between different arts and disciplines are extremely important, also underlay one of the major achievements of early modern scholars, their development of techniques for detecting forgeries. These techniques of detection depended on an increasingly sharp awareness of anachronism. From Lorenzo Valla's exposure of the so-called *Donation of Constantine* in the middle of the fifteenth century to the rejection of the poems of 'Ossian' at the end of the eighteenth century, there was a long series of debates on the authenticity of particular texts, or more rarely, artefacts such as medals or 'Doctor Woodward's Shield'.[38] In these debates the protagonists were forced to formulate their criteria more and more precisely.

Valla, for example, noted anachronisms in the *Donation*'s style or mode of expression (*stilus, modus loquendi*). Richard Bentley, in his *Dissertation upon the Epistles of Phalaris* (1697), that famous exposure of a forged classical text, went into rather more detail on the history of Greek, noting that the 'idiom and style' of the letters 'by the whole thread and colour of it betrays itself to be a thousand years younger' than the ruler to whom they had been attributed. Thomas Warton discusses his criteria still more fully in his exposure of the 'medieval' poems Chatterton sent to Horace Walpole, *An Enquiry into the Authenticity of the Poems attributed to Thomas Rowley* (1782). Warton used his knowledge of what he called 'the progression of poetical composition' to show up the forgery, noting anachronisms both in the language ('optics', for example) and in the style

[37] Haskell (1993).
[38] Levine (1977).

(full of abstractions and 'sophistications' impossible in the fifteenth century).

The view that a culture forms a whole, a view implicit in
demonstrations such as these, was gradually formulated more
and more clearly. The French scholar Étienne Pasquier was one
of the first to make the point explicit when he remarked in his
Recherches de la France (1566, book 4, chapter 1), that 'any
intelligent man' would 'virtually be able to imagine the humour
of a people by reading its ancient statutes and ordinances', and
conversely, to predict the laws of a people on the basis of its
'style of life' (*manière de vivre*).

The spread of the idea can be documented from the increasingly common use of such terms as the 'genius', 'humour' or
'spirit' of an age or people. In later seventeenth-century English
texts, for example, we find phrases such as 'the temper and
geniuses of times' (Stillingfleet); 'the genius of every age'
(Dryden); 'the general vein and humour of ages' (Temple). In
France in the age of Montesquieu and Voltaire, references to
changes in the *esprit général*, or *esprit humain*, or *génie*, are frequent. The same goes for the Scots in the age of Hume and
Robertson: 'the spirit of the nation', 'the spirit of enquiry', 'the
humour of the nation', 'the reigning genius', 'the genius of
government', and so on.

When the term *Kultur* came into general use in Germany in the
1780s, it may, like the term *Geist*, have marked a sharper awareness of the links between changes in language, law, religion, the
arts and sciences on the part of Johann Gottfried Herder and
other writers (such as Adelung and Eichhorn) who used these
expressions. All the same, this awareness was not something
completely new. After all, Herder's famous *Ideas on the
Philosophy of the History of Mankind* (1784–91) made considerable use of the work of such earlier historians of ideas and of the
arts as Sainte-Palaye and Goguet.[39]

Where the Germans spoke of culture, the French preferred the
phrase, *les progrès de l'esprit humain*. Employed by Fontenelle,
the phrase was taken up in the 1750s by Voltaire, by Estève in
his history of astronomy and by Montucla in his history of mathematics. At the end of the century it became the organizing concept for a history of the world, Condorcet's *Esquisse d'un*

[39] Bruford (1962), ch. 4.

tableau historique des progrès de l'esprit humain (1793), a history of the world divided into periods according to cultural as well as economic criteria, with writing, printing and the philosophy of Descartes marking epochs.

In other words, it is not quite accurate to assert – as Sir Ernst Gombrich did in a famous lecture – that cultural history was built on 'Hegelian foundations', however influential Hegel's concept of the *Zeitgeist* was to be in the nineteenth and twentieth centuries.[40] Hegel built his own structure on the foundations of work of the previous generation of German intellectuals, notably Johann Gottfried Herder, while they built on that of the French, and so on. This regress leads us back to Aristotle, who discussed the internal development of literary genres such as tragedy in his *Poetics*, while his teleological views might entitle him to be called the first recorded Whig historian.

All the same, it is appropriate to end this essay on the origins of cultural history around the year 1800. By this time the idea of a general history of culture and society had established itself in some intellectual circles at least from Edinburgh to Florence, from Paris to Göttingen. In the next generation, this style of history would be marginalized by the rise of Leopold von Ranke in the early nineteenth century and of the document-based narrative political history associated with him and his school.

This is not to say that cultural history completely disappeared in the nineteenth century. Jules Michelet's conception of history was broad enough to include culture (notably in his volume on the French Renaissance). So indeed was Ranke's. His *History of England* (1859–68), which concentrated on the seventeenth century, found space for an account of the literature of the time. Studies concentrating on culture include François Guizot's lectures on the *General History of Civilisation in Europe* (1828) and the *History of Civilisation in France* (1829–32), which went through many editions in French and other languages. Jacob Burckhardt's classic study of *The Civilization of the Renaissance in Italy* (1860) was much appreciated in the later nineteenth century, although it attracted relatively little notice at the time of publication. In the German-speaking world, the importance of cultural history and the way in which cultural history should be written remained topics for debate. It has been argued that in the

[40] Gombrich (1969).

later nineteenth century the reaffirmation of allegiance to tradition of cultural history was a way of expressing opposition to the post-1871 regime.[41]

All the same, the nineteenth century witnessed a widening gap between cultural history, virtually abandoned to the amateur, and professional or 'positivist' history, increasingly concerned with politics, documents and 'hard facts'. Despite the changes which have taken place in the last generation, among them the rise to academic respectability of 'cultural studies', it may still be too soon to assert that this gap has been bridged. To contribute to the construction of such a bridge is one of the aims of the essays which follow.

[41] Gothein (1889); Schäfer (1891); cf Elias (1989), 118, 127, 129.

2

The Cultural History of Dreams

❧

In the last generation or so, many areas of human life which were once thought to be unchanging have been claimed as territories of the historian. Madness, for instance, thanks to Michel Foucault; childhood, thanks to Philippe Ariès; gestures (below, chapter 4); humour (chapter 5); and even smells, studied by Alain Corbin and others, have been incorporated into history.[1] In this movement of colonization, historians – with distinguished exceptions such as Reinhart Koselleck and Jacques Le Goff – have paid relatively little attention to dreams.[2] This essay presents a historical reconnaissance of this territory. The evidence is drawn almost entirely from the English-speaking world in the seventeenth century, but the real point of the essay is to argue for the possibility of a cultural history of dreaming. Not a history of interpretations of dreams, interesting as this may be.[3] A history of the dreams themselves.

Theories of Dreams

The idea that dreams have a history is denied, at least implicitly, by what might be called the 'classical' theory of dreams put

---

[1] Foucault (1961); Ariès (1960); Corbin (1982).
[2] Koselleck (1979); Le Goff (1971, 1983, 1984).
[3] Price (1986); Kagan (1990), 36–43.

forward by Freud and Jung.[4] According to them, dreams have two levels of meaning, the individual and the universal. At the individual level, Freud viewed dreams as expressions of the unconscious wishes of the dreamer (a view he later modified to account for the traumatic dreams of the shell-shocked). For his part, Jung argued that dreams performed a variety of functions, such as warning the dreamer about the dangers of his way of life or compensating for his conscious attitudes. At the universal level, Freud was especially concerned to pierce beneath the manifest content of the dream to its latent content. He suggested, for example, that in dreams 'all elongated objects ... may stand for the male organ,' and all boxes for the uterus; that kings and queens usually represent the parents of the dreamer; and so on. He accounted for manifest content in terms of day residues, but this point was marginal to his main concern.

Jung was more interested than Freud in the manifest content of dreams, but he too treated some dream symbols as universals; the Wise Old Man, for example, and the Great Mother were in his view 'archetypes of the collective unconscious'. Both men drew attention to the analogy between dream and myth, but Freud tended to interpret myths in terms of dream, whereas Jung normally interpreted dreams in terms of myth. Neither Freud nor Jung treated dream symbols as fixed, although they have often been criticized for so doing. They were too much concerned with the individual level to freeze meanings in this way. Where the classical theory is more vulnerable to criticism is in its neglect of a third level of meaning, intermediate between the individual and the universal: the cultural or social level.

The case for ascribing social or cultural meanings to dreams was first made by anthropologists, in particular by psychological anthropologists, trained in two disciplines as well as working in two cultures. In a pioneering study, Jackson S. Lincoln suggested that two kinds of dream could be found in primitive cultures, both with social meanings. The first kind was the spontaneous or 'individual' dream, the manifest content of which reflected the culture while the latent content was universal. The second kind he called the 'culture pattern' dream, which in each tribe conformed to a stereotype laid down by the culture. In these cases even the latent content of the dream was influenced by the

---

[4] Freud (1899); Jung (1928, 1930, 1945).

culture. In short, in a given culture people tend to dream particular kinds of dream.[5]

These are strong claims, but the evidence in their support is also strong. The best-known examples of the culture pattern dream come from the Indians of North America, and in particular from the Ojibwa, who lived in what is now Michigan and Ontario. Dreams played an important part in their culture, at least before 1900 or so. Boys could not come of age without taking part in what was called a 'dream fast'. They would be sent into the wilderness for a week or ten days in order to wait for dreams. The Ojibwa believed that supernatural beings would take pity on the boys when they saw them fasting and come to their aid, give them advice and become their guardian spirits for life. These supernatural beings would appear in the form of an animal or bird. The remarkable thing is that the appropriate dreams seem to have come when required, at least after a few days of hunger, a state apparently conducive to visions. To take an example recorded by the American anthropologist Paul Radin:

> I dreamt that I was alongside a lake and had not had anything to eat for some time. I was wandering in search of food for quite a time when I saw a big bird. This bird came over where I was staying and spoke to me, telling me that I was lost and that a party was out searching for me and that they really intended to shoot me instead of rescuing me. Then the bird flew out into the lake and brought me a fish to eat and told me that I would have good luck in hunting and fishing; that I would live to a good old age; and that I would never be wounded by shot-gun or rifle. This bird who had blessed me was the kind that one rarely has the chance of shooting. From that time on the loon was my guardian spirit.

In this case the informant was not a boy but an old man remembering his boyhood, and perhaps hindsight made the dream clearer than it originally had been. The wish-fulfilment element in the dream will be obvious. The statement that 'they really intended to shoot me' is interesting as an expression of aggressive feelings towards the adults who had made him fast in the wilderness.

Assuming that this first-hand account of a dream-fast is fairly accurate and reasonably typical, the problem remains of

[5] Lincoln (1935); cf. D'Andrade (1961).

explaining why the culture pattern dream actually occurred. No doubt the fasting helped, and also the expectation that a dream of this kind was going to make its appearance. A vague dream might well be assimilated to the stereotype and both recounted and remembered in a culturally appropriate way. Boys unlucky enough to have no dreams of the right kind presumably resorted to fabrication, though it is not clear in the ethnographies whether or not they would have been able to find out in advance what kind of dream the adults wanted to hear. The wrong kind of dream sometimes occurred, and it would be rejected. In another story retailed to Radin, 'The boy's father came and asked him of what he had dreamt. The boy told him, but it was not what the father wanted him to get, so he told him to go right on fasting.'[6] Sooner or later the right kind of dream made its appearance, which is not too surprising, since what the fathers wanted to hear was a dream about the central symbols of the culture.

Only a few peoples have the dream-fast among their cultural practices, but elsewhere too dreams follow the stereotypes of the local culture. A water serpent played an important part in the dreams of the Hopi Indians, as studied by the anthropologist Dorothy Eggan. For example, 'I come toward my home village. People are frightened. Children run toward where I am and tell me there is a big Water Serpent in the pond standing out of it four feet high, making an awful noise.'

Dreams of snakes and serpents are not uncommon in other cultures, and Freud interpreted them as symbols of the male genitals. However, the Water Serpent plays an important part in Hopi myths, where it represents authority. Hopi children were taught these myths, which were made easy to visualize by means of dramatic rituals. Hence it is hardly surprising to find that this imagery recurs in Hopi dreams, although no one was required to dream dreams of a particular kind. It is plausible to suggest that the Water Serpent has the same meaning in Hopi dreams as in Hopi myths: authority.[7]

The hypothesis that dreams have a cultural meaning has been confirmed by studies of the Zulu, of the villagers of Rajastan, of blacks in São Paulo, and of students in Tokyo and Kentucky.[8]

[6] Radin (1936); cf. Hallowell (1966).
[7] Eggan (1966).
[8] Carstairs (1957), 89ff.; Bastide (1966); Griffith et al. (1958).

Taken together, these studies suggest, as J. S. Lincoln's work does, that dreams are shaped in two ways by the dreamer's culture.

In the first place, dream symbols may have particular meanings in a given culture, as in the example of the Water Serpent among the Hopi. When a dreamer dreams a myth, we should not take it for granted, as Jung and his followers appear to do, that this is a spontaneous re-creation of the myth, an 'archetype of the collective unconscious'. We should begin by asking whether or not the dreamer is in fact aware of the myth. It may be objected that variations in the manifest content of dreams are not important; the sociology of dreams is a superficial one if it leads only to the conclusion that the same basic themes or problems are symbolized in different ways in different societies. This question of the relative importance of the manifest content of dreams is a controversial one among psychologists, in which historians should not meddle. However, they may be allowed to point out that if people in a given culture dream the myths of that culture, then their dreaming in turn supports belief in the myths, particularly in cultures in which dreaming is interpreted as 'seeing' another world. Myths shape dreams, but dreams in turn authenticate myths, in a circle which facilitates cultural reproduction or continuity.

In the second place, it may be argued that the latent content too is shaped in part by the dreamer's culture. A brief justification for this hypothesis, which is at once more fundamental and more controversial than the previous one, might run as follows. Dreams are concerned with the stresses, anxieties and conflicts of the dreamer. Typical or recurrent stresses, anxieties and conflicts vary from one culture to another. One cross-cultural study of 'typical dreams' showed that the relative frequency of different anxiety dreams varied considerably. Americans, for example, dreamed more often of arriving late for appointments and of being discovered naked, while Japanese dreamed of being attacked. The contrast suggests what other evidence confirms, that Americans are more concerned with punctuality and with 'body shame', while Japanese are more anxious about aggression.[9]

[9] Griffith et al. (1958).

Dreams in History

What have these findings to do with cultural history? The fact that people have dreamed in the past and have sometimes recorded their dreams is a necessary but not a sufficient condition for historians to take an interest in them. If dreams are meaningless, they need not concern themselves any further. If the universal meaning of dreams were the only meaning, historians could confine themselves to noting the recurrence in their period of dreams of flying, pursuit, or loss of teeth, and they could immediately pass on to other topics.

If, however, dreams tell us something about the individual dreamer, then historians need to pay them more attention. They become a potential source, to be approached, like other sources, with caution, as Freud himself noted on occasion.[10] Historians need to bear constantly in mind the fact that they do not have access to the dream itself but at best to a written record, modified by the preconscious or conscious mind in the course of recollection and writing (for the problem of 'memory', see chapter 3 below). However, such 'secondary elaboration' probably reveals the character and problems of the dreamer as clearly as the dream itself does.

Historians also need to remember that unlike psychoanalysts they do not have access to the associations of the dreamer to the incidents of the dream, associations which enable analysts to avoid a mechanical decoding and help them discover what dream symbols mean to the dreamers themselves. The best that historians can do is to work with a series of dreams by the same individual and to interpret each one in terms of the others. For example, the Swedish theologian Emmanuel Swedenborg recorded over 150 dreams in a single year, 1744.[11] In favourable cases like these, dreams provide biographers with evidence which cannot be obtained by any other means.

If, as we have argued above, dreams have a cultural layer of meaning as well as a personal and a universal layer, still more exciting possibilities open up for historians. In the first place, the study of changes in the manifest content of dreams should reveal changes in the myths and images which were psychologically

[10] Freud (1929).
[11] Freud (1929).

effective at the time (as opposed to the myths which were merely in circulation). In the second place, dreams, like jokes (below, chapter 5), deal obliquely with what is inhibited or repressed, and this varies from period to period. Repressed wishes, anxieties and conflicts are likely to find expression in the latent content of dreams, which must therefore change over time, and may help historians reconstruct the history of repression.

All the same, until quite recently it was a rare historian who was prepared to take dreams seriously as evidence. Take the case of Archbishop William Laud, for example, who recorded some thirty dreams in his diary between 1623 and 1643. One of his biographers, W. H. Hutton, referred in 1895 to the 'quaint humour' which made Laud record 'the curious visions which came to him as he slept', visions which 'do not read seriously'. In her *Strafford* (1935), C. V. Wedgwood was even more dismissive, writing that Laud 'set down in his diary the silliest dreams as though they had some profound significance'. The most recent biographer of Laud, on the other hand, uses dreams as evidence of the Archbishop's state of mind.[12]

A pioneering historian in this field, as in others, was the classical scholar E. R. Dodds, who wrote about the dreams of ancient Greeks.[13] He was more concerned with Greek dream interpretation (Artemidorus, for example) than with the dreams themselves, but he discussed culturally stereotyped dreams and also the cultural practice of 'incubation', in other words sleeping in a holy place in order to obtain an oracle dream advising the dreamer what to do, a practice not unlike the Ojibwa dream-fast. Among historians of the Middle Ages, Jacques Le Goff has paid particular attention to dreaming.[14] Early modern historians are moving in the same direction.[15] So are historians of the nineteenth and twentieth centuries. Alain Besançon, for example, has argued that the dreams of a culture can and should be interpreted like the dreams of an individual and he has offered analyses of dreams in Russian literature, such as Grinev's in Pushkin's *The Captain's Daughter* and Raskolnikov's in *Crime and Punishment*.[16]

---

[12] Carlton (1987), 56, 144–5, 148–53.
[13] Dodds (1951); cf. Dodds (1965) and Miller (1994).
[14] Le Goff (1983, 1984); cf. Dutton (1994).
[15] Macfarlane (1970); Kagan (1990).
[16] Besançon (1971); Koselleck (1979); Theweleit (1977).

Let us now examine some early modern examples. In Europe in the sixteenth and seventeenth centuries, as in antiquity and the Middle Ages, dreams were taken seriously for what they revealed about the future. Manuals of dream interpretation abounded and there were practices equivalent to incubation, notably sleeping in cemeteries and sleeping with the Bible under the pillow.[17] The examples which follow are divided into two groups, following Lincoln's classification. In the first place, the 'individual' dreams, and then the 'culture pattern' dreams.

Individual Dreams

On 11 November 1689, the Paris *Gazette* offered 20,000 louis reward for the interpretation of a dream of Louis XIV's (it is not known whether any successful Joseph appeared before Pharaoh). It is a pity to evade this challenge, but the danger of misinterpreting isolated dreams is an obvious one. It is better to concentrate on dream series.

In the seventeenth century, series of dreams were recorded by at least three Englishmen (Elias Ashmole, Ralph Josselin and William Laud) and, across the Atlantic, by the New Englander Samuel Sewall.[18] Between them these four men recorded 120 dreams (42 for Ashmole, 31 each for Josselin and Laud, and 16 for Sewall). This sample is of course a ridiculously small one for the analysis of the dreams of a whole culture (or rather, two related cultures), but it may at least be sufficient to illuminate the principal problems of method. In a study of the cultural meanings of dreams it remains necessary to bear in mind that there are other levels of analysis and that the dreams of all four men were related to their private lives and problems. A few biographical details are therefore in order. The eldest of the group, William Laud (1573–1645), Archbishop of Canterbury, recorded most of his dreams in the years 1623–8, when he was in his fifties. Contemporaries remarked on his 'arrogant pride' when he was in power, his insistence on authority, obedience and discipline in church and state. Since Laud was a man of low birth and low stature, he looks like a classic case of an inferiority complex. He

---

[17] Cardano (1557), ch. 44.
[18] Ashmole (1966); Josselin (1976); Laud (1847–60); Sewall (1878).

was the son of a prosperous Reading cloth merchant, but in the circles in which he came to move this origin was a humble one, often mocked by his political opponents. That Laud felt insecure even when in power is suggested by some of his dreams. His enemies thought him close to King Charles I, but 'I dreamed marvellously, that the King was offended with me, and would cast me off, and tell me no cause why.' Or more vividly, 'I brought him drink, but it pleased him not. I brought him more, but in a silver cup. Thereupon His Majesty said: you know that I always drink out of glass.' Elias Ashmole (1617–92), a professional astrologer, recorded dreams between 1645 and 1650, when he was in his late twenties and early thirties. From 1647 onwards he was courting the woman who became his second wife in 1649, and several dreams were concerned with this relationship. Ralph Josselin (1617–83), an Essex parson, was the only one of the four not to have a distinguished career. He recorded most dreams in the 1650s, when he was in his thirties and early forties. Samuel Sewall (1652–1730), the youngest of the group, as well as the only American, was a judge. The sixteen dreams he recorded are thinly spread over a long period, 1675–1719, beginning just before his first marriage.

In order to analyse the manifest content of these 120 dreams, it is necessary to distinguish categories or themes. Ideally, these categories would not only be appropriate to the dreams analysed, but also allow comparisons with the dreams of other cultures. Such categories are not easy to devise. A content analysis of 10,000 American dreams made by Calvin Hall in the late 1940s grouped the dreams by (1) settings, (2) characters, (3) action, (4) the interaction of the characters, and (5) the emotion felt by the dreamer. This is excellent if the analyst can make use of a questionnaire, but our four dreamers do not often provide information under all five heads.[19]

By contrast Dorothy Eggan's analysis of Hopi dreams employed seven more concrete categories as follows: (1) security, (2) persecution and conflict, (3) physical hazard, (4) heterosexual elements, (5) crops and stock, (6) water, and (7) religion.[20] These categories may well be the most useful for the study of Hopi dreams, but 'water' and 'crops' are not recurrent themes in the

---

[19] Hall (1951).
[20] Eggan (1952).

dreams to be considered here. Until a set of cross-cultural categories is worked out, it seems best to work with categories
which will (like Eggan's) apply at least to the culture being studied, paying the price of making comparison more difficult.

In our seventeenth-century cases, the most important recurrent
themes are those of (1) death and burial, (2) the church, (3)
kings, (4) wars, (5) politics, and (6) injury to the dreamer or to
something associated with the dreamer. These themes are in
strong contrast to the central themes found by Hall in twentieth-
century American dreams.

There are nineteen death and burial dreams among the 120 in
our sample, although nine of them come from one dreamer, Elias
Ashmole. In three cases the dream refers to the death of the
dreamer's wife; in three cases to the death of another close relative (mother, father or children); and in four cases the death is
that of the dreamer himself. Josselin and Sewall both dreamed of
their trial and condemnation to death, while Ashmole dreamed
that he was actually beheaded (and on another occasion, that he
was poisoned). Curiously enough, the only one of the four who
did not have a dream of this kind, William Laud, was also the
only one to be condemned and executed in real life.

There are also five cases of references to a grave, a tomb or
monument or a burial. In contrast to this preoccupation, the
theme of death and burial was not important enough in the
1940s to be mentioned in Hall's analysis. It looks as if seventeenth-century Englishmen were more anxious about death than
twentieth-century Americans, an anxiety which reflected their
lower expectation of life. If seventeenth-century people dreamed
more of burials and tombs than we do, this is surely related to
the greater emphasis placed in their waking lives on the public
and ceremonial aspects of death.

Turning to our second category (in order of frequency), there
are fourteen dreams of the church in the sample; six dreams
located in a church or churchyard, and eight dreams of clergy-
men and ecclesiastical affairs. In Hall's analysis of twentieth-
century dreams, the church setting is so rare that it is placed
(together with bars) in a 'miscellaneous' category. This makes
another obvious contrast between the two centuries. It is necessary to bear in mind that thirteen out of the fourteen dreams of
the church come from our two clerical dreamers – the exception
being Ashmole dreaming that he was in Litchfield Minster – and

so to be cautious in drawing conclusions about general attitudes to the church. One might indeed regard churches as the clergy's place of work – but in the United States in the 1940s, to dream of one's place of work was itself unusual, so that contrasts between the centuries remain.

As for the eight dreams of the church as an institution, it is worth noting that both the Anglican clerics were attracted to Rome in their sleep. Laud dreamed that he was 'reconciled to the church of Rome', and feeling guilty about this in the dream itself, went to beg pardon of the church of England. As for Josselin, he dreamed that he was 'familiar with the pope'. There are of course all too many ways to interpret these dreams, from simple wish-fulfilment, not so implausible in Laud's case, to compensation for hostility to Rome in waking hours. It is intriguing to discover that both Laud and Josselin recorded versions of what might be called the 'classic' clerical dream. Laud dreamed that when he was officiating at a wedding 'I could not find the order for marriage' in his book, while Josselin dreamed that when he was conducting a service, he 'could not read the psalms, or sing', or find his Bible. Again, Laud dreamed 'that I put off my rochet [surplice] all save one sleeve; and when I would have put it on again, I could not find it.' It might be interesting to attempt a sociology of anxiety dreams of this kind among people of different occupations. Besides the fourteen dreams of the church, there were three more concerned with the supernatural. Laud and Sewall dreamed of Jesus Christ, and Sewall of going up to heaven.

Turning to the third category, we find eight dreams of kings (one of James I, six of Charles I, and one of Charles II). It is of course common for psychoanalysts to claim, following Freud, that a king in a dream symbolizes the father of the dreamer. However, like a literal-minded historian, I am convinced that in the sample, at least on one level and on some occasions, 'the king' meant the king. After all, Laud, who dreamed of the king most (four times) frequently saw and spoke to Charles I. Ashmole dreamed of the king three times in 1645–6, in other words at the height of the Civil War. Josselin dreamed of the deposition of Charles II. On the other hand Sewall, far away in America, was the only one of the four not to dream of a king at all.

This point about kings is a special case of a more general contrast between the seventeenth century and the twentieth. Calvin

Hall found that only 1 per cent of the dreams he collected were of what he called 'famous or prominent public figures', while seventeen of the dreams studied here (about 14 per cent) fall into this category. Once again, distinctions between our four dreamers are in order. Laud, who is responsible for nine out of the seventeen dreams of public figures, knew some of them very well. The Duke of Buckingham, for example, was a personal friend, and the Bishop of Lincoln a personal enemy. However, Josselin, who had no celebrated friends or acquaintances, dreamed not only of Charles II but also of the Pope, Oliver Cromwell and Mr Secretary Thurlow. In similar fashion, Swedenborg dreamed of King Charles XII, the King of Prussia, the King of France, the King of Poland and the Tsar.[21] A similar contrast between the seventeenth century and the twentieth emerges from the eight dreams in the fourth category, wars. Laud did not record any dreams of this kind, but Ashmole dreamed of Charles I marching out of Oxford and of the king besieged; Josselin, of the defeat of the Scots, of an English army in France, and of civil war; Sewall of the French (twice) and once of what he called 'a military flame'.

Another eight dreams were concerned with politics. Laud dreamed once of parliament, for example, while Josselin (who was not a member of parliament) dreamed of it twice. Ashmole dreamed of taking the Negative Oath, and Sewall that he was chosen Lord Mayor. In contrast to this, Hall found that in his sample, dreams had 'little or nothing to say about current events', though a study of German dreams during the Nazi period came to opposite conclusions.[22] How can this contrast be explained? Eleven of the sixteen dreams concerned with war and politics in the seventeenth century dated from 1642–55, a period of civil war and other conflicts when people might be expected to have been more anxious than usual about political affairs. Yet Hall collected his sample from Americans at the very time when the atom bomb was dropped on Japan, without it making much impact on their dreams. His conclusion was that political concern 'does not go very deep nor is it emotionally relevant for us'. For the seventeenth century, exactly the opposite conclusion seems in

---

[21] Swedenborg (1744), 1–2 Apr., 19–20 Apr., 24–25 Apr., 28–29 Apr., 16–17 Sept., 17–18 Sept., 6–7 Oct., 20–21 Oct.
[22] Beradt (1966).

order. The relative frequency of political dreams suggests that political concern did go deep and also – to employ Hall's useful term – that it was emotionally relevant.

Exactly how deep and how relevant it is of course impossible to say. It may be that these seventeenth-century dreamers were making use of political events and figures to symbolize private anxieties. We have returned to the problem of distinguishing manifest from latent content, the problem whether 'the king' in Laud's dreams really meant Charles I or not. However, if seventeenth-century dreamers were more likely to symbolize their private anxieties by political images than twentieth-century dreamers are, that fact already tells us something about the emotional relevance of politics in the seventeenth century. A similar point might be made about religion. Even if a dream of the church or of Christ had a latent private meaning, it remains evidence of the emotional relevance of Christianity.

The last of our six categories, overlapping with the first, is that of injury to the dreamer, which occurs in eight dreams in the sample. Laud dreamed twice of his teeth falling out. Dreams of the loss of teeth are common to many cultures, as anthropologists testify and as an inspection of dream-books from Artemidorus onwards will confirm. The dream-books usually say that this dream portends the loss of a relative. Freud, on the other hand, treated teeth as a symbol for the genitals, while some more recent psychoanalysts interpret this dream as an expression of defencelessness against aggression. In both cases, a loss of power or potency is involved.

As for other dreams of injury, Ashmole dreamed that he was going bald, that his hand had rotted off, and that his head was cut off, while Josselin and Sewall dreamed, as already noted, that they were condemned to death. Laud also dreamed of damage to St John's College, Oxford, his old college and one which he had partly rebuilt. The category of injury does not ocur at all in Hall's analysis, so the only comparison which can be made is an extremely vague one, the proportion of pleasant and unpleasant dreams in the two samples. Hall claimed that 64 per cent of dream emotions in his sample were unpleasant: apprehension, anger and sadness were the dominant emotions. In the case of the seventeenth-century sample, it was difficult to place half the dreams in either the 'pleasant' or the 'unpleasant' category. Of those which remained, about 70 per cent were unpleasant. Given the small size of the sample, the difference between 70 per cent and 64 per cent should not be taken too seriously. In other words, the evidence of these dreams cannot be used to show that seventeenth-century people were either more or less anxious than moderns, although the objects of their anxiety may well have differed.

Culture-Pattern Dreams

The 120 dreams discussed above belong to Lincoln's category of 'individual' dreams which draw elements from the dreamer's culture. It may also be possible to identify in early modern Europe what Lincoln called 'culture-pattern' dreams, as stereotyped as the dreams of Ojibwa boys. A number of recorded dreams lend themselves to interpretations in these terms. For example:

> In the year 1525, after Whitsuntide, in the night between Wednesday and Thursday, I saw this vision in my sleep, how many big waters fell from the firmament. And the first hit the earth about four miles from myself with great violence and with enormous noise, and drowned the whole land. So frightened was I that I woke before the other waters fell.

Albrecht Dürer, for it was he, drew a picture of the 'big waters' beside his text. It is hardly surprising to find a dream of destruction occurring at the time of the German Peasants' War, nor, given the Christian tradition, is it odd to find the dreamer symbolizing destruction by a flood, especially at a time of heavy rains. In Germany at this time there were a number of texts in circulation predicting disasters of this kind and at this time.[23]

A second vivid example of a culturally stereotyped dream is provided by another sixteenth-century artist, Benvenuto Cellini. According to his autobiography (part 1, section 89), when Cellini was seriously ill he dreamed that 'a terrifying old man appeared at my bedside and tried to drag me by force into his enormous boat.' Cellini resisted, and he recovered from his illness. A curious feature of the story is that the teller does not name the old man – yet who else could he be but Charon? We need have no

[23] Dürer (1956), 214.

recourse to a theory of archetypes to explain the appearance of Charon to an Italian Renaissance artist, familiar with Dante (if not with Lucian and his recent imitators) and with the figure of Charon in Michelangelo's *Last Judgement* (which existed in 1550, when he was writing, though not at the time of the illness he wrote about).

It may also be argued that two phenomena which are well documented for the early modern period but have often puzzled historians may be explained in terms of culturally stereotyped dreams; religious visions and the witches' sabbath.

Historians have carried out some fascinating research on visions since this essay was first published.[24] Of these the most relevant to the present chapter is that of David Blackbourn. His book concentrates on a single story, that of the apparition of the Virgin Mary to some children in the village of Marpingen in the age of Bismarck and the pilgrimages to the 'German Lourdes' which followed. However, the author places this story in a much wider context, that of a 'great wave of visions' of the Virgin Mary which took place after 1789. Blackbourn explains this wave not only in religious terms (the 'Marianization' of popular Catholicism), but also by war and political upheaval, including Bismarck's campaign against the Catholic church.

Blackbourn's point about the link between visions and political upheaval is confirmed by what might be called an 'epidemic' of visions in Silesia (at that time part of the Kingdom of Bohemia) in the early to middle seventeenth century, a time when the Thirty Years' War was raging in the region and the belief in the imminent end of the world was unusually widespread.[25] The visionaries included Mikulas Drabic, Christoph Kotter, Christiana Poniatowska and Stephan Melisch.[26] The texts of these 'revelations' appeared in several languages but probably achieved their widest currency as a result of the Latin translations of the visions of Drabic and Kotter by the famous Czech scholar Jan Amos Comenius. What follows will concentrate on Melisch.

An example from his revelations runs as follows:

---

[24] Christian (1981); Dinzelbacher (1981); Gurevich (1984); Kagan (1990); Sallmann (1992); Blackbourn (1993).
[25] Haase (1933).
[26] Benz (1969), 300ff., 460ff., 501ff. on Kotter, and 113ff., 145ff., 171ff., 300ff., 599ff. on Poniatowska.

I saw red foxes come from the east, every one having a great tooth.
And a gold yellowish lion stood upon a green place, about whom
the foxes were leaping. Instantly after came a fiery man like a
flame, with a black sword of iron; and against him a bright shining
man, like the sun, with such a sword like a flash of lightning.
Betwixt these there was such a fight, that many thousands did fall
in the place, and none was left remaining but very few. Between
them stood a white eagle . . . I saw that the bright sun-shining man
had cut off the head of the white eagle, and that head was given
with the crown to the North; but the body of the eagle was given
to a red eagle, and the wings to the East.[27]

This vision dates from 1656, and it is not difficult to identify
the theme, even without the glosses provided, as the invasion and
division of Poland by Russian, Swedish and Prussian forces from
1654 onwards, an episode which the Poles still describe as the
'Deluge'. The vision might be described as 'apocalyptic' in tone,
and many of Melisch's visions do indeed echo the Apocalypse.
There are references to the 'Babylonish beast'; to the Lamb, the
book, the seals; and to a time, times, and half of half a time. The
images which do not come from Revelation are often heraldic
beasts like the Polish eagle and the Swedish lion. In other words,
Melisch's visions have literary and visual sources, and the same is
true of the other visionaries mentioned above. What might be
called the 'iconography' of visions deserves further study.[28]

It may seem natural to conclude that the visions are all conscious fabrications, to be classified with a well-known literary
genre, of which Francisco de Quevedo's *Sueños* and Johan
Kepler's *Somnium* are famous seventeenth-century examples. In
favour of this conclusion is the fact that the visions, when read
one after another, do not give the impression of dreams. They are
too coherent. They do not keep changing the subject or the scene
as dreams so often do, and their political or religious meaning is
consistent and clear. They read like allegories, and some of them
even use the literary device of the dreamer asking someone what
the vision means, and having it all explained.

Implicit in this argument, however, is a dichotomy which is
open to criticism. The assumption is that a given text must be
either an accurate transcript of a dream or a literary effusion

---

[27] Melisch (1659), no. xv; the translation in his *Twelve Visions* (1663), no. 4.
[28] Cf. Benz (1969), 311–410.

couched in the form of a dream. However, the discovery of the culture-pattern dream suggests that this dichotomy is a false one. Melisch and the other visionaries clearly studied Revelation with care, and it meant a great deal to them. The French Calvinist pastor Moïse Amyraut used their studies against them, arguing that the images from biblical prophecies were 'painted in their minds' (*peintes dans l'esprit*), persuading them that they had genuine visions when they did not.[29] The comment is an acute one, but a sharp distinction between a 'genuine' vision and a false one can only be justified on theological grounds.

It is likely that reading the Apocalypse of St John produces apocalyptic dreams in some people. Ralph Josselin and Emmanuel Swedenborg both recorded dreams of this kind in their diaries. Josselin, for example, dreamed of a black cloud in the shape of a stag, with a man riding it. His wife dreamed of lights blazing in the sky, 'flames exceeding terrible', and 'three smokes like pillars out of the earth'. On waking, she thought of Revelation 19: 3.[30] In similar fashion, Swedenborg once dreamed of thrusting a sword into the jaws of a great beast, and recorded that he had been 'thinking during the day about the woman and the dragon in the Apocalypse'.[31] A Freudian would doubtless interpret Swedenborg's dream in a quite different way, and might well be right in doing so, but this should not stop us from seeing the dream's cultural component. Like the Hopi and the Ojibwa, Swedenborg was dreaming one of the central myths of his culture.

These analogies suggest what cannot of course be verified or falsified, that the 'revelations' of Melisch and the others were dream experiences, stimulated by literary sources, interpreted in terms of literary models, and finally elaborated and made more coherent for publication. Drawing a parallel with some seventeenth-century autobiographies, for example John Bunyan's *Grace Abounding*, may be illuminating. It has been shown that this work has literary sources, St Paul for example, and that it follows a pattern of development from sinfulness to conversion which can be found in many spiritual autobiographies of the period. It would therefore be unwise to accept it as a completely accurate account of Bunyan's life. However, it would be equally

[29] Amyraut (1665).
[30] Josselin (1976).
[31] Swedenborg (1744).

unwise to dismiss the text as nothing but fiction. It is more likely to be an account of genuine experiences perceived and ordered in terms of cultural schemata or stereotypes (cf. p. 50 below).[32]

A similar approach may help us understand a well-known series of less orthodox visions, visions of the 'witches' sabbath'. As is well known, there were many trials in early modern Europe in which the accused confessed to flying to nocturnal feasts and dances at which the devil presided. The interpretation of these confessions was and remains controversial.[33] Writers of treatises on witchcraft discussed in learned detail whether the witches went to their sabbaths 'in the body' or 'in the spirit'. One suggestion was that the witches dreamed that they went. The problem with this suggestion, as the Italian physician Girolamo Cardano pointed out, was the implication that different people dreamed the same dream, which seemed contrary to experience.[34] The anthropologists have answered Cardano's objection. The sabbath dream, if it is a dream, is no more stereotyped than the Ojibwa puberty dream. If the notorious ointment which witches were supposed to use contained narcotics, as has been suggested more than once, this would explain how the so-called witches dreamed of flying.[35]

It is of course perfectly possible, and even likely, that the accused elaborated their dreams during interrogation, or interpreted them in the way they thought the interrogators wanted. It is less likely that they manufactured the whole story of the sabbath in order to satisfy the inquisitors, because in some cases at least their story ran counter to the expectations of their interrogators. The best-known examples of confessions which disconcerted the inquisitors are those discussed in Carlo Ginzburg's well-known study of the so-called 'good walkers' or *benandanti* of Friuli.[36] When Piero Gasparutto was interrogated on suspicion of witchcraft at Cividale in Friuli in 1580, he burst out laughing. How could he be a witch? He was, he explained, a *benandante*, and that meant that he fought witches. He and others went out to fight on certain nights of the year armed with sticks of fennel, while their enemies, the witches, carried sticks of sorghum. 'And

[32] Tindall (1934).
[33] Ginzburg (1990); Muchembled (1990).
[34] Cardano (1557).
[35] Clark (1921); cf. Castaneda (1968), 43ff.
[36] Ginzburg (1966).

if we are the victors,' another *benandante* declared, 'that year is abundance, but if we lose there is famine.'

These imagined night battles were more than a local custom. Ginzburg himself drew a parallel with the phenomenon of the good werewolf in seventeenth-century Livonia, while a Hungarian historian has compared the *benandante* to the Hungarian *táltos* or shaman.[37] The reference to shamans suggests comparisons with much of Asia and the Americas. In East Africa too there is a parallel to the *benandanti*. Among the Nyakyusa of Tanganyika (as it then was) in 1951, it was 'thought that in every village there were defenders [*abamanga*] who see the witches in dreams and fight them and drive them off'.[38]

Ginzburg's book has attracted much attention as a contribution to witchcraft studies. However, it also deserves attention as a contribution to the study of dreams and visions. Indeed, the history of witchcraft itself needs to be viewed, as it has been in recent years, from the perspective of the history of the collective imagination. The activities of the *benandanti* make fine examples of culturally stereotyped dreams. It is in this context that we should consider two points made by the *benandanti* in the course of explaining their activities to the inquisitors. The first point is that they went out not in the body but 'in the spirit', so that

> if by chance while we were out someone should come with a light and look for a long time at the body, the spirit would never re-enter it until there was no one around to see it that night; and if the body, seeming to be dead, should be buried, the spirit would have to wander around the world until the hour fixed for that body to die.[39]

The second point is that of the suggestibility of the new recruits, who testified that they were 'summoned' to the night battles and had no choice but to go. Bastiano Menos, for example, declared that one night a certain Michele 'called me by name and said, "Bastiano, you must come with me,"' and he did.[40] The parallel with the more indirect suggestions made to the Ojibwa boys enduring the dream-fast discussed above is clear enough.

This essay has emphasized analogies between seventeenth-

[37] Klaniczay (1984).
[38] Wilson (1951).
[39] Ginzburg (1966), ch. 1, section 11.
[40] Ginzburg (1966), ch. 4, section 13.

century dreams and the dreams of some tribal societies. Among the Ojibwa and the Hopi, as in early modern Europe, dreams, like myths, were often concerned with religion and dreamers often made contact with supernatural beings. In twentieth-century American dreams, by contrast, supernatural elements are almost entirely lacking. In his study of Ojibwa puberty dreams, the anthropologist Paul Radin pointed out that as long as traditional culture remained strong, the dreams were concerned with the myths. When the traditional culture disintegrated, around 1900, Ojibwa dreams became personal in theme.[41] The same process of transition from public symbols to private ones seems to have taken place in the West between the seventeenth century and the present, as is shown not only by dreams but also by the changing subjects of plays and stories.

At the level of manifest content, then, a cultural interpretation of dreams does seem possible. At the more interesting level of latent content it is obviously more difficult to give a confident answer. An attractive hypothesis, impossible to verify, is that in the early modern period repression was more concerned with political and religious temptations and less with sexual ones than is the case today. This is not to say that sex was unimportant in the period or even that it was unimportant in the dreams of the period. Sexual problems are explicit in two dreams of Ashmole's (wanting to make love to two ladies, and being frustrated). Laud dreamed that the Duke of Buckingham got into his bed. Other dreams discussed here for their manifest content could be given sexual interpretations, like the dream of Swedenborg's mentioned above.

However, many other dreams refer to public problems, such as the unconscious attraction of Catholicism for some Protestants. The high proportion of public themes, whether religious or political, in the dreams discussed here ought to give historians food for thought. It seems plausible to suggest that seventeenth-century Englishmen, at least, were more anxious about public issues than seems to be the case with twentieth-century Americans. The German classical scholar Werner Jaeger once remarked on the 'public conscience' of the ancient Greeks.[42] His point seems valid for seventeenth-century England as well.

[41] Radin (1936).
[42] Jaeger (1933).

3

History as Social Memory

The traditional view of the relation between history and
memory is a relatively simple one. The historian's function
is to be the custodian of the memory of public events
which are put down in writing for the benefit of the actors, to
give them fame, and also for the benefit of posterity, to learn
from their example. History, as Cicero wrote in a passage which
has been quoted ever since (*De oratore*, ii. 36), is 'the life of
memory' (*vita memoriae*). Historians as diverse as Herodotus,
Froissart and Lord Clarendon all claimed to write in order to
keep alive the memory of great deeds and great events.

Two Byzantine historians made the point particularly fully in
their prologues, utilizing the traditional metaphors of time as a
river and of actions as texts which may be obliterated. The
Princess Anna Comnena described history as a 'bulwark' against
the 'stream of time' which carries everything away into 'the
depths of oblivion', while Procopius declared that he wrote his
history of the Gothic, Persian and other wars 'to the end that the
long course of time may not overwhelm deeds of singular importance through lack of a record, and thus abandon them to oblivion and utterly obliterate them'. The idea of actions as texts can
also be seen in the notion of the 'book of memory', employed by
Dante and Shakespeare, who wrote of 'blotting your name from
books of memory' (*Henry VI, Part 2*, Act 1, Scene 1).

This traditional account of the relation between memory and
written history, in which memory reflects what actually happened

and history reflects memory, now seems much too simple. Both history and memory have come to appear increasingly problematic. Remembering the past and writing about it no longer seem the innocent activities they were once taken to be. Neither memories nor histories seem objective any longer. In both cases historians are learning to take account of conscious or unconscious selection, interpretation and distortion. In both cases they are coming to see the process of selection, interpretation and distortion as conditioned, or at least influenced, by social groups. It is not the work of individuals alone.

The first serious explorer of the 'social framework of memory', as he called it, was of course the French sociologist or anthropologist Maurice Halbwachs, in the 1920s.[1] Halbwachs argued that memories are constructed by social groups. It is individuals who remember, in the literal, physical sense, but it is social groups who determine what is 'memorable' and also how it will be remembered. Individuals identify with public events of importance to their group. They 'remember' a great deal that they have not experienced directly. A news item, for example, can become part of one's life. Hence memory may be described as a group reconstruction of the past.

Like a faithful pupil of Émile Durkheim, Halbwachs couched his arguments about the sociology of memory in a strong if not an extreme form. Halbwachs did not assert (as the Cambridge psychologist Frederick Bartlett once accused him of asserting) that social groups remember in the same literal sense that individuals remember.[2] As we shall see (below, p. 170), a similar misunderstanding of Durkheim's position was shown by those British historians who claimed that the 'collective mentalities' studied by their French colleagues stand outside individuals rather than being shared by them.

However, Halbwachs was more vulnerable to the more precise criticisms of the great French historian Marc Bloch. It was Bloch who pointed out the danger of borrowing terms from individual psychology and simply adding the adjective 'collective' (as in the cases of *représentations collectives*, *mentalités collectives*, *conscience collective*, as well as *mémoire collective*).[3] Despite this

---

[1] Halbwachs (1925); cf. Halbwachs (1941, 1950); Lowenthal (1985), 192ff.; Hutton (1993), 73–90.
[2] Bartlett (1932), 296ff.; Douglas (1980), 268.
[3] Bloch (1925); cf. Connerton (1989), 38.

critique, Bloch was prepared to adopt the phrase *mémoire collective* and to analyse peasant customs in these interdisciplinary terms, noting for example the importance of grandparents in the transmission of traditions (a later historian of the *Annales* school has criticized this 'grandfather law', in the seventeenth century at least, on the grounds that grandparents rarely survived long enough to teach their grandchildren, but he does not cast doubt on the importance of the social transmission of tradition).[4]

Halbwachs made a sharp distinction between collective memory, which was a social construct, and written history, which he considered – in the traditional manner – to be objective. However, many recent studies of the history of historical writing treat it much as Halbwachs treated memory, as the product of social groups such as Roman senators, Chinese mandarins, Benedictine monks, university professors and so on. It has become commonplace to point out that in different places and times, historians have considered different aspects of the past to be memorable (battles, politics, religion, the economy and so on) and that they have presented the past in very different ways, concentrating on events or structures, on great men or ordinary people, according to their group's point of view.

It is because I share this view of the history of history that this chapter is entitled 'History as social memory'. The term 'social memory', which has established itself in the last decade, has been chosen as a useful piece of shorthand which sums up the complex process of selection and interpretation in a simple formula and stresses the homology between the ways in which the past is recorded and remembered.[5] The phrase raises problems which need to be addressed at the start. The analogies between individual and group thought are as elusive as they are fascinating. If we use terms like 'social memory' we do risk reifying concepts. On the other hand, if we refuse to use such terms, we are in danger of failing to notice the different ways in which the ideas of individuals are influenced by the groups to which they belong.

Another serious problem is raised by the historical relativism implicit in this enterprise. The argument is not that any account of the past is just as good (reliable, plausible, perceptive, and so on) as any other. Some investigators can be shown to be better informed or more judicious than others. The point is that all of

---

[4] Goubert (1982), 77.
[5] Connerton (1989); Fentress and Wickham (1992).

us have access to the past (like the present) only via the categories and schemata – or as Durkheim would say, the 'collective representations' – of our own culture (discussed in chapter 11).

Historians are concerned, or at any rate need to be concerned, with memory from two different points of view. In the first place, they need to study memory as a historical source, to produce a critique of the reliability of reminiscence on the lines of the traditional critique of historical documents. This enterprise has in fact been under way since the 1960s, when historians of the twentieth century came to realize the importance of 'oral history'.[6] Even historians who work on earlier periods have something to learn from the oral history movement, since they need to be aware of the oral testimonies and traditions embedded in many written records.[7]

In the second place, historians are concerned with memory as a historical phenomenon; with what might be called the social history of remembering. Given the fact that the social memory, like the individual memory, is selective, we need to identify the principles of selection and to note how they vary from place to place or from one group to another and how they change over time. Memories are malleable, and we need to understand how they are shaped and by whom, as well as the limits to this malleability.

These are topics which for some reason attracted the attention of historians only in the late 1970s. Since that time, books and articles and conferences about them have multiplied, including the multivolume survey of 'realms of memory' edited by Pierre Nora, developing the insights of Halbwachs into the relation between memory and its spatial framework and offering a survey of French history from this point of view.[8]

The social history of remembering is an attempt to answer three main questions. What are the modes of transmission of public memories and how have these modes changed over time? What are the uses of these memories, the uses of the past, and how have these uses changed? Conversely, what are the uses of oblivion? These broad questions will be examined here only from

[6] Thompson (1978).
[7] Davis (1987).
[8] Nora (1984–92); cf. Le Goff (1988); Hutton (1993), esp. 1–26; Samuel (1994).

the relatively narrow point of view of a historian of early modern Europe.

Transmission of the Social Memory

Memories are affected by the social organization of transmission and the different media employed. Let us consider for a moment the sheer variety of these media, five in particular.

(1) Oral traditions, discussed from a historian's point of view in a famous study by Jan Vansina. The transformations of this study between its original publication in French in 1961 and the much revised English version of 1985 make useful indicators of the changes which have taken place in the discipline of history in the last generation, notably the decline of the hope of establishing the objective 'facts' and the rise of interest in symbolic aspects of narrative.[9]

(2) The traditional province of the historian, memoirs and other written 'records' (another term related to remembering, *ricordare* in Italian). We need of course to remind ourselves that these records are not innocent acts of memory, but rather attempts to persuade, to shape the memory of others. We also need to keep in mind, as historians have not always done, the warning of a perceptive literary critic: 'As we read the writings of memory, it is easy to forget that we do not read memory itself but its transformation through writing.'[10] However, a similar point could be made about oral tradition, which has its own forms of stylization. Hence it is difficult to justify a sharp contrast like Pierre Nora's between the spontaneous 'memory' of traditional societies and the self-conscious 'representation' of modern ones.[11]

(3) Images, whether pictorial or photographic, still or moving. Practitioners of the so-called 'art of memory' from classical antiquity to the Renaissance emphasized the value of associating whatever one wanted to remember with striking images.[12] These were

[9] Vansina (1961).
[10] Owen (1986), 114; cf. Fussell (1975).
[11] Nora (1984–92), vol. 1, xvii–xlii.
[12] Yates (1966); cf. Bartlett (1932), ch. 11.

immaterial, indeed 'imaginary' images. However, material images have long been constructed in order to assist the retention and transmission of memories – 'memorials' such as tombstones, statues and medals, and 'souvenirs' of various kinds. Historians of the nineteenth and twentieth centuries in particular have been taking an increasing interest in public monuments in the last few years, precisely because these monuments both expressed and shaped the national memory.[13]

(4) Actions transmit memories as they transmit skills, from master to apprentice for example. Many of them leave no traces for later historians to study, but ritual actions at least are often recorded, including rituals of 'commemoration': Remembrance Sunday in Britain, Memorial Day in the USA, 14 July in France, 12 July in Northern Ireland, 7 September in Brazil, and so on.[14] These rituals are re-enactments of the past, acts of memory, but they are also attempts to impose interpretations of the past, to shape memory and thus to construct social identity. They are in every sense collective re-presentations.

(5) One of the most interesting observations in Halbwachs's study of the social framework of memory concerned the importance of a fifth medium in the transmission of memories: space.[15] He made explicit a point which had been implicit in the classical and Renaissance art of memory, the value of 'placing' images that one wishes to remember in impressive imaginary locations, such as memory palaces or memory theatres, thus exploiting the association of ideas. One group of Catholic missionaries in Brazil, the Salesian fathers, were apparently aware of the link between spaces and memories. One of their strategies for the conversion of the Bororo Indians, as Claude Lévi-Strauss has reminded us, was to move them from their traditional villages, in which houses were arranged in a circle, to new ones in which the houses were arranged in rows, thus wiping the slate clean and making the Indians ready to receive the Christian message.[16] We might ask ourselves whether the European enclosure movement may not have had similar effects (however unintentional) in wip-

[13] Nipperdey (1981); Ozouf (1984).
[14] Warner (1959); Amalvi (1984); Larsen (1982).
[15] Hutton (1993), 75–84.
[16] Lévi-Strauss (1955), 220–1.

ing the slate clean for industrialization, especially in Sweden, where the enclosure decree of 1803 was followed by the destruction of traditional villages and the dispersal of their inhabitants.[17]

Yet in certain circumstances, a social group and some of its memories may resist the destruction of its home. An extreme example of uprooting and transplantation is the case of the black slaves transported to the New World. Despite this uprooting, the slaves were able to cling to some of their culture, some of their memories, and to reconstruct them on American soil. According to the French sociologist Roger Bastide, the Afro-American rituals of *candomblé*, still widely practised in Brazil, involve a symbolic reconstruction of African space, a kind of psychological compensation for the loss of a homeland. Bastide thus uses evidence from Afro-American religious practices to criticize and refine the ideas of Halbwachs. The loss of local roots was compensated, to some degree at least, by a more general African consciousness.[18]

From the point of view of the transmission of memories, each medium has its own strengths and weaknesses. I should like to place most emphasis on an element common to several media which has been analysed by investigators as different as the social psychologist Frederick Bartlett, the cultural historian Aby Warburg, the art historian Ernst Gombrich, and the Slavist Albert Lord, who studied oral poetry in Bosnia.[19] This common feature is the 'schema'. The schema is associated with the tendency to represent – and sometimes to remember – a given event or person in terms of another.

Schemata of this kind are not confined to oral traditions, as the following chain of written examples may suggest. In his fine study of *The Great War and Modern Memory*, the American critic Paul Fussell noted what he calls 'the domination of the Second War by the First', not only at the level of the generals, who are supposed always to be fighting the previous war, but at the level of ordinary participants as well.[20] The First World War in its turn was perceived in terms of schemata, and Fussell notes

[17] Pred (1986).
[18] Bastide (1970).
[19] Bartlett (1932), 204ff., 299; Warburg (1932); Gombrich (1960b); Lord (1960).
[20] Fussell (1975), 317ff.

the recurrence of imagery from Bunyan's *Pilgrim's Progress*, especially the Slough of Despond and the Valley of the Shadow of Death, in descriptions of life in the trenches in memoirs and newspapers.[21] To go back a little further, Bunyan's own writing – including his autobiography, *Grace Abounding* – also made use of schemata (cf. p. 140 above). For instance, Bunyan's account of his conversion is clearly modelled, consciously or unconsciously – it is difficult to say which – on the conversion of St Paul as described in the Acts of the Apostles.[22]

In early modern Europe, many people had read the Bible so often that it had become part of them and its stories organized their perceptions, their memories and even their dreams (above, chapter 2). It would not be difficult to cite scores of examples of this process. For example, the French Protestant community viewed the sixteenth-century wars of religion through biblical spectacles, including the Massacre of the Innocents. In the nineteenth and twentieth centuries they 'remembered' the houses of Protestants as having been marked for the slaughter by the Catholics at the time of the Massacre of St Bartholomew in 1572.[23] To go back still further, Johan Kessler was a Swiss Protestant pastor of the first generation. In his memoirs, he tells the story of how, as he puts it, 'Martin Luther met me on the road to Wittenberg.' When he was a student, he and a companion stayed the night in the Black Bear at Jena, where they shared a table with a man who was dressed as a knight but was reading a book – which turned out to be a Hebrew psalter – and was eager to talk about theology. 'We asked, "Sir, can you tell us whether Dr Martin Luther is in Wittenberg just now, or where else he may be?" He replied, "I know for certain that he is not at Wittenberg at this moment" . . . "My boys," he asked, "what do they think about this Luther in Switzerland?"' The students still don't get the point until the landlord drops a hint.[24] My own point, however, is that consciously or unconsciously, Kessler has structured his story on a biblical prototype, in this case that of the disciples who met Christ at Emmaus.

The chain of examples could be stretched still further back, since the Bible itself is full of schemata, and some of the events

[21] Fussell (1975), 137ff.
[22] Tindall (1934), 22ff.
[23] Joutard (1976).
[24] Kessler (1540), 23ff.

narrated in it are presented as re-enactments of earlier ones.[25] However, the examples already given are perhaps sufficient to suggest some features of the process by which the remembered past turns into myth. It should be emphasized that the slippery term 'myth' is being used here not in the positivist sense of 'inaccurate history' but in the richer, more positive sense of a story with a symbolic meaning involving characters who are larger than life, whether they are heroes or villains.[26] These stories are generally made up of a sequence of stereotyped incidents, sometimes known as 'themes'.[27]

There is an obvious question for a historian to ask at this point. Why do myths attach themselves to some individuals (living or dead) and not to others? Only a few European rulers have become heroes in popular memory, or at least remained heroes over the long term: Henri IV in France, for example, Frederick the Great in Prussia, Sebastian in Portugal, William III in Britain (especially Northern Ireland), and Matthias Corvinus in Hungary, of whom it was said that 'Matthias died, justice perished.' Again, it is not every holy man or woman who becomes a saint, official or unofficial. What is it that determines success?

The existence of schemata does not explain why they become attached to particular individuals, why some people are, shall we say, more 'mythogenic' than others. Nor is it an adequate answer to do what literal-minded historians generally do and describe the actual achievements of the successful rulers or saints, considerable as these may be, since the myth often attributes qualities to them which there is no evidence that they ever possessed.[28] The transformation of the cold and colourless William III into the popular Protestant idol 'King Billy' can hardly be explained in terms of his own personality alone.

In my view, the central element in the explanation of this mythogenesis is the perception (conscious or unconscious) of a 'fit' in some respect or respects between a particular individual and a current stereotype of a hero or villain – ruler, saint, bandit, witch, or whatever. This 'fit' strikes people's imagination, and stories about that individual begin to circulate, orally in the first instance. In the course of this oral circulation, the ordinary

[25] Trompf (1979).
[26] Burke (1996).
[27] Lord (1960).
[28] Burke (1982, 1984).

mechanisms of distortion studied by social psychologists, such as 'levelling' and 'sharpening', come into play.[29] More speculatively, one might suggest that processes like condensation and displacement, described by Freud in his *Interpretation of Dreams*, are also to be found in these collective dreams or quasi-dreams. These processes assist the assimilation of the life of the particular individual to a particular stereotype from the repertoire present in the social memory in a given culture.[30] A process of what might be called 'crystallization' occurs in which traditional free-floating stories are attached to the new hero.

Thus bandits (Jesse James, for instance) turn into Robin Hoods, robbing the rich to give to the poor. Rulers (Harun al-Rashid, Henri IV of France, Henry V of England, and so on) are perceived as travelling their kingdom in disguise to learn about the condition of their subjects. The life of a modern saint may be remembered as a re-enactment of the life of an earlier one: St Carlo Borromeo was perceived as a second Ambrose, and St Rose of Lima as a second Catherine of Siena. In similar fashion the emperor Charles V was perceived as a second Charlemagne (his name helping in the process), while William III of England was perceived as a second William the Conqueror, and Frederick the Great as a new 'Emperor Frederick'.

Explanations of the process of hero-making in terms of the media are of course insufficient in themselves. To present them in this way would be politically naive. It is equally necessary to consider the functions or uses of the social memory.

Uses of the Social Memory

What are the functions of the social memory? It is hard to get a purchase on such a large question. A lawyer might well discuss the importance of custom and precedent, the justification or legitimation of actions in the present with reference to the past, the place of the memories of witnesses in trials, the concept of 'time immemorial', in other words time 'whereof the memory of man . . . runneth not to the contrary', and the change in attitudes to the evidence of memory consequent on the spread of literacy

---

[29] Allport and Postman (1945).
[30] Freud (1899); cf. Allport and Postman (1945).

and written records. Custom was indeed discussed in the article on *mémoire collective* by Bloch, cited above, and a few medievalists have pursued these questions further.[31]

The examples of rulers as popular heroes, discussed above, also illustrate the social uses of collective memories. In the stories, disasters follow the death or disappearance of the hero. However, there is a case for turning this point around and arguing that a ruler whose reign is followed by disasters, from foreign invasion to steep rises in taxation, stands a good chance of turning into a hero, since the people will look back with nostalgia to the good old days under his rule.

For example, the Ottoman invasion of Hungary in 1526, a generation after the death of Matthias, and the Spanish takeover of Portugal soon after the death of Sebastian were good for the posthumous reputation of these two kings. In similar fashion, Henri IV may well have seemed a hero to the French people not only because he followed the disorder of the wars of religion but also because the reign of his son and successor Louis XIII was marked by a sharp rise in taxes. The appeal to memories of this kind is one of the main ideological resources of rebels, at any rate in traditional societies. Thus the Spanish rebels of the 1520s, the *comuneros*, appealed to the memory of the late King Ferdinand, while the Normans who rose against Louis XIII in 1639 expressed their desire to return to the 'golden age' of Louis XII, who was said to have wept whenever he had to tax the people.[32]

Another approach to the uses of social memory is to ask why some cultures seem to be more concerned with recalling their past than others. It is commonplace to contrast the traditional Chinese concern for their past with the traditional Indian indifference to theirs. Within Europe, contrasts of this kind are also apparent. Despite their reverence for tradition and concern for 'the national heritage', the social memory of the English is relatively short. The same point has been made about the Americans, notably by a penetrating French observer, Alexis de Tocqueville.[33]

The Irish and the Poles, on the other hand, have social memories which are relatively long. In Northern Ireland, it is possible

[31] Guénée (1976–7); Clanchy (1979); Wickham (1985).
[32] Foisil (1970), 188–94; cf. Fentress and Wickham (1992), 109.
[33] Schudson (1992), 60.

to see portraits of William III on horseback, chalked on a wall, with the inscription, 'Remember 1690'.[34] In the south of Ireland, people still resent what the English did to them in Cromwell's time as if it were yesterday.[35] As the American bishop Fulton Sheen once put it, 'The British never remember it: the Irish never forget it.'[36] In Poland, Andrzej Wajda's film *Ashes* (1965), translating into cinematic terms a classic novel of 1904 about the Polish Legion in the army of Napoleon, provoked national controversy about what Wajda presented as the Legion's futile heroism.[37] In England, on the other hand, at much the same time, Tony Richardson's film *The Charge of the Light Brigade* (1968) was viewed as little more than a costume picture. The English seem to prefer to forget. They suffer from, or rejoice in, what has been called 'structural amnesia'.[38] Since structural amnesia is the complementary opposite to the concept 'social memory', I shall refer to it henceforth as 'social amnesia'.

Why should there be such a sharp contrast in attitudes to the past in different cultures? It is often said that history is written by the victors. It might also be said that history is forgotten by the victors. They can afford to forget, while the losers are unable to accept what happened and are condemned to brood over it, relive it, and reflect how different it might have been. Another explanation might be given in terms of cultural roots. When you have these roots you can afford to take them for granted, but when you lose them you feel the need to search for them. The Irish and the Poles have been uprooted, their countries partitioned. It is no wonder that they seem obsessed by their past. We have returned to that favourite theme of Halbwachs, the relation between place and memory.

The Irish and the Poles offer particularly clear examples of the use of the past, the use of the social memory and the use of myth in order to define identity. The point of remembering 1690 (in a particular way), or re-enacting the 12th of July, or of blowing up Nelson's Pillar in Dublin – as the IRA did in 1966 – or of reconstructing the old centre of Warsaw, after the Germans had blown it up – as the Poles did after 1945 – the point of all this is surely

[34] Cf. Larsen (1982), 280.
[35] Macdonagh (1983), ch. 1.
[36] Quoted Levinson (1972), 129; cf. Buckley (1989).
[37] Michalek (1973), ch. 11.
[38] Barnes (1947), 52; Watt and Goody (1962-3).

to say who 'we' are, and to distinguish 'us' from them. Such examples could be multiplied. In the case of Europe, they are particularly easy to find in the nineteenth century.

The later nineteenth century has been provocatively described by Eric Hobsbawm as the age of the 'invention of tradition'.[39] It was certainly an age of a search for national traditions, in which national monuments were constructed and national rituals (like Bastille Day) devised, while national history was given a more important place in European schools than ever before or since. The aim of all this was essentially to justify or 'legitimate' the existence of the nation-state; whether in the case of new nations like Italy and Germany, or of older ones like France, in which national loyalty still had to be created, and peasants turned into Frenchmen.[40]

The sociology of Émile Durkheim, with its emphasis on community, consensus and cohesion, itself bears the stamp of this period. It would be unwise to follow Durkheim and his pupil Halbwachs too closely in this respect, and to discuss the social function of the social memory as if conflict and dissent did not exist. Northern Ireland has made its appearance several times already and the region offers a classic example, though far from the only one, of both memories of conflict and conflicts of memory. The seventeenth-century siege of Londonderry ('Derry') and the battle of the Boyne are re-enacted every year by the Protestants who identify with the victors and apply the phrases of the past ('No Surrender', for example) to the events of the present.[41] In the south of Ireland, the memory of the rising of 1798 against the British is still very much alive. For a French parallel, one might turn to western France, especially Anjou, where the memory of the Vendée, the peasant rising of the 1790s, remains alive and controversial, so much so that a recent historian has described the situation as a 'war over memory'.[42]

Given the multiplicity of social identities, and the coexistence of rival memories, alternative memories (family memories, local memories, class memories, national memories, and so on), it is fruitful to think in pluralistic terms about the uses of memories to different social groups, who may well have different views about

[39] Hobsbawm and Ranger (1983).
[40] Weber (1976), esp. 336ff.
[41] Larsen (1982); Bell (1986); Buckley (1989).
[42] Martin (1987), ch. 9.

what is significant or 'worthy of memory'.[43] The American literary critic Stanley Fish has coined the phrase 'interpretative communities' in order to analyse conflicts over the interpretation of texts. In a similar way, it might be useful to think in terms of different 'memory communities' within a given society. It is important to ask the question, who wants whom to remember what, and why? Whose version of the past is recorded and preserved?

Disputes between historians presenting rival accounts of the past sometimes reflect wider and deeper social conflicts. An obvious example is the current debate about the importance of history from below, a debate which goes back at least as far as Aleksandr Pushkin, a historian as well as a poet, who once told the Tsar that he wanted to write about the eighteenth-century peasant leader Pugachev. The Tsar's reply was brutally simple: 'Such a man has no history.'

Official and unofficial memories of the past may differ sharply and the unofficial memories, which have been relatively little studied, are sometimes historical forces in their own right; the 'Good Old Law' in the German Peasant War of 1525, the 'Norman Yoke' in the English Revolution, and so on. Without invoking social memories of this kind, it would be hard to explain the geography of dissent and protest, the fact that some Calabrian villages, for example, take part in different protest movements century after century, while their neighbours do not.

The systematic destruction of documents which is such a common feature of revolts – think of the English peasants in 1381, the German peasants in 1525, the French peasants in 1789, and so on – may be interpreted as the expression of the belief that the records had falsified the situation, that they were biased in favour of the ruling class, while ordinary people remembered what had really happened. These acts of destruction broach the last theme of this chapter, the uses of oblivion or social amnesia.

The Uses of Social Amnesia

It is often illuminating to approach problems from behind, to turn them inside out. To understand the workings of the social memory it may be worth investigating the social organization of

[43] Wickham (1985); cf. Fentress and Wickham (1992), 87–143.

forgetting, the rules of exclusion, suppression or repression, and the question of who wants whom to forget what, and why. In a phrase, social amnesia. Amnesia is related to 'amnesty', to what used to be called 'acts of oblivion', the official erasure of memories of conflict in the interests of social cohesion.

Official censorship of the past is all too well known, and there is little need to talk about the various revisions of the Soviet Encyclopaedia, with and without the entry on Trotsky. Many revolutionary and counter-revolutionary regimes like to symbolize their break with the past by changing the names of streets, especially when these names refer to the dates of significant events. When I visited Bulgaria in the mid-1960s, the only guidebook I had with me was a Guide Bleu of 1938. Despite the useful street-maps it provided I sometimes lost my way, and so I had to ask passers-by how to find 12 November Street, or whatever it was. No one looked surprised, no one smiled, they simply directed me, but when I arrived, 12 November Street turned out to be 1 May Street, and so on. In other words, I had been quoting dates associated with the fascist regime without knowing it. This incident may be taken as a reminder of the strength of unofficial memories and the difficulty of erasing them, even under the so-called 'totalitarian' regimes of our own day.

As it happens, what might be called the 'Soviet Encyclopaedia syndrome' was not the invention of the Communist Party of the Soviet Union. In early modern Europe too, events could become non-events, officially at least. King Louis XIV and his advisers were very much concerned with what we would call his 'public image'. Medals were struck to commemorate the major events of the reign. These medals included one of the destruction of the city of Heidelberg in 1693, complete with inscription HEIDELBERGA DELETA. However, when the medals were collected together to form a 'metallic history' of the reign, this particular medal disappeared from the catalogue. It seems that Louis had come to realize that the destruction of Heidelberg had not added to his reputation, his glory, and so the event was officially suppressed, erased from the book of memory.[44]

The official censorship of embarrassing memories, 'organized oblivion' as it has been called, is well known.[45] What is in greater

[44] Burke (1992), 110–1.
[45] Connerton (1989), 14.

need of investigation is their unofficial suppression or repression in post-Nazi Germany, post-Vichy France, Franco's Spain and so on.[46] This topic raises once more the awkward question of the analogy between individual and collective memory. Freud's famous metaphor of the 'censor' inside each individual was of course derived from the official censorship of the Habsburg Empire. In a similar manner, a social psychologist, Peter Berger, has suggested that we all rewrite our biographies all the time in the manner of the Soviet Encyclopaedia.[47] But between these two censors, public and private, there is space for a third, collective but unofficial. Can groups, like individuals, suppress what it is inconvenient to remember? If so, how do they do it?[48]

Consider the following story, recorded by the anthropologist Jack Goody. The origin of the territorial divisions of Gonja, in northern Ghana, was said to have been the act of the founder, Jakpa, who divided the kingdom among his sons.

> When the details of this story were first recorded at the turn of the present century, at the time that the British were extending their control over the area, Jakpa was said to have begotten seven sons, this corresponding to the number of divisions ... But at the same time as the British had arrived, two of the seven divisions disappeared ... sixty years later, when the myths of state were again recorded, Jakpa was credited with only five sons.[49]

This is a classic case of the past being used to legitimate the present, of what the anthropologist Bronislaw Malinowski described as myth functioning as the 'charter' of institutions (borrowing the term 'charter' from the historians of the Middle Ages).

I would not care to assert that this adjustment of the past to the present is to be found only in societies without writing. Indeed, it is often quite easy to show major discrepancies between the image of the past shared by members of a particular social group, and the surviving records of that past. A recurrent myth (to be found in many forms in our own society, today) is that of the 'founding fathers'; the story of Martin Luther founding the Protestant church, of Émile Durkheim (or Max Weber)

[46] Rousso (1987).
[47] Cf. Erikson (1968), esp. 701ff.
[48] Reik (1920).
[49] Watt and Goody (1962–3), 310.

founding sociology, and so on. Generally speaking, what happens in the case of these myths is that differences between past and present are elided, and unintended consequences are turned into conscious aims, as if the main purpose of these past heroes had been to bring about the present – our present.

Writing and print are not powerful enough to stop the spread of myths of this kind. What they can do, however, is to preserve records of the past which are inconsistent with the myths, which undermine them – records of a past which has become awkward and embarrassing, a past which people for one reason or another do not wish to know about, though it might be better for them if they did. It might, for example, free them from the dangerous illusion that the past may be seen as a simple struggle between heroes and villains, good and evil, right and wrong. Myths are not to be despised, but reading them literally is not to be recommended. Writing and print thus assist the resistance of memory to manipulation.[50]

Historians also have a role to play in this process of resistance. Herodotus thought of historians as the guardians of memory, the memory of glorious deeds. I prefer to see historians as the guardians of the skeletons in the cupboard of the social memory, the 'anomalies', as the historian of science Thomas Kuhn calls them, which reveal weaknesses in grand and not-so-grand theories.[51] There used to be an official called the 'Remembrancer'. The title was actually a euphemism for debt collector. The official's job was to remind people of what they would have liked to forget. One of the most important functions of the historian is to be a remembrancer.

[50] Schudson (1992), 206.
[51] Kuhn (1962), 52–3.

4

The Language of Gesture in Early Modern Italy

❧

The knowledge of gestures is necessary to the historian.
Bonifacio, *L'arte dei cenni* (1616)

T his chapter will discuss, with special reference to Italy, the problems involved in writing the history of gesture, or better, in integrating gesture into history. It will be concerned with the problem of conceptualization, distinguishing conscious and unconscious, ritualized and spontaneous gestures, with the sources (visual as well as literary), with regional and social variations, and above all with changes over time, notably the increasing emphasis on bodily discipline or self-control, recommended in treatises by authors as different as Baldassare Castiglione and Carlo Borromeo. What was the significance of this new emphasis? What difference did it make to everyday life? Who was supposed to show this control, and in what situations? What forms did this discipline take? What possible relation can it have to the foreign travellers' stereotype of the wildly gesticulating Italian?

In the last generation, as was noted in chapter 2 above, the territory of the historian has expanded to include many new topics, such as the history of the body, including gesture.[1] Here as elsewhere Jacques Le Goff has been among the pioneers.[2] Opponents of this 'new history', as it is often called, assert that historians of this school trivialize the past. Three responses to this charge seem

[1] Barasch (1987); Schmitt (1981, 1990); Bremmer and Roodenburg (1991).
[2] Le Goff (1982, 1985).

appropriate. The first is to recognize the very real danger of trivialization whenever one of these topics is pursued for its own sake without any attempt to connect it with the surrounding culture. For an example of this approach one might cite Câmara Cascudo's historical dictionary of Brazilian gestures, a scholarly and fascinating book (and a good basis for future work), but a study which collects information without raising questions.[3]

A second response might be to argue that the notion of the 'trivial' needs to be problematized and relativized and more specifically that gestures were not taken lightly in early modern Europe. In England, the Quakers refused to observe what they called 'hat honour', in other words the custom of raising the hat to social superiors. In Russia, the question whether the act of blessing should be performed with two fingers or three was one of the issues leading to the schism in the Orthodox Church in the middle of the seventeenth century. Early modern Italy may lack spectacular debates over gesture of this kind. All the same, a Genoese patrician, Andrea Spinola, a crusader for the vanishing ideal of republican equality (below, p. 120), claimed that he had been imprisoned unjustly on account of his *gesti del corpo*, such as his proud way of walking into the room and his failure to stand up straight before the chancellor.[4] These gestures were regarded by the Genoese government as a form of 'dumb insolence', a phrase still current in the British army and a reminder that in some quarters at least, the rules of gesture continue to be taken seriously.

The third response might be to follow Sherlock Holmes, Sigmund Freud and Giovanni Morelli – not to mention Carlo Ginzburg, who first linked the three of them – and to assert the importance of the trivial, on the grounds that it so often provides clues to what is more significant.[5] Historians, like anthropologists and psychologists, can study gesture as a subsystem within the larger system of communication which we call 'culture'. This assumption is currently shared by many social and cultural historians. It may even seem obvious. So it may be useful to remind the reader at this point of the existence of a 'universalist' approach to gesture, reincarnated in the well-known books by

[3] Câmara Cascudo (*c*.1974).
[4] Spinola (1981), 126.
[5] Ginzburg (1990), 96–125.

Desmond Morris – despite the unresolved tension in his work
between universalizing zoological explanations of the gestures of
the 'naked ape' and attempts to map their cultural geography.[6]

As an example of more rigorous analysis pointing in the opposite direction, we may cite Ray Birdwhistell's famous demonstra-
tion that even unconscious gestures, such as modes of walking,
are not natural but learned, and so vary from one culture to
another. The same point had been made in the 1930s in a famous
essay by the anthropologist Marcel Mauss, who claimed to be
able to detect which Frenchwomen had been educated at convent
schools by observing the position of their hands when they were
walking.[7] It is this 'culturalist' approach which will be pursued
here, in the case of a society in which – according to its northern
visitors, at least – the language of gesture was and is particularly
eloquent: Italy.

To follow this road to the end it would first be necessary to
reconstruct the complete repertoire of gestures available in Italian
culture, the 'langue' from which individuals choose their individual 'paroles' according to their personalities or social roles. The
way would then be clear for a general discussion of the relation
between that repertoire and other aspects of the culture, including the local contrasts between public and private, sacred and
profane, decent and indecent, spontaneous and controlled behaviour, male and female decorum, and so on.

The surviving sources are inevitably inadequate for these tasks,
although they are quite as rich as any early modern historian has
a right to hope. They include contemporary encyclopaedias of
gestures such as *The Art of Gesture* (1616) by the lawyer
Giovanni Bonifacio and, at the end of the period, Andrea di
Jorio's *The Imitation of the Ancients Investigated in the Gestures
of the Neapolitans* (1832), which compares the evidence of classical vases and statues with what could be seen in the streets of
Naples in his own day.[8] More ambitious still, a book by Scipione
Chiaramonti, published in 1625, discussed gesture as part of a
general study of signs or 'semiotics', as he already called it.
Chiaramonti also devoted a few pages to the peculiarities of the
Italians.[9]

[6] Morris (1977, 1979).
[7] Birdwhistell (1970); cf. Mauss (1935).
[8] Bonifacio (1616); Jorio (1832); cf. Knowlson (1965); Chastel (1986).
[9] Chiaramonti (1625), 70ff.

To these systematic compilations may be added a number of observations by foreign travellers, casual but vivid and direct. The Catholic Montaigne, passing through Verona, and the Protestant Philip Skippon, passing through Padua, were both impressed by the lack of reverence shown by Italians in church, chatting during Mass, standing with their hats on and their backs to the altar or 'discoursing and laughing with one another'.[10] In Venice, John Evelyn recorded at least one insulting gesture which the two lexicographers mentioned above seem to have missed, biting one's own finger (presumably as a symbol of the adversary's penis). Shakespeare was already familiar with this insult, to which he gave an Italian context: 'I will bite my thumb at them; which is a disgrace to them if they bear it' (*Romeo and Juliet*, Act 1, scene 1).

Italian judicial archives are another important source. Courts often note the gestures leading to cases of assault and battery, including staring at one's adversary, *bravando* (strutting in a provocative manner) and of course offering insults such as 'making horns', publicly displaying one's private parts, and so on. Among other things, the archives confirm the existence of the finger-biting gesture mentioned by Evelyn, *mittendosi la dita in bocca*.[11] The Inquisition archives are of particular value because interrogators and clerks were instructed to observe and record with care the gestures of the accused.[12] It was for instance the Inquisition which recorded another gesture absent from both Bonifacio and Jorio, the denial of Christianity by pointing the index figure of the right hand heavenwards.[13] The art of the period can also be utilized as a source, despite the difficulty of measuring the distance between painted gestures and their equivalents in everyday life. A few art historians have commented on the representation of gestures of respect, submission, greeting, prayer, silence, admonition, despair, pride, aggression, and so on.[14]

The task of reconstructing the complete repertoire of Italian gestures is clearly too ambitious for a short chapter. All that can

[10] Montaigne (1992), 64; Skippon (1732), 534.
[11] Evelyn (1955), vol. 2, 173; Rome, Archivio di Stato, Tribunale del Governatore, Processi Criminali, '600, busta 50.
[12] Masini (1621), 157.
[13] Bennassar and Bennassar (1989), 313.
[14] Baxandall (1972), 56ff.; Heinz (1972); Chastel (1986); Barasch (1987); Spicer (1991); Fermor (1993).

reasonably be done is to discuss what appear to be the major changes in the system between 1500 and 1800. Unlike earlier work on the topic, this chapter will focus on everyday life rather than the ritualized gestures of kissing the Pope's foot, walking in procession, and so on.[15] Following the bias of the sources, it will be difficult to avoid devoting disproportionate attention to the upper classes and also to males, since one of the rules of the culture was that respectable women did not gesture, or at least not very much.

The changes to be emphasized here may be summed up in three hypotheses. The first is that of an increasing interest in gestures in this period, not only in Italy but in Europe more generally. The second hypothesis is that this self-consciousness was encouraged by a movement for the 'reform' of gesture which occurred in both Catholic and Protestant Europe in the age of the Reformations. The third and last hypothesis attempts to link this reform to the rise of the northern stereotype of the gesticulating Italian.

A New Interest in Gestures

The French historian Jean-Claude Schmitt has noted a new interest in gestures in the twelfth century. A similar point might be made about Western Europe in the early modern period, especially in the seventeenth century, as Schmitt himself admits.[16] In the case of England, for example, this interest can be seen in the writings of Francis Bacon; in John Bulwer's guide to hand gestures, the *Chirologia* (1644), which argued that these gestures 'disclose the present humour and state of the mind and will'; and in the observations of travellers abroad, including John Evelyn, Thomas Coryate and Philip Skippon.

In the case of France, penetrating analyses of gesture can be found in the writings of Montaigne, Pascal, La Bruyère, La Rochefoucauld, and Saint-Simon, as well as in the art theory of Charles Lebrun. The history of gesture and posture attracted the attention of scholars and of artists such as Nicolas Poussin, whose *Last Supper* reveals his awareness of the ancient Roman

[15] Trexler (1980), 87–94, 99–111, etc.; Muir (1981).
[16] Schmitt (1990), 362–3.

custom of reclining to eat. More practical advice was offered in Antoine Courtin's *Nouveau traité de la civilité* (1671), which told readers not to cross their legs or to make 'grand gestures with the hands' when speaking. Crossed legs, incidentally, had a variety of meanings. In some contexts they signified power, but in others lack of dignity. The posture was forbidden to women, but it was not always permitted to men either.[17]

The contrast between Spanish gravity and French vivacity made by Baldassare Castiglione in his *Courtier* (book 2, chapter 37) became a commonplace in the seventeenth century. For example, Carlos García's treatise of 1617 on the 'antipathy' between the French and the Spaniards drew attention to the different ways in which they walked, ate, or used their hands. According to García, the Frenchman walks with his hand on the pommel of his sword and his cloak on one shoulder, while the Spaniard throws out his legs like a cock and pulls at his moustache. 'When Frenchmen walk the streets in a group they laugh, jump, talk and make such a noise that they can be heard a league away; the Spaniards on the contrary walk straight ahead, gravely and coolly, without speaking or engaging in any immodest or extravagant action.'[18]

García's work is not without relevance to Italy. Indeed, it went through thirteen Italian editions between 1636 and 1702, besides being translated into English and German. At a time when France and Spain were the leading European powers, the book had political relevance. García's influence, or at least that of the commonplaces which he articulated with unusual vivacity and detail, can be seen in an anonymous manuscript account of the Venetian Republic written in the late seventeenth century, the *Historical-Political Examination*, which divided a hundred leading politicians into those with the grave 'Spanish genius' (*genio spagnuolo*), and those with a livelier *genio francese*.[19] There was a similar conflict between the French and Spanish styles in mid seventeenth-century Rome. The architect Francesco Borromini, for example, wore Spanish dress (unfortunately his gestures are not recorded).[20] No wonder then that the Englishman Richard Lassels described 'the Italian humour' as 'a middling humour

[17] Barasch (1987), 180–1.
[18] García (1617), ch. 14.
[19] Venice, Biblioteca Marciana, MS Gradenigo 15.
[20] Wittkower (1967).

between the too much of the French and the too little of the Spaniard'.[21]

Linguistic evidence points in the same directions. In the first place, towards an increasing interest in gesture, revealed by the development of an increasingly rich and subtle language to describe it. In the second place, towards the Spanish model, for the language of gesture developed in early modern Italy by borrowing from Spanish such terms as *etichetta*, *complimento*, *crianza* (good manners), *disinvoltura* (negligence) and *sussiego* (gravity or calm).[22]

The multiplication of Italian texts discussing gesture from the Renaissance onwards (a century or so earlier than in other countries) confirms the impression of increasing interest in the topic. The literature of morals and manners contains many relevant observations on appropriate gestures for women as well as for men. For example, the anonymous *Decor puellarum* (1471), a vernacular text despite its Latin title, tells girls to keep their eyes on the ground, to eat and speak with gravity, to walk and stand with the right hand over the left, and to keep their feet together, so as not to look like the prostitutes of Venice. The gesture of one hand clasping the other was a 'formula of submission' to be found for example in some of Giotto's female figures.[23] Castiglione's *Courtier* (1528) also comments on the appropriate posture (*lo stare*) and gestures (*i movimenti*) for both women and men, emphasizing the need for 'supreme grace' in women, and also a kind of timidity which reveals their modesty.[24]

Alessandro Piccolomini's dialogue *La Rafaella* (1539) follows in the footsteps of Castiglione but is concerned exclusively with the education of women, including their movements and 'carriage' (*portatura*). Ladies are told to walk slowly, but also 'to flee affectation' and 'to show a certain negligence and a certain don't think much about it' [*mostrar un certo disprezzo e un certo non molto pensare*], a close relative of Castiglione's famous *sprezzatura*.[25] Angelo Firenzuola's dialogue *Delle bellezze delle donne* (1541) is concerned with grace as well as beauty. The speakers

[21] Lassels (1654), 150.
[22] Beccaria (1968), 161–207.
[23] Barasch (1987), 42, 46.
[24] Burke (1995), 29–30.
[25] Piccolomini (1539), 56–7.

recommend 'elegance' (*leggiadria*) defined in terms of grace, modesty, nobility, measure and good manners. They also praise the 'air' of a beautiful woman and the 'majesty' of a woman who 'sits with a certain grandeur, speaks with gravity, smiles with modesty and behaves like a queen'. Giovanni Della Casa's *Galateo* (1558) and Stefano Guazzo's *Civile conversatione* (1574) also make a number of points about appropriate gesture and the eloquence of the body. So does the literature of the dance, notably the treatise *Il ballarino* (1581) by Fabrizio Caroso, which discusses not only the various kinds of step but also tells gentlemen how to deal with their cloak and sword, how to make a proper bow, how to take a lady's hand, and so on.

In the seventeenth century, as we have seen, a lawyer from Verona, Giovanni Bonifacio, produced the first encyclopaedia of gesture. Bonifacio based himself mainly on the Bible and on classical authors, which makes him less useful than he might have been as a source for Italian social history. All the same, his book bears eloquent witness to contemporary interest in the topic. So do the books about the theatre which begin to appear at this period. G. D. Ottonelli's *The Christian Moderation of the Theatre* (1652) and A. Perrucci's *Art of Representation* (1699) were both concerned with what they call the 'art' or 'rules' of gesture. The relation between happenings on and off the stage is not a simple one, but to foreign visitors at least actors appear to stylize and perhaps to exaggerate the gestures current in their culture.

In their different ways, the texts cited above reveal considerable interest not only in the psychology of gestures, as the outward signs of hidden emotions, but also – and this is the innovation – in what we might call their 'sociology'. It was frequently asserted that gestures formed a universal language, but this 'universalist' position was opposed by a 'culturalist' one. A number of authors were concerned with the way in which gestures vary, or ought to vary, according to what might be called the various 'domains' of gesture (the family, the court, the church and so on), and also to the actors – young or old, male or female, respectable or shameless, noble or common, lay or clerical. One might say therefore that early modern texts bear witness to an increasing interest not only in the vocabulary of gesture, exemplified by Bonifacio's dictionary, but also in its 'grammar', in the sense of the rules for correct expression, and finally in its various 'dialects' (to use di Jorio's term) or 'sociolects' as modern linguists would put it.[26]

It is worth emphasizing the connections between this interest in gesture and contemporary concerns with social variations in language and costume, and more generally with the study of men and animals in the so-called 'age of observation'. For an example of the practical value of this knowledge, we may turn to an English visitor to Italy, Fynes Morison. Morison wanted to see Cardinal Bellarmine in Rome and paid him a visit, 'being attired like an Italian and careful not to use any strange gesture' which might have given him away as an English Protestant.[27]

The Reform of Gesture

The increasing consciousness of gesture was linked to attempts by some people to change the gestures of others. Protestants were concerned with behaviour as well as belief, while in Catholic countries a reform of gesture formed part of the moral discipline of the Counter-Reformation.[28] For example, in the *Constitutions* which he issued for his diocese of Verona around the year 1527, Gianmatteo Giberti, who came to be regarded as a model bishop, ordered his clergy to show gravity 'in their gestures, their walk and their bodily style' ('in gestu, incessu et habitu corporis'). The term 'habitus' was of course well known in this period thanks to Latin translations of Aristotle, long before Marcel Mauss and Pierre Bourdieu made it their own. San Carlo Borromeo, another model bishop, also recommended *gravitas* and decorum to the clergy of his diocese, 'in their walking, standing, sitting' and in 'the lowering of their eyes'. He told preachers to avoid 'histrionic' gestures, such as throwing out their arms like a 'gladiator' or making indecorous movements of the fingers.[29] San Carlo would not have approved of the preachers described by Giraldi in his discourse on comedies, whose gestures resembled those of actors or charlatans.

San Carlo, however, concerned himself with the laity as well, recommending decorum, dignity and 'moderation' (*misura*) and

---

[26] Jorio (1832), xxii; cf. Bremmer and Roodenburg (1991), 3, 36.
[27] Quoted in Mączak (1978), 191.
[28] Knox (1990), 113–14.
[29] Borromeo (1758), 23, 87, 90.

warning them against laughing, shouting, dancing and tumultuous behaviour.[30] At much the same time, his episcopal colleague at Tortona concerned himself with behaviour in church. 'Let no one dare to stroll through the church ... or lean on the altars, holy water stoup or font. Or sit irreverently with their backs turned to the Blessed Sacrament,' make 'dishonourable signs' to a woman, or talk of secular business.[31] A little later, the anonymous *Discourse against Carnival* discussed the need for order, restraint, prudence and sobriety and underlined the dangers of *pazzia*, a term which might in this context be translated not as 'madness' but as 'loss of self-control'.[32]

The reform of Italian gesture should not be tied too closely to the Counter-Reformation. Cicero had already discouraged what he called 'theatrical' movements or walking too quickly (or too slowly), and from the Renaissance onwards his authority was taken as seriously in the domain of gesture as in that of speech.[33] In the case of women, there is a long tradition of texts advising restraint. In the fourteenth century, young women were recommended to show timidity and modesty in their gestures. They were to take small steps when they walked. They were not to support their head with their hands, not to show their teeth when they smiled and not to weep loudly.[34] The humanist Francesco Barbaro's treatise *On Marriage* (1416) told wives to show restraint 'in the movements of the eyes, in their walking, and in the movement of their bodies; for the wandering of the eyes, a hasty gait, and excessive movement of the hands and other parts of the body cannot be done without loss of dignity, and such actions are always joined to vanity and are signs of frivolity.'[35] Similar recommendations for unmarried girls were made in the fifteenth-century treatise *Decor puellarum*, discussed above.

On the other hand, it was relatively rare before 1500 to advise boys or men to restrain their behaviour in this way. The fifteenth-century humanist Matteo Vegio was unusual in warning boys (in a treatise on education, *De liberorum educatione*, book 5, chapter 3) to concern themselves with the modesty of their

[30] Taviani (1969), 5–43; *San Carlo* (1986), 911, 926–7.
[31] Quoted Tacchella (1966), 75–6.
[32] Taviani (1969), 67–81.
[33] Bremmer and Roodenburg (1991), 28–9.
[34] Lazard (1993).
[35] Kohl and Witt (1978), 202.

gestures ('verecundia motuum gestuumque corporis'). It was the sixteenth-century reform of gesture which extended to males, first the clergy and then the upper-class laity, ideals of restraint which had earlier been formulated with women in mind.

In his treatise *On the Position of Cardinal* (1510), the clerical humanist Paolo Cortese warned against ugly movements of the lips, frequent hand movements and walking quickly, recommending what he called a senatorial gravity. Again, Baldassare Castiglione warned his readers against affected gestures and recommended the courtier to be 'restrained' (*ritenuto, rimesso*). Although Castiglione's dialogue deals with men and women separately and might thus be taken as a guide to the construction (or reconstruction) of masculinity and femininity, his stress on restraint may be viewed as an example of the feminization of polite behaviour at a time when the nobility was losing its military role.

The most detailed as well as the best-known Italian recommendations for the reform of gesture are those to be found in Giovanni Della Casa's *Galateo*. The ideal of this Counter-Reformation prelate is almost as secular as that of Castiglione or Firenzuola. It is to be 'elegant' and 'well bred' (*leggiadro, costumato*) 'in walking, in standing, in sitting, in movements, in carriage and in clothing' (chapter 28). To achieve elegance, it is necessary to be aware of one's gestures in order to control them. The hands and legs in particular need discipline. For example, in chapter 6 of the treatise noblemen are advised, in the author's version of the classical topos, not to walk too quickly (like a servant), or too slowly (like a woman), but to aim at the golden mean.

A number of Italian writers of this period contributed to the chorus urging restraint. For example, Giovanni Battista Della Porta, whose activities as scientist and dramatist should have given him a double interest in the subject, recommended the readers of his *On Human Physiognomy* (1586) not to make hand gestures while speaking (in Italy!). Stefano Guazzo, whose book on conversation and deportment was cited above, discussed the need to find the golden mean, as he put it, between 'the immobility of statues' and the exaggerated movements of monkeys ('l'instabilità delle simie'). As for Caroso's treatise on dancing, it has been argued that it expresses a more restrained ideal than its predecessors, suggesting that the court dance was diverging more and more from the peasant dance in this period.[36] After one reads this corpus of texts, not to mention the observations on movement made by contemporary art critics such as Giorgio Vasari and Ludovico Dolce, many Italian portraits of this period begin to look like translations into visual terms of the recommendations of the treatises. Whether a given portrait expresses the ideals of the artist, the self-image of the sitter or the artist's image of the sitter's self-image, the gestures portrayed – which to post-romantic eyes often seem intolerably artificial – may be read as evidence of attempts to create new habits, a second nature.

Movement was represented as gender-specific, with female delicacy complementing male vivacity.[37] It should be added that the range of female gestures in Renaissance portraits (one hand holding a fan or a book, or one hand on the breast, or the hands clasped in the submissive gesture already discussed) is much narrower than that available to males. The gestures portrayed in portraits of men in this period include the hand on the hip or sword, the hand supporting the cheek (a sign of melancholy), the hand pressed to the heart, and the hand extended in the orator's pose recommended by Cicero and Quintilian, while full-length portraits of standing figures began to show them with crossed legs, now a sign of ease rather than of lack of dignity.[38] However, the rejection by the priests who had commissioned it of Caravaggio's painting of St Matthew because it showed the saint sitting with his legs crossed (*le gambe incavalcate*) reminds us that the clergy had to be almost as sensitive to decorum as women.[39] In eighteenth-century Venice, anonymous verses about the fashionable ladies of the time were still mocking *el sentar a la sultana*, in other words crossing the legs when seated.[40] The verses may express a reaction against the relaxation of manners characteristic of the European nobility in the age of Rousseau, but the values they express are traditional.

Della Casa's points are mainly negative. One suspects that this inquisitor kept in mind, if not in his study, an index of forbidden gestures (including the hand on the hip, which he interpreted as a

[36] *Dizionario Biografico degli Italiani* (43 vols, in progress, Rome 1960–), s.v. 'Caroso'.
[37] Fermor (1993).
[38] Heinz (1972); Burke (1987); Spicer (1991).
[39] Bellori (1672), 219.
[40] Molmenti (1879), 3, 311–12.

sign of pride). Yet it would be a mistake to discuss the reform of gesture in purely negative terms, as part of the history of repression. It can also be viewed more positively as an art, or a contribution to the art of living. This is the way in which Castiglione saw it, not to mention the dancing-masters – and in the seventeenth century, if not earlier, dancing formed part of the curriculum of some Italian colleges for nobles. It was a festive mode of inculcating discipline.[41]

If the reformers of gesture had a positive ideal in mind, what was it? The ideal might be (and sometimes was, as we have seen) described as a Spanish model, influential in central Europe as well as Italy and including language and clothes as well as gesture. If this ideal had to be summed up in a single word, that word might well be 'gravity'. The German humanist Heinrich Agrippa testified in 1530 that the Italians 'walk rather slowly, are dignified in their gestures'.[42] Another German, Hieronymus Turler, made the same point (whether from observation or copying Agrippa) in the 1570s; 'the Italian has a slow gait, a grave gesture' ('incessum tardiusculum, gestum gravem').[43] Joseph Addison, arriving in Milan (still part of the Spanish Empire) from France, found the Italians 'stiff, ceremonious and reserved' by contrast to the French.[44]

The Italians were or had been closer to the French style of vicacity, so much so that they sometimes perceived Spanish gesture as an absence. Thus Pedro de Toledo, Viceroy of Naples in the middle of the sixteenth century, surprised the local nobility by the fact that when he gave audience he remained immobile, like a 'marble statue'.[45] The phrase was, or became, a topos. One of Toledo's successors was described by the political theorist Traiano Boccalini, who viewed him in Naples in 1591, as so grave and motionless 'that I should never have known whether he was a man or a figure of wood'. According to Boccalini, the viceroy did not even blink. The Venetian ambassador to Turin in 1588 described the prince's wife, a Spanish Infanta, as 'brought up in the Spanish style ... she stands with great tranquillity [*sussiego*], she seems immobile.' Guazzo's remark about the need

[41] Brizzi (1976), 254–5; cf. Lippe (1974); Braun and Gugerli (1993).
[42] Quoted Knox (1995), 33–4.
[43] Turler (1574), book 1, ch. 4.
[44] Addison (1705), 373.
[45] Caraffa (1880).

to avoid the immobility of statues, quoted above, must have had a topical ring to it.[46]

The employment of the term 'model' is not intended to imply that the Italians of the period always idealized the Spaniards. On the contrary, they were much hated and frequently mocked, the mockery extending on occasion to their gestures. Their gravity was sometimes interpreted as the stiffness of arrogance. The charge of arrogance was incarnated in the figure of 'Capitano' on the Italian stage. This figure from the Commedia dell'Arte was often given a Spanish name such as 'Matamoros', together with stylized *bravure*, in other words aggressive, macho gestures intended to challenge or provoke his neighbours. An eighteenth-century description of Naples under Spanish hegemony, the *Massime del governo spagnolo* written by the nobleman Paolo Matteo Doria (a friend of Vico's), gave a highly critical account of the hispanized gestures of the upper nobility, notably an 'affected negligence' (*affettata disinvoltura*) and 'determined, arrogant movements' (*movimenti risoluti e disprezzanti*), displaying superiority over others.

This discussion of Italian perceptions of Spain makes no claim that Spaniards of this period always followed the model just described. It was probably restricted to upper-class males, or to some of them, and it may also have been limited to particular situations, notably rituals – although, curiously enough, the notoriously rigid rituals of the court seem to have reached Spain from Burgundy only in the mid-sixteenth century.[47] As for the explanation of change in Italy, it would be facile and superficial to attribute it to Spanish 'influence'. The appeal of the Spanish model in the sixteenth and seventeenth centuries was surely that it met a pre-existing demand for stricter bodily control, the reform of gesture discussed in this section.

The history of that demand has been written by the sociologist Norbert Elias in his famous study of the 'process of civilization' (by which he generally means self-control, more especially table manners), concentrating on northern Europe but including a few observations on the Italians, who were, after all, pioneers in the use of the fork.[48] More recently, Michel Foucault offered an alternative history of the body, examining the negative aspects in

[46] Burke (1987); cf. Knox (1989).
[47] Hofmann (1985).
[48] Elias (1939).

his *Discipline and Punish*, the more positive ones in his *History of Sexuality*, and emphasizing control over the bodies of others as well as over the self. Elias and Foucault were concerned with the practice as well as the theory of gesture and bodily control. It is time to ask whether the Italian reformers of gesture succeeded in their aims.

The Gesticulating Italian

The reform discussed in the previous section was not peculiarly Italian, but part of a general Western 'process of civilization' (there are parallels in other parts of the world, such as China and Japan, but their history remains to be written). The hypothesis to be presented here is that the reform of gesture, if not more rigorous, was at least more successful in the northern Protestant parts of Europe, such as Britain, the Netherlands and the German-speaking regions, than in the Catholic south. The result was to increase the gap between northern and southern behaviour and in particular to make northerners more critical of Italians. The stereotype of the gesticulating Italian seems to have come into existence in the early modern period, reflecting the contrast between two gestural cultures, associated with two styles of rhetoric (laconic versus copious) and other differences as well.

The contrast is not one between the presence and the absence of gesture, though it was sometimes perceived as such. Nor is it an opposition between a natural and an artificial style, for all body languages are artificial in the sense that they have to be learned.[49] What we observe in this period – at second hand – is rather the increasing distance between two body languages, which might be described as the flamboyant and the disciplined. If the Italians perceived the Spaniards as gesturing too little, the northerners came increasingly to perceive the southerners as gesturing too much. Their criticisms echoed and perhaps exaggerated the criticisms of the Italian reformers, some of which have been quoted above.

In the Netherlands, the critique of gesticulation goes back at least as far as Erasmus and his textbook of good manners for boys, *De civilitate morum puerilium*. An eighteenth-century

---

[49] Birdwhistell (1970).

Dutch manual of etiquette condemned the Italians 'who speak with their head, arms, feet and the whole body', and claimed that the French, the English and the Dutch had all abandoned such gesticulations.[50] It might be more accurate to say that France was divided between the northern and the southern styles, just as it was split between Catholics and Protestants. In this context it is interesting to find a French Calvinist, the printer Henri Estienne, criticizing the exaggerated gestures of the Italians in a dialogue he published in 1578, and claiming that the French 'n'aiment les gesticulations'.[51] In the nineteenth century, a French book on etiquette warned its readers, 'Gardez-vous de gesticuler comme un Gascon.'[52]

In English, the pejorative term to 'gesticulate', defined by the *Oxford English Dictionary* as the use of 'much' or 'foolish' gestures, is documented from 1613 onwards.[53] From about this time onwards, we find British observers commenting with surprise or disdain on what they regard as the excessive gesticulations of the Italians – or the Greeks, or the French, mocked by *The English Spy* in 1691 for their 'Apish Gestures' and their 'Finger-Talk as if they were conversing with the Deaf'. For example, Thomas Coryat, in Venice in 1608, noted what he called the 'extraordinary' greeting customs of the natives, striking the breast or kissing one another. In the church of San Giorgio, he noted 'one kind of gesture which seemeth to me both very unseemly and ridiculous', that of people who 'wag their hands up and down very often'.[54]

The gestures of preachers attracted particularly unfavourable attention from Protestant observers. William Bedell, in Venice at the same time as Coryat, condemned the friars for 'the antics of their gesture more than player- or fencer-like'. Philip Skippon, in Rome in 1663, described a Jesuit preaching on Piazza Navona 'with much action and postures of his body', while Gilbert Burnet, who visited Italy in the 1680s, complained of the 'many comical expressions and gestures' of a Capuchin preacher in Milan.[55] Burnet would not have appreciated being told that he

[50] Bremmer and Roodenburg (1991), 160.
[51] Quoted Knox (1990), 103.
[52] Montandon (1995), 62.
[53] Cf. Schmitt (1981).
[54] Coryat (1611), 399, 369.
[55] Bedell quoted in Chambers and Pullan (1992), 195; Skippon (1732), 665; Burnet (1686), 110, cf. 197.

was echoing the recommendations of San Carlo Borromeo, just as Borromeo would not have appreciated learning that resistance to his decrees had lasted more than a century.

In Naples, the language of the body was even more visible than it was elsewhere, at least to the British visitor: to John Moore in 1781, for example, noting the 'great gesticulation' of a storyteller, or to J. J. Blunt in the 1820s, observing 'infinite gesticulation' during a reading of Ariosto.[56] In the early nineteenth century, an American writer, Washington Irving, was still more explicit in his diagnosis of the symptoms of the Italian national character, as he viewed from his café table on Piazza San Marco a conversation conducted 'with Italian vivacity and gesticulation'.[57] Stendhal too commented on the southern love of 'pantomime' and the preference for gesturing over speaking.[58]

The texts quoted here remain insufficient to support any grand hypotheses, but at least they may give a fascinating problem more visibility. The simple contrast between north and south, Protestant and Catholic, will of course have to be refined. Where, for example, should one place Poland? In what ways did Spanish gravity differ from British self-control? To what extent were these stereotypes of national character generalizations about a single social group, the noblemen?

[56] Moore (1781), letter 60; Blunt (1823), 290.
[57] Irving (1824), vol. 1, 103.
[58] Crouzet (1982), 90, 106.

5

Frontiers of the Comic in Early Modern Italy

❧❧❧

ike gestures, discussed in the previous chapter, joking – or laughter – has its place among the objects of the new socio-cultural history. In the 1960s, Mikhail Bakhtin made the topic central to his study of Rabelais, emphasizing what he described as the liberating function of 'folk laughter'. In the 1970s, Keith Thomas devoted a lecture to 'the place of laughter' in early modern England. In the 1980s, Robert Darnton retold the story of 'the great cat massacre', a grisly practical joke played by some eighteenth-century Paris apprentices on their master and mistress.[1]

What is the point of the history of jokes? There are actually two points to make about change. In the first place, attitudes to joking have changed over time. Bakhtin, for example, suggested that the subversive laughter institutionalized in carnival was tolerated by the authorities in church and state in the Middle Ages and the Renaissance, but repressed thereafter. Another cultural theorist, Norbert Elias, might also be invoked here (although he had little explicit to say about laughter), because his idea of the rise of self-control and the raising of the 'threshold of embarrassment' is as applicable to joking as it is to table manners. In early modern Europe, jokes which had once been acceptable in dignified public places such as churches and courts were officially banished from them.

[1] Bakhtin (1965); Thomas (1977); Darnton (1984).

In the second place, the jokes themselves change over the centuries. They are difficult to translate from one period to another just as they are difficult to translate from one culture to another. What makes one generation laugh has little effect on the next. Hence there is a place for the history of laughter as there is for the sociology or anthropology of laughter.[2] Freud, of course, believed that jokes reveal underlying unconscious wishes or anxieties, which he viewed as unchanging.[3] His view of jokes was similar to his view of dreams, discussed in chapter 2 above. His emphasis on humour as an expression of anxiety offers us an important alternative to Bakhtin's view of liberating laughter (which had actually been put forward as an alternative to Freud).

The challenge to the cultural historian is to historicize Freud's theory. At the deepest psychological level he may well be right. All the same, changes in jokes over the long term suggest that a case can be made for the existence of a level intermediate between the worlds of consciousness and unconsciousness. At this level jokes change over time because the objects of anxiety change over time. For example, jokes about cuckoldry fall flat today, as revivals of Elizabethan or Restoration comedy demonstrate, although they seem to have made the contemporaries of Shakespeare and Wycherley dissolve into laughter. Joking may also be analysed in terms of displaced or sublimated aggression: class war, ethnic war or the war between the sexes conducted by other means. An anthropologist once described accusations of witchcraft as a social 'strain-gauge' which revealed the tensions specific to particular cultures.[4] Jokes are another such gauge.

Hence the need for cultural historians to ask: When is a joke not a joke? When, where, for whom is a given joke funny or unfunny? What are the limits, the boundaries, the frontiers of the comic? How different do jokes appear from different viewpoints and how do their meanings shift in the course of time? The aim of this chapter is to address such problems by focusing on a single comic genre, the practical joke or *beffa*, reinserting it into what might be called the contemporary 'system of the comic', in other words the varieties of humour recorded in Italy in the late medieval and early modern period, their definitions, their functions, their genres and so on.

[2] Propp (1976); Apte (1985); Mulkay (1988).
[3] Freud (1905).
[4] Marwick (1964).

The approach adopted here will be an anthropological one, in the sense of keeping close to indigenous categories and distinctions between jest and earnest. This is the justification for the many Italian words which will appear below. An attempt will be made to follow Darnton's advice to 'capture otherness', in other words to concentrate on what is most alien to us in the past and to try to make it intelligible.[5] Hence the emphasis here will fall on what is funny no longer, rather than on cultural continuities, important as they are.

The System of the Comic in Italy, 1350–1550

To begin with a sketch of this 'system' from Boccaccio to Bandello, or more generally from the Black Death to the Counter-Reformation. Despite the fact that Jacob Burckhardt, in his famous essay on the Renaissance, devoted some perceptive pages to what he called 'modern mockery and humour' ('der moderne Spott und Witz'), the subject has not attracted many historians.[6] Yet it certainly interested contemporaries, as the language of the period quickly reveals.

In the Italian of this time, there was a rich variety of terms available to distinguish varieties of play and humour. Words for the joke itself included *baia, beffa, burla, facezia, giuoco, leggerezza, pazzia, piacevolezza* and *scherzo*, while the joker was known as a *beffardo, beffatore, buffone, burlona, giuocatore* or *scherzatore*. Verbs included *burlare, giocare, uccellare*, while a distinction was made between *beffare* and the milder but more continuous *beffeggiare*, which we might translate as 'to tease'. Adjectives were richest of all: *beffabile, beffevole, burlesco, faceto, festevole, giocoso, grottesco, mottevole, scherzoso, sciocco*, and so on. The richness of vocabulary suggests that Italians were indeed connoisseurs in this domain.

The variety of comic genres deserves to be emphasized. They included comedy itself, whether 'learned' or popular, including the original 'slapstick' comedy of Harlequin in the Commedia dell'Arte. Stories (*novelle*) were often comic, while jokes often took the form of stories, *facezie*, which were collected and

[5] Darnton (1984), 4.
[6] Burckhardt (1860), ch. 2, section 4.

printed. Famous collections include the stories attributed to the Tuscan priest Arlotto Mainardi and those collected by the humanists Poggio Bracciolini and Angelo Poliziano, the latter published in 1548 under the name of the editor, Ludovico Domenichi.[7] Sermons often contained funny stories of this kind, thus combining the serious with the comic.

Paradox was much appreciated, as in the mock eulogies by Francesco Berni and Ortensio Lando.[8] So was nonsense-verse. The Florentine barber-poet Burchiello's contributions to this genre were immortalized by a new verb, *burchielleggare*. Parody was another favoured genre. Pulci's *Morgante*, for instance, mocked romances of chivalry. Aretino's *Ragionamenti* mocked courtesy books. The *Aeneid* and the epitaph were parodied in now-forgotten works of the seventeenth century such as Gianbattista Lalli's *L'Eneide travestite* (1618) or the Venetian patrician Gianfrancesco Loredan's *Il cimiterio* (1680) or A. M. del Priuli's *Epitafi giocosi* (1680).[9]

There were also a number of comic forms in the visual arts. In the Palazzo del Te in Mantua, designed by Giulio Romano, there are visual shocks like the frieze in which some pieces seem to be slipping and the frescoed ceilings which appear to be crashing down on the visitor.[10] They should perhaps be understood as a kind of practical joke. The portraits of the Milanese painter Arcimboldo, who made faces out of fruit, or fish, or books, were demonstrations of his wit. The imitation of the recently rediscovered classical 'grotesques' included statues for gardens, like Grand Duke Cosimo de' Medici's court dwarf Morgante (named after a famous giant) in the Boboli Gardens in Florence, represented naked, paunchy and sitting astride a turtle with his penis hanging down onto the shell.[11] Gardens were a place for play, for liberation from social conventions. In what we might describe as the private 'theme park' of Bomarzo, constructed a few miles from Viterbo for one of the Orsini family in the late sixteenth century, there was, for instance, a gigantic stone hell mouth which apparently functioned as a cool site for picnics. That this part of the 'Sacred Wood' was a joke, even if a joke on the edge

---

[7] Luck (1958); Fontes (1987).
[8] Grendler (1969); Borsellino (1973), 41–65.
[9] Rochon (1975), 83–102; Larivaille (1980).
[10] Gombrich (1984).
[11] Battisti (1962), 278ff.; Barolsky (1978), 153ff.

of blasphemy, is suggested by the inscription, 'lasciate ogni pensiero' ('leave behind every thought'), parodying Dante, and confirmed by the remarks in a contemporary discussion of grottos that they should be furnished with 'frightful or ridiculous masks'.[12]

No discussion of medieval or early modern humour would be complete without reference to the professional fools who could be found at court and elsewhere. A number of Italians of the time achieved inter-regional if not international fame in this profession, among them Dolcibene, the two Gonellas, Borso d'Este's Scocola at Ferrara (immortalized in the frescoes at Schifanoia), Beatrice d'Este's Diodato at Milan, and Isabella d'Este's Fritella at Mantua.[13]

The idea of the comic or the playful was not sharply defined in this period but shaded into entertainment, or diversion – *spasso, diporto, trattenimento, trastullo* – at one end of the spectrum, and at the other into tricks and insults – *inganni, truffe, affronti, diffamazioni, offese, scherni*. Two sixteenth-century informants bear witness to the difficulty of marking the boundary. In his dialogue *The Courtier* (1528), Baldassare Castiglione defined the *burla* as a 'friendly deceit' which 'does not give offence, or at least not very much' (book 2, section 85). Again, in his conduct book the *Galateo* (1558), Giovanni Della Casa distinguished *beffe* from insults only in terms of the intention of the perpetrator, since the effects on the victim were more or less the same (chapter 19). This ambiguity, or ambivalence, raises the question of the limits of the permissible. How far could one go without going too far, in what direction, with whom, about what? Although the idea of transgression is central to the comic, the limits or boundaries transgressed are always unstable, varying with the locale, region, moment, period, and the social groups involved.

Looking back at Renaissance Italy from our own time, or even from the seventeenth century, what appears most striking, or strange, is the generosity or permeability of the limits. Religious matters might be the object of jokes without causing offence, at least on occasion. Mattello, a court fool at Mantua, dressed as a

---

[12] Battisti (1962), 125ff.; Barolsky (1978); Bredecamp (1985); Lazzaro (1990), 137, 142, 306.
[13] Luzio and Renier (1891); Malaguzzi Valeri (1913–23), vol. 1, 563–4; Welsford (1935), 8–19, 128–37.

friar and parodied ecclesiastical rituals.[14] In the introduction to the stories of Antonfrancesco Grazzini, set at carnival, a lady says that even friars and nuns are allowed to enjoy themselves at this time and to dress as members of the opposite sex. Priests might be jesters, like Fra Mariano at the court of Leo X.[15] Boundaries existed all the same. In Castiglione's *Courtier* (book 2, section 93), for instance, Bernardo Bibbiena criticizes Boccaccio for a joke which 'goes beyond the limits' (*passa il termine*).

Ambiguity also leads to the question of function. Was laughter always an end in itself, or might it be a means to another end? One possibility to be taken seriously is the Russian folklorist Vladimir Propp's idea of laughter on certain occasions as a kind of ritual. Easter laughter in particular may be interpreted as ritual laughter. A case has been made for the presence of ritual elements in the humour of a sixteenth-century comic figure, Bertoldo.[16] We shall soon see examples of laughter as an instrument of vengeance.

The *Beffa*

The practical joke, trick or *beffa*, otherwise known as the *burla*, *giarda* or *natta* and frequently described in Italian jest-books, stories and other sources, was not of course unique to the peninsula or to the period under discussion. Whether or not practical jokes are a cultural universal, the recurrent figure of the trickster in world folklore (including that of China, West Africa, and the Indians of North America) suggests that they are at the very least extremely widespread. Such figures as Panurge and Till Eulenspiegel (not to mention medieval *fabliaux*) bear witness to the love of *beffe* in northern and central Europe, while in parts of the Mediterranean world, from Andalusia to Crete, anthropologists find the custom very much alive among young adult males.[17]

All the same, there was apparently an unusual emphasis on this kind of humour in Italy, especially in Florence, 'la capitale de la *beffa*'.[18] Boccaccio's *Decameron* makes an obvious starting-

---

[14] Malaguzzi Valeri (1913–23), vol. 1, 563.
[15] Graf (1916).
[16] Propp (1976), ch. 9; Bernardi (1990), 153; Camporesi (1976), 92.
[17] Brandes (1980); Herzfeld (1985).
[18] Rochon (1972), 28.

point for the study of the genre. The tricks occur in twenty-seven stories altogether, and the terms *beffa*, *beffare*, and *beffatore* are used eighty times.[19] Later in the century, *beffe* recur in the stories of Francesco Sacchetti. In the fifteenth century, they can be found in the tales of Masuccio Salernitano and Sabadino degli Arienti.[20] There is also the anonymous fifteenth-century story of a joke played on a fat carpenter by the architect Filippo Brunelleschi. This example is all the more interesting because it plays with the idea of identity in a period which Burckhardt has described as an age of individualism.[21]

As for *beffe* in the sixteenth-century *novella*, one finds them everywhere. In the stories of Antonfrancesco Grazzini (died 1584), 'the *beffa* is the key,' as a French critic puts it, occurring in eighteen stories.[22] They are even more important in Matteo Bandello, seventy *beffe* in 214 *novelle*.[23] The sixteenth-century material also includes plays, such as Machiavelli's *Mandragola* and Pietro Aretino's *Il Marescalco*, a carnival entertainment in which the Master of the Horse at the court of the Duke of Mantua is informed that the duke wishes him to marry. Bad news for him, since his tastes were not for the opposite sex, but he goes through the ceremony only to discover that his 'bride' is a page. The incident is described in the play as a '*burla*' (Act 5, Scene 11).[24]

To sum up this evidence and place it in comparative perspective, we might compare the American folklorist Stith Thompson's world survey of folktales with a specialized motif-index of the Italian *novella* by D. P. Rotunda. For category X 0–99, 'Humor of Discomfiture', for instance, Thompson gives four examples, Rotunda twenty. In the case of category K 1200–99, 'Deception into a Humiliating Position', Thompson gives twenty-seven examples (including eight from Boccaccio), while Rotunda offers no fewer than seventy-two.[25] The Italians, more exactly the Tuscans, appear to have been obsessed by this theme.

Needless to say there are problems for a cultural historian in handling such literary evidence. The stories are stylized, indeed

---

[19] Cf. Mazzotti (1986).
[20] Rochon (1975), 65–170.
[21] Varese (1955), 767–802; Rochon (1972), 211–376.
[22] Rochon (1972), 45–98; cf. Rodini (1970), 153–6.
[23] Rochon (1972), 121–66.
[24] Rochon (1972), 99–110.
[25] Thompson (1955–8); Rotunda (1942).

they were subject to a double stylization as they circulated through two media, oral and printed. They are full of *topoi*. The same stories have different heroes. Fiction is of course good evidence of fantasy, of the collective imagination. But can we draw conclusions about social life from this evidence? Was the *beffa* a social custom or just a literary game? Practical jokes are known to have been played in some courts in Renaissance Italy, for example in Milan under the Sforza or in Ferrara under the Este.[26] Other evidence comes from judicial records regarding joking which gave offence and so led to legal proceedings. These records suggest that taverns were a favourite locale for *beffe*, as in the case of the trick played on a certain Furlinfan in the village of Lio Maggiore in 1315, for instance.[27] They also suggest that carnival was a favourite time for *beffe*, witness the case of a mysterious coil of rope, from Rome in 1551, when seven Jews pretended to arrest a Neapolitan, at the time of their carnival (Purim), not the carnival of the Christians. This 'case' could have been made into a *novella*.[28]

Material culture also provides evidence of joking. Let us return for a moment to the Renaissance garden, where there might be hidden fountains activated at a sign from the host, taking the guests by surprise and soaking them to the skin. This mild form of *beffa* was current in aristocratic circles, and can be documented at Caprarola, for instance, designed by Vignola for the Farnese, as well as at Pratolino, designed by Buontalenti for Francesco I de' Medici, where Montaigne was among the victims.[29] It was not very different from the common Italian practice of throwing water at carnival.

Some of the examples cited above raise the problem of the limits of joking, the frontier between relatively harmless or disinterested deception and more serious trickery or aggression. In northern Italy in the sixteenth century, *dare la burla* was a standard phrase employed to describe false promises of marriage.[30] Again, in an age when jokes were often insulting and insults sometimes took playful forms, it was inevitable that someone would overstep the customary limits and that some cases would

[26] Malaguzzi Valeri (1913–23), vol. 1, 560ff.; Prandi (1990), 78.
[27] Ortalli (1993), 67.
[28] Cohen (1988).
[29] Robertson (1992), 128; Lazzaro (1990), 65–8.
[30] Muir and Ruggiero (1990), 351.

end up in court. The difficulty of defining the frontiers of the comic is apparent in these records. In sixteenth-century Bologna, one victim of a verbal assault (by means of a sonnet) complained to the tribunal, but they considered the letter not to be defamatory but only 'a joke, containing something laughable'.[31] On the other hand, the painter Michelangelo di Caravaggio, who had a gift for getting himself into trouble, was called before the Tribunal of the Governor of Rome in 1603 (in company with other painters), charged with what their colleague Baglioni called 'verses in my dishonour'.[32]

Turning to the world of politics, think of Cesare Borgia and the famous trick he played on his enemies at Sinigaglia, a 'torpedo' (as Italo-American gangsters would have called it in the age of Al Capone). The story is told by Machiavelli in his famous 'Description of the way in which Duke Valentino (Cesare) assassinated Vitelozzo Vitelli', inviting Vitelozzo and his companions to enter his lodgings unarmed and having them strangled there. Machiavelli wrote in a cool deadpan manner, but elsewhere he expresses his enormous admiration for Cesare. It may not be too far from the point to suggest a link between his politics and his dramatic interest in *beffe*. His play *Mandragola* is 'Machiavellian' in its interest in stratagems, while his history of Florence is presented in dramatic terms.

Five further comments may place the *beffa* more firmly in its cultural context.

(1) The *beffa* was often presented as a 'work of art', to adapt Burckhardt's view of the Renaissance in general. It was supposed to give aesthetic pleasure, as well as the more obvious *Schadenfreude*, and it was sometimes described as *bella*. The titles of stories, Bandello's for instance, refer to a 'giocosa astuzia' (book 2, no. 45), or a 'piacevole e ridicolo inganno' (book 2, no. 47). Pleasant, that is, from the point of view of the joker or the bystanders, which is the point of view the reader is generally encouraged to take. Unless of course the victim turns the tables on the aggressor, for special pleasure is taken in what is called 'il contracambio', in other words the theme of *beffatore beffato*, the biter bit (Bandello, book 1, no. 3, for instance).

[31] Evangelisti (1992), 221.
[32] Friedlaender (1955), 271–2.

(2) The *beffa* was an appropriate form of joking in a competitive culture which was also what might be called a 'culture of trickery', in which the rulers were often civilians rather than soldiers, or in Machiavellian language foxes rather than lions. Even today, Italians explicitly approve of people who are cunning (*furbo*), witness the account of daily life in a small town in southern Italy in the 1970s by a British anthropologist who describes a father repeatedly asking his small son, 'Sei furbo?' The answer he wanted, expected and rewarded was of course 'yes'.[33]

(3) The *beffa* was often not 'pure' amusement but a means of humiliating, shaming, and indeed of socially annihilating rivals and enemies. This was a culture in which honour and shame were leading values. The titles of some stories reinforce this perception, as in the case of Sabadino degli Arienti, for instance, in which a recurrent phrase is 'se trova vergognato' (no. 1), 'remase vergognato' (no. 16), or 'resta vergognato' (nos 31, 35). The culture of Renaissance Italy was an agonistic one, most vividly exemplified in Florence.[34] Revenge (*bella vendetta*, as it is sometimes called) is another recurrent motif in the *novelle* (Bandello, book 4, no. 6; Grazzini, book 2, no. 9, etc.). So is cuckoldry. Aggression and sadism also recur, for instance in two famous stories in which what is supposed to be so funny is the castration of the victim (Bandello, book 2, no. 20; Grazzini, book 1, no. 2). These examples underline a point which Bakhtin's famous discussion of festive aggression seems to forget, that jokes were not amusing for everyone, that there were victims as well as spectators or listeners.

(4) That brings us to what Bakhtin called the 'lower bodily stratum'. In a story told by Sabadino (no. 16), a craftsman goes to the barber to be shaved and sees that the barber's shoes are very large. 'He felt an urge to piss in them,' and he did so. In a story by Bandello (book 1, no. 35), Madonna Cassandra has an affair with a friar, the husband discovers, dresses as the friar, takes laxative pills and shits all over her in the bed. Readers will probably find the story quite revolting. That is precisely why it is quoted here, at the price of transgressing the boundaries of the

---

[33] Davis (1973), 23; cf. Brandes (1980), 115ff.; Herzfeld (1985), 148.
[34] Burckhardt (1860), part 2.

acceptable in our own culture, in order to remind us of the 'otherness' of sixteenth-century Italy.

(5) The sense of cultural distance becomes still greater if we call to mind the fact that the last story was not only told about a lady but also dedicated to another lady, Paola Gonzaga, by a priest, at the time of the Council of Trent. Today, we tend to think of priests as serious or even as solemn people, at least in public. However, fifteenth-century Tuscans enjoyed the jests they attributed to a rural parish priest of the region, Arlotto Mainardi, and as we have seen Fra Mariano played the fool at the court of Pope Leo X. Again, we tend to think of Renaissance rulers such as Isabella d'Este of Mantua and Cosimo I of Tuscany as if they were always serious, although they are known to have enjoyed the wit and the antics of dwarves and fools.[35] The point to underline, at least for the period 1350–1550, is the widespread participation – both as jokers and victims – of princes and peasants, men and women, clergy and laity, young and old. Archive evidence confirms the testimony of fiction in this respect. At the court of Milan in 1492, for instance, Princess Beatrice d'Este played a trick on the ambassador of Ferrara, causing his garden to be invaded by wild animals, which killed his chickens, to the amusement of Beatrice's husband, Lodovico Sforza, the ruler of the state.[36] However, this situation would not last. It is time to turn to change.

Changes in the System

What then were the major changes in the system, in attitudes to jokes among Italians? Although a shift is perceptible by the 1520s, if not before, it is more obvious in the period 1550–1650, supporting Enid Welsford's point about 'the decline of the court-fool' in the seventeenth century, and Bakhtin's assertion about the 'disintegration of folk laughter' in the same period.[37] In reflecting on the reasons for these changes, it may be useful to distinguish between the religious and the secular aspects of what Norbert Elias called the 'process of civilization', a European

[35] Luzio and Renier (1891).
[36] Malaguzzi Valeri (1913–23), vol. 1, 560–1.
[37] Welsford (1935), 182–96; Bakhtin (1965).

movement of self-control (more precisely, 'the social constraint towards self-constraint'), considered here in its Italian Counter-Reformation version.

Some traditional forms of joking which had already been criticized by foreign clergy, from Erasmus on carnival to the Swiss reformer Oecolampadius on Easter laughter, were now condemned by Italians on religious or moral grounds. Aretino joined Luther and Calvin on the Index of Prohibited Books (compiled in Italy though binding on the whole church). The stories of the jester-priest Arlotto, first published in 1516 or thereabouts, were expurgated from 1565 onwards, with an introductory note explaining the need to remove the jokes 'which seemed to the inquisitor to be too free'. Bandello published his stories only just in time, in 1554, while the stories of the Florentine writer Antonfrancesco Grazzini, written around 1580, remained unpublished till the eighteenth century. Oral tales could not easily be censored, but all the same the storyteller Straparola was once summoned before the Venetian Inquisition.

Printed *beffe* were increasingly edited in order to point a moral, underlined by means of metaphors such as 'cures', 'lessons' and 'punishments'. Arlotto had already been described as curing someone of his bad habit of spitting near the altar, and teaching a lesson to the young men who want a quick 'hunter's Mass' (nos 5, 6). Bandello drew attention to the ethical implications of his stories (in book 1, nos 3, 35, etc.), although readers may not find this moral packaging altogether convincing. The editor Ludovico Domenichi made cuts in the 1548 edition of the *facezie* compiled by the humanist Angelo Poliziano, and revised them still further for the 1562 edition, changing the title to the more serious *Detti e fatti*, removing blasphemies and anticlerical remarks, and adding morals to each joke.[38] A collection of jokes by Luigi Guicciardini were also described on the title page as 'moralized' ('ridotti a moralità').

The changing reception of the *Decameron* makes an illuminating case-study in changing attitudes. Boccaccio's stories might have been prohibited altogether by the Council of Trent if the Duke of Florence, Cosimo de' Medici, had not sent an ambassador to the Council to beg for a reprieve. The stories reappeared in expurgated form in 1582. One story, concerning the hypocrisy

[38] Richardson (1994), 135.

of an inquisitor, had disappeared entirely from the collection, while other stories which mocked the clergy suffered drastic revision. Terms like 'friar' and 'archangel' were removed, at the price of making one story completely meaningless – that of Friar Alberto, who pretended to be the archangel Gabriel in order to seduce a pious Venetian lady.[39] The jokes in book 2 of Castiglione's *Courtier* were subjected to similar treatment in the expurgated edition of 1584.[40]

The Counter-Reformation clergy had embarked upon a 'cultural offensive', not to ban joking altogether but to reduce its domain. Jokes were increasingly considered indecorous if told by the clergy, whose behaviour should be marked by *gravitas*, or in church, because it was a holy place, or on sacred subjects. The careers of the jester-priests Arlotto and Fra Mariano began to seem indecorous – and later, almost unimaginable.

In his provincial council of 1565, San Carlo Borromeo denounced Easter plays for provoking laughter. He would not have agreed with Vladimir Propp about ritual laughter. As Borromeo saw it, the pious custom of representing the lives of Christ and the saints had been corrupted by human perversity, resulting in scandal, laughter, and contempt. He also instructed preachers not to tell funny stories.[41] Pope Pius V issued a decree against 'immoderate' laughter in church.[42] The Index of Sixtus V (1590), stricter than its predecessors, included the collections of *facezie* edited by Domenichi and Guicciardini, despite their claims to be moralists.[43] In a letter of 1608, Robert Bellarmine, another leading figure of the Counter-Reformation, expressed his opposition to revealing details about the lives of saints which might encourage laughter rather than edification ('quae risum potius quam aedificationem pariant'). Perhaps he was thinking of the traditional image of St Joseph, cuckolded by the Holy Ghost.

This clerical offensive needs to be seen as part of a wider movement, or at least of a wider shift in attitudes (among the upper classes at any rate), extending from the rise of classicism in the arts to the withdrawal from participation in popular culture, a shift which Elias described in terms of increasing self-control or

[39] Sorrentino (1935); Brown (1967).
[40] Cian (1887).
[41] Bernardi (1990), 256, 259; Taviani (1969); Borromeo (1758), 44.
[42] Azpilcueta (1582), 42–3.
[43] Reusch (1886), 481.

'civilization'.[44] For example, the *Discourses on What is Appropriate for a Young Noble who Serves a Great Prince* (1565) by Gianbattista Giraldi Cinthio (better known as a playwright) told its readers not to be the first to joke, since this might be construed as disrespect for the prince. The Genoese patrician Ansaldo Cebà emphasized the need for moderation in jokes, which should be adapted to places, times and persons and should not be unworthy of a gentleman ('che non disdicano ad huom libero e costumato').[45]

Changes in the *Beffa*

To return to the *beffa*. From the 'civilization' point of view, it is surely significant that among the critics of the *beffa*, as we have seen, are two authors whose conduct books became famous: the *Cortegiano* of Baldassare Castiglione and the *Galateo* of Giovanni Della Casa. Castiglione's speakers criticize *beffe* on moral grounds, preferring verbal jokes to practical ones, while the author censored some of his own jokes in the third manuscript version of his treatise. The criticisms may seem anodyne today, but in the context of the early sixteenth century they look almost puritanical, or revolutionary.[46] As for the Counter-Reformation moralist Della Casa, he admitted the need for people to play tricks on one another because life in this vale of tears needed some kind of solace (*sollazzo*), but he also criticized some kinds of *beffa*.[47]

Other evidence also points in the direction of the sharper definition of standards and a shrinking in the area of the publicly permissible. A noble dramatic society of Siena, the Intronati, now took care not to offend the modesty of ladies by their *burle*. In the case of the *beffe* recounted by Grazzini, probably in the 1580s, it has been claimed by a recent critic that there was a change of perspective from joker to victim.[48] Another recent writer on Italian literature has remarked on the seventeenth-

---

[44] Elias (1939); Burke (1978), 270–80.
[45] Cebà (1617), ch. 43.
[46] Grudin (1974); Rochon (1975), 171–210.
[47] Della Casa (1554), chs 11, 19.
[48] Plaisance (1972), 46.

century 'crisis' and decline of the *beffa*.[49] At the very least, it was purified.

What replaced the traditional *beffa*? Typical of the new regime of humour is Girolamo Parabosco's relatively mild *beffa* in which 'a large jar of water and hot ash' falls on the head of a lover as he arrives at the house of his lady. The tricks played by Bertoldo, the hero of a late sixteenth-century cycle of jests written by Giulio Cesare Croce, include violence but no scatology. There also seems to have been a shift among the upper classes in the direction of wit and verbal humour. This shift may be illustrated from the life of the academies, an increasingly important form of upper-class sociability in Italian cities of the sixteenth and seventeenth centuries. These discussion groups, which went back to the early Renaissance, now became at once increasingly formal and increasingly playful, in a respectable way. The change may be illustrated from the humorous names which became virtually *de rigueur* for members and for the academies themselves – the 'Sleepyheads' (Addormentati); the 'Confused' (Confusi); the 'Frozen' (Gelati); the 'Immature' (Immaturi); the 'Thoughtless' (Spensierati); the 'Uncivilized' (Incolti); and so on – as well as from mock lectures and parodies which figured largely on their programmes, some of which are reproduced in Gianfrancesco Loredan's *Bizarrie academiche* (1638).[50]

The seventeenth-century rhetorician Emmanuele Tesauro (who might be described in the language of today as a literary theorist), expressed a new ideal of elegance, dismissing 'popular jokes' (*facetie popolari*). He did not reject the *beffa* altogether, but he was much more concerned with verbal than practical jokes.[51] In this respect he was a typical representative of the cultural movement we now call 'baroque'. It does not seem unreasonable to suggest that the baroque obsession with word-play was a form of psychological compensation, a reaction to the shrinking of the domain of the comic. Another form of compensation was the rise of the caricature, which was invented in the circles of the Carracci and Bernini in the early to mid-seventeenth century. In other words, it was the work of artists famous for their classicism, suggesting that they needed some respite from

[49] Rochon (1972), 179–202.
[50] Quondam (1982), 823–98.
[51] Tesauro (1654), 38, 223, 583ff., 682.

idealization, while earlier forms of comic relief were now denied them.[52]

Of course the Elias thesis of the rise of self-control or 'civilization' should not be enunciated in too simple a manner. The trend was gradual not sudden, it provoked resistance, and it was successful only to varying extents and at different moments in different places, among different groups, or even in different kinds of situation. For example, Adriano Banchieri, a Benedictine monk, published comic works in the seventeenth century, although he did so under a pseudonym, thus revealing as well as breaking the Counter-Reformation taboo. The Florentine patrician Niccolò Strozzi in the mid-seventeenth century told the story of a *beffa* in which the victim was left on Piazza della Signoria all night.[53] At Pratolino, the fountains were still at work in the seventeenth century or even later, as two English travellers (among others) testify. John Evelyn, visiting in 1645, says that he and his companions were 'well washed for our curiosity'.[54] Richard Lassels recorded visiting 'the Grotto of Cupid with the wetting-stools upon which, sitting down, a great Spout of Water comes full in your face'.[55]

In the eighteenth century we find a return to the Renaissance, but with a difference. Several sixteenth-century comic texts reappeared at this time, but in revised forms. *Bertoldo*, for instance, was republished in 1736, rewritten by twenty men of letters, in verse, with allegories. G. C. Becelli rewrote the exploits of the famous medieval jester as *Il Gonnella* (1739). Grazzini's *beffe*, written about 1580, were published for the first time in 1756. A life of the celebrated jester-priest Arlotto Mainardi was published in Venice in 1763. Thus the eighteenth-century revival of the Renaissance was accompanied by – and perhaps depended on – a kind of cultural distanciation.

To pursue this theme of distanciation, we may turn to a mid twentieth-century story told by the novelist Vasco Pratolini in his novel *The Girls of San Frediano* (1949), an evocation of traditional working-class culture in the years following the Second World War. The punishment of 'Bob', the local Don Giovanni, by a gang of six girls whom he has tried to seduce individually,

[52] Kris (1953), chs 6–7; Lavin (1983).
[53] Woodhouse (1982).
[54] Evelyn (1955), vol. 2, 418.
[55] Lassels (1670), 134.

takes the form of a *beffa* in the Florentine tradition, in which he is tied up and paraded through the streets with his genitals exposed. Pratolini is not only placing himself in a high literary tradition, but also in a popular tradition, that of Florentine working-class culture, out of which he came and which he celebrates throughout his work. We do not seem to have moved very far in the 400 years separating Pratolini from Pratolino, or even the 600 years separating him from Boccaccio. The 'gang', or *brigata*, is central in both instances. However, the social frontiers of the comic have changed. What was represented in the fourteenth century as a general social custom is now associated with young adults of the working class.

At this point it may be useful to go back to Darnton's comments about otherness. Are we less cruel and more civilized, as he suggests? Is a cat massacre impossible today? In the *Cambridge Evening News* in the early 1990s, an incident was reported in which a young man who had quarrelled with his girlfriend revenged himself on her by putting her cat in the microwave. The example suggests that it might be prudent to speak not so much of a deep change in human psychology as of changes in social conventions, in the rules of the game, in the frontiers of the comic. Like sex, laughter is impossible to repress altogether. Rather than speaking of the 'decline' of traditional forms of humour from the later sixteenth century onwards, we might employ Bakhtin's more precise term 'distintegration'. What we find in the period 1550–1650 in particular are increasing restrictions on the public participation of clergy, women, or gentlemen in certain kinds of joke, a reduction of comic domains, occasions, and locales; a raising of the threshold; an increase in the policing of the frontiers.

6

The Discreet Charm of Milan: English Travellers in the Seventeenth Century

If we can only learn how to use them, travelogues will be among the most eloquent sources for cultural history. By a 'travelogue' I mean a journal or diary kept by a traveller, usually in a foreign country, or a series of letters describing his or her impressions. The temptation to historians as to other readers is to imagine ourselves looking through the writers' eyes and listening through their ears and so perceiving a now remote culture as it really was.

The reason we should not succumb to this temptation is not that travellers differ, since it is relatively easy to check one account against another. The point to emphasize is the rhetorical aspect of their descriptions, notably the importance of commonplaces and schemata. The texts are no more completely spontaneous and objective descriptions of new experiences than autobiographies are completely spontaneous and objective records of an individual life (above, p. 39). Some of these descriptions at least were written with publication in mind, and all follow certain literary conventions. Others simply reflect prejudices, in the literal sense of opinions formed before the travellers left their own country, whether these opinions were the result of conversation or reading.

An anthropological study of the 'man-eating myth' notes how common it is for travellers to perceive the inhabitants of a culturally distant society as cannibals. 'The cannibal epithet at one time or another has been applied by someone to every human group.' Another well-known example of prejudice, most carefully studied in the case of Europeans in the Far East, has been christened 'the myth of the lazy native'. Time and time again Europeans comment on the 'idleness', 'indolence', or 'disinclination to work' of the Malays, Filipinos, Javanese and so on.[1] Again, from the days of Herodotos onwards, the schema of the world turned upside down has appealed to travellers in what they regard as exotic places as a way of oganizing their observations. More than one of the characters in the novels of E. M. Forster see foreign parts as the reverse of their own country. In both *A Room with a View* (1908), set in Italy, and *A Passage to India* (1924), someone complains about the terrible lack of privacy.

How to Travel

It also turns out that a number of travelogues follow the recipes given in books on the 'art of travel'. Instructions 'how to travel' were an established literary genre by the seventeenth century. Contributions to what was sometimes called the 'apodemic art', in other words methodical travel, include Hieronymus Turler's *De peregrinatione* (1574), Hilarius Pyrckmair's *De arte apodemica* (1577), Theodor Zwinger's *Methodus apodemica* (1577), Justus Lipsius's *De ratione peregrinandi* (1578), Albert Meier's *Methodus* (1587), Salomon Neugebauer's *De peregrinatione* (1605), and Henrik Rantzau's *Methodus peregrinandi* (1608).[2]

In texts like these, intending travellers were advised to observe in each place they visited the funeral monuments; the paintings; the buildings, public and private, religious and secular; the fortifications; the fountains; the political system; and the manners and customs of the inhabitants. They were also advised to carry a guidebook and to take careful notes on what they saw. Englishmen who could not read Latin still had access to the texts by Turler (translated into English in 1575), Meier (translated 1589) and Lipsius (translated 1592), as well as to Francis Bacon's essay 'Of Travel', first published in 1612. Although some

---

[1] Arens (1979), 13; Alatas (1977).
[2] Stagl (1980, 1990); Rubiès (1995).

travellers, notably Michel de Montaigne, used their eyes and ears
to produce original accounts, the writers of many travel journals
followed the advice given in these 'apodemic' texts, simply privi-
leging one category rather than another according to taste. Thus
the Englishman Thomas Coryat anticipated the criticism that he
was 'a tombstone traveller' who copied too many epitaphs and
said too little about forms of government, his defence being that
he was 'a private man and no statist'.[3]

Despite occasional expressions of scepticism, travellers also
followed the assertions made in books published by earlier travellers, including the guidebooks to foreign countries which were
being published in increasing numbers in the seventeenth century.
As a result, many of their descriptions have a formulaic quality.
In their relatively brief notes on Genoa, for example, one
Englishman comments on the 'kingly magnificence' of the city
and another on the 'kingly luxury' (cf. chapter 7 below).[4]
'Magnificence' was an overworked word in these descriptions.

Not only brief formulae but also topics or themes occur again
and again.[5] They include processions (especially of flagellants)
and ex-votos, signs of Catholic 'superstition' which fascinated the
Protestant visitors. They also include violence, vengeance, the
guarding of women by their menfolk, and *lazzaroni*. Accounts of
Italy written by English, French and German travellers in the
seventeenth, eighteenth and nineteenth centuries offer a European
version of the myth of the lazy native in their recurrent descriptions of the *lazzaroni* of Naples, able-bodied men lying in the sun
and doing nothing, the *dolce far niente* being an indispensable
part of the Italian *dolce vita* as northerners saw it.[6] The
Englishman Samuel Sharp wrote of 6,000 *lazzaroni* who sleep in
the streets and 'are suffered to sun themselves a great part of the
day under the palace walls'. A fellow-countryman of his extended
the idea, claiming that 'the wants of nature are so easily satisfied
here that the lower class of people work but little: their great
pleasure is, to bask in the sun and do nothing.'[7] French and
German writers made the same point – apart from Goethe, who

[3] Coryat (1611), 11–12.
[4] Moryson (1617), 167; Raymond (1648), 13.
[5] Lord (1960).
[6] Crouzet (1982), 112, 114; Burke (1987), 15–19; cf. Comparato (1979); De'
    Seta (1981).
[7] Sharp (1766), letter 24; Martyn (1787), 264; cf. Croce (1895); Michéa
    (1939).

dismissed the idea as an example of the northern stereotype of the south.[8]

These descriptions are not necessarily pure plagiarism. It is likely that the travellers actually saw men lying in the sun, whether or not resting after work, interpreting them as *lazzaroni* because they fulfilled expectations created either by books or by oral tradition. By the eighteenth century (if not before) the travellers were looking for the 'picturesque', a new and fashionable word which reveals the habit of viewing everyday life through the spectacles of the old masters. A little later, in 1814, the English poet Samuel Rogers described the balconies in Milan 'from which a female figure is always looking as in P. Veronese and Tintoret'.[9] It is not only in the case of visionaries, discussed in chapter 2 above, that paintings have the power to modify perceptions of reality. In any case, entering an alien or semi-alien culture turns the traveller into a spectator, a viewer if not a voyeur. As Henry James put it in his *Italian Hours* (1877), 'To travel is, as it were, to go to the play.'

After so many critical observations, the reader may be expecting me to throw these travel narratives into the wastebasket, or to describe the Italy of their authors as pure 'invention'. As elsewhere in this volume, however, I shall try to avoid the opposite dangers of positivism and constructivism. The narratives will be analysed here as sources for the history of attitudes or mentalities.[10] They are precious documents of cultural encounters, revealing both the perception of cultural distance and the attempt to come to terms with or 'translate' it into something more familiar.

Views of Italy

For concrete examples of such perception of distance, we may turn to the case of northern European and more especially British travellers in early modern Italy.[11] In the early modern period northerners already tended to see Italy as the Other. It is tempting but too facile to explain this cultural distance in religious

[8] Goethe (1951), 28 May 1787.
[9] Rogers (1956), 165.
[10] Harbsmeier (1982).
[11] Stoye (1952); Sells (1964); Comparato (1979); De' Seta (1981).

terms as the result of the Reformation. Too facile, because a case could be made for explaining the Reformation in terms of this very cultural distance. Two leading reformers, Erasmus and Luther, visited Italy and recorded their dislike of some Italian customs, such as the carnival in Siena which Erasmus witnessed in 1509. All the same, the rejection of images, rituals, saints and so on at the Reformation can only have increased the distance from Italian culture experienced by northern Protestant travellers.

Despite their contempt for, or fear of, Catholicism (or 'Popery' as they put it), a considerable number of the British upper classes took a lively interest in Italian culture. Philip Sidney, William Harvey, John Milton, John Evelyn, Joseph Addison and Tobias Smollett are among the most famous of the many Englishmen who spent time in Italy in the early modern period. Italian art and architecture was quite well known in Britain, not only that of the Renaissance but also the work of seventeenth-century artists such as the Caracci, Guido Reni, Guercino and Salvator Rosa.[12] Sir Henry Wotton, who spent many years as ambassador in Venice, was an important mediator between his fellow-countrymen and Italian culture. So was the famous connoisseur Thomas Howard, Earl of Arundel, who took Inigo Jones with him on a visit to Italy in 1613. More than thirty years later, in 1646, the Earl gave Evelyn 'remembrances' of what to see in Italy.[13]

Italian was probably the best-known foreign language of the English at this time, overtaken by French only in the course of the eighteenth century. Italian literature was much admired, notably the poetry of Petrarch, Ariosto and Tasso (whose *Jerusalem Delivered* was published in an English translation by Edward Fairfax in 1600). A number of works by seventeenth-century Italian writers were translated into English without delay, including Paolo Sarpi's *History of the Council of Trent* (1620), Virgilio Malvezzi's *Romulus and Tarquin* and *David Persecuted* (both 1637), Enrico Davila's *History of the Civil Wars in France* (1647), Traiano Boccalini's *Advertisements from Parnassus* (1656), and Galileo's *System of the World* (1661).

It is not surprising, then, that there was a substantial number

[12] Hale (1954), 65–75
[13] Hervey (1921); White (1995).

of British travellers to Italy in the early modern period. As Addison put it, 'There is certainly no place in the world where a man may travel with greater pleasure and advantage than Italy.'[14] The arts of travel described above, notably the works by Pyrckmair, Turler and Lipsius, had referred to Italy in particular detail. Italy was the principal goal of the 'Grand Tour', a phrase just coming into use to describe a sojourn abroad by one or more young noblemen, often accompanied by a tutor.[15] One of our informants, John Ray, wrote in his preface of his plan of 'making Grand Tour (as they there call it)' in France. The tour, which was an important European cultural institution between the late sixteenth and late eighteenth centuries, often lasted for years. A considerable proportion of the time was spent in Italy, not only by British 'grand tourists' but also by Dutchmen, Danes and Poles.[16] The demand was sufficient to generate a number of guidebooks, whether to Italy in general or to major cities such as Venice or Rome.

Differences in religion, language, climate and customs gave the travellers an acute sense of cultural distance. John Ray, who devoted more than ten pages to Italian manners and morals, emphasized revenge, lust and jealousy. Elias Veryard came to similar conclusions (or copied those of Ray): 'The Italians are generally ... lascivious, jealous and revengeful.'[17] Richard Lassels, a Catholic priest who spent a long time in Italy, presented Italian manners as 'most commendable', but even he noted that Italians were vengeful, as well as 'sensible of their honour' and 'strict to their wives even to jealousy'.[18]

Another aspect of Italy which impressed the foreign visitors was the concern with display. Lassels made the point more sympathetically when he described Italians as 'sparing in diet that they may both love and live handsomely; spending upon the back what we spend on our bellies'. Ray thought the houses 'rather great and stately than commodious for habitation', and noted that 'the inferior gentry affect to appear in public with as much splendour as they can, and will deny themselves many satisfactions at home that they may be able to keep a coach and therein

[14] Addison (1705), 357.
[15] Black (1985); Chaney (1985).
[16] Mączak (1978); Frank-van Westrienen (1983).
[17] Veryard (1701), 263.
[18] Ray (1673), 150–1.

make the tour à la mode about the streets of their city every eve.'
In similar fashion, Veryard asserted that the nobles 'spend their
estates ... in making the greatest figure their degree and dignity
will permit'. Italy was already perceived as the land of appear-
ances and façades. Given the similarity of the last phrase to the
consecrated Italian expression *fare bella figura*, we may hazard
the guess that Veryard and other foreign visitors often recorded
observations which they had originally heard from the Italians
themselves. Travelogues include what Bakhtin would call a 'het-
eroglossic' dimension, recording not pure observation but the
interaction between travellers and 'travelees', as a recent critic
calls them.[19] The relation between the stereotypes of national
character current inside and outside a given country is a topic
deserving systematic investigation.

The sense of distance was sometimes acute enough for visitors
to employ the topos of the world turned upside down. Thus
Gilbert Burnet, Bishop of Salisbury, a Scottish Calvinist, viewed
the Italy through which he travelled in the 1680s as the converse
of the enlightenment, freedom and industriousness which he
attributed to his own country. He too contributed to the myth of
the lazy native with his reference to 'the sloth and laziness of this
people'.[20] Addison did the same, blaming 'idleness' on the number of monasteries and hospitals to be found in Italy and operating with a similar system of binary oppositions to Burnet (whose
analysis he praised), contrasting Catholics and Protestants,
tyranny and liberty, idleness and industry, Self and Other.[21]

These writers were influenced by and also contributed to what
has been called the 'myth' of Italy, part of a stereotyped contrast
between north and south (culture and nature, civilization and
savagery), which became even sharper in the nineteenth century.[22] Italy had formerly been viewed as the centre of civilization, but in the eighteenth century it was turning into an Arcadia.
In both cases we find a myth of place not so unlike the myths of
time discussed in chapter 3 above, a vision in which everything
was larger (or sharper) than life. If the northerners found the
south of Europe exotic, the reverse was also the case. It was at
this time, for example, that count Maiolino Bisaccioni, a prolific

[19] Pratt (1992), 135–6.
[20] Burnet (1686), 108.
[21] Addison (1705), 420–1.
[22] Crouzet (1982), 2, 38–49, 75, 79, 120, 242.

writer of history and fiction, published books on *Demetrius the Muscovite* (1639) and *Historical Memoirs of Gustavus Adolphus* (1642) as well as locating one of the stories in his collection *The Ship* (1643) in Norway and another in Russia.

The myth of Italy did not prevent some visitors from carefully observing the local customs, as the guides to travel advised. As we saw in chapter 4, northern visitors became increasingly conscious of the theatricality of Italian gestures (whether or not assisted in this process by the criticisms of Italian reformers). Fynes Morison, in Venice in the 1590s, was impressed by the 'variety of apparel, languages and manners'.[23] Thomas Coryat observed the uses of fans, forks and umbrellas, all alien objects in England at the time he was writing. Philip Skippon, who was in Italy in the 1660s, made careful notes on food ('they strew scraped cheese on most of their dishes'), clothes (with a sketch of a doge's cap), flagellants ('whippers'), funerals, blasphemies, silk production, the guillotine used in Milan, the voting system in Venice (complete with a diagram of a ballot box), the way in which the washing was hung out to dry on iron bars across the streets, and much else. Skippon is an unjustly neglected travel writer, with eyes and ears perhaps sharpened by his scientific training at Cambridge, where he studied with the famous botanist John Ray. It is a pity that his account of his journey to Italy has not been reprinted since 1732, while one of the few studies devoted to English travellers in Italy in the seventeenth century omits him altogether.[24]

Views of Milan

For a more precise case-study of the interaction between cultural stereotype and personal observation we may turn to the views of Milan recorded by British travellers in the course of a long seventeenth century, from the 1590s to the early 1700s. By this time, the British had a fairly clear impression of at least four Italian cities. Rome was of course associated both with the ruins of antiquity and with the papacy. Venice was known for its carnival as well as for its long-lived 'mixed constitution'.[25]

[23] Moryson (1617), 90.
[24] Skippon (1732); Sells (1964).
[25] Gaeta (1961); Bouwsma (1990); Haitsma Mulier (1980).

Florence was famous for its works of art, and Naples for its natural beauty.

By contrast, the British view of Milan was rather vague. According to the common saying, Rome was the Holy, Venice the Rich, Naples the Gentle (in the sense of noble), Florence the Fair, Genoa the Superb (in the sense of 'proud'), Bologna the Fat, Padua the Learned, and Milan the Great – in other words, large. For anyone interested in reading something in English about the city or state of Milan, there was little material available, especially in the first half of the century. Two plays performed on the London stage at this time provided a little information on the history of the city. Philip Massinger's *The Duke of Milan* (1621) and Robert Gomersall's *The Tragedie of Lodovick Sforza Duke of Milan* (1628) were both set in the late fifteenth century and based on the English translation of Francesco Guicciardini's *History of Italy*. The only concrete reference to contemporary Milan occurs in Thomas Dekker's *Honest Whore*, in which a scene takes place in a shop selling fine cloth.[26] The seventeenth century was the age of the first newspapers, but it was rare for them to report events from the region, apart from the plague of 1630 and the earthquake of 1680. At the beginning of our period, travellers are unlikely to have associated Milan with much more than St Ambrose and San Carlo Borromeo. Later, they could read the descriptions by earlier travellers such as Thomas Coryat (published in 1611), Fynes Morison (published in 1617), Raymond (1648), and so on.

Then as now, the British generally visited Milan on the way to somewhere else, if they did not omit it from their itineraries altogether. Milton, for example, spent a good deal of time in Florence, Rome, Naples and Venice in the years 1638–9, but there is no evidence of his having set foot in Milan (he approached Florence via Genoa and Livorno).[27] As for Edward Lord Herbert of Cherbury, who was there in 1615, all he could find to say about the city in his autobiography was that he had heard a famous nun sing there to the accompaniment of an organ.

The British travellers whose testimonies will be used below deserve to be introduced to the reader. They were virtually all members of the upper classes. In chronological order, they are

[26] Cf. Rebora (1936).
[27] Arthos (1968).

the gentleman Fynes Morison, who was in Milan in 1594; Thomas Coryat, who visited the city in 1608; Sir Thomas Berkeley (1610); the Earl of Arundel, who was there in 1613 and 1622; Peter Mundy, who visited in 1620 and recorded his impressions in sketches as well as texts; John Raymond, who was there in the 1640s; John Evelyn, gentleman and virtuoso (1646); Richard Symonds, another art-loving gentleman (*c*.1650); the Catholic priest Richard Lassels, who spent many years in the peninsula, and wrote a description of Milan in 1654; the Cambridge don John Ray and his pupil Philip Skippon, who were there together in 1663; the extremely Protestant Gilbert Burnet (1686); William Bromley, later a secretary of state (the 1680s); William Acton, a tutor who accompanied a young nobleman on the Grand Tour (*c*.1690); the physician Elias Veryard, who was in Italy at the end of the century; and Joseph Addison, who was there from 1701 to 1703. Of these sixteen visitors, nine published accounts of their travels in their lifetimes. Two different accounts have, somewhat implausibly, been attributed to Bromley. For convenience I will call the account of 1692 'Bromley' and the account of 1702 'pseudo-Bromley', without prejudice to what future research may reveal.

In general, British visitors tended to spend only a few days in Milan, compared to weeks or months in Venice or Rome. John Raymond spent four days and Richard Lassels, six. There was no ambassador in Milan as there was in Venice and official contacts were rare, although British diplomats and other important people might be received by the Spanish governor. For information about Milan the British relied on unofficial agents, or not to put too fine a point on it, spies. The importance of the information provided by these underground agents is revealed by the fact that in order to discover the plans of the governor of Milan, the doge once consulted the British ambassador in Venice.[28]

What follows is a collective portrait of Milan as seen by the British travellers. The method is to juxtapose or superimpose different images. The object of the exercise is to describe not the city itself so much as the impression it made on visitors – the sense of cultural distance, the mixture of attraction and repulsion. These visitors were all individuals with their own particular interests – Addison and Burnet in the Italian economy, Evelyn in the arts,

[28] Wotton (1907), 359, 399, 404; Brown (1864), vol. 10, nos 658, 673.

Lassels and Burnet in religion, Ray in science, Skippon in every-day life. On the other hand, they were often aware of their prede-cessors, if only to claim their unwillingness to 'transcribe the travels of others'.[29] Both commonplaces and individualized obser-vations will be studied not so much for what they tell us about Milan as for what they tell us about the attitudes of the travellers themselves. Particular attention will be given to what they found surprising or disconcerting.

The first point to make is that the British regarded Milan, at least in the early part of the century, as a sinister, dangerous place, much as their descendants viewed Eastern Europe in the 1950s, with the Inquisition in the place of the KGB. There was indeed a kind of 'cold war' in progress at this time. The rebel Earl of Tyrone received a warm welcome from the governor of Milan after he fled from Ireland in 1608. The man who attempted to assassinate King James I in 1613 came from Milan. In 1617, a possible attack on Milan by the joint British, Venetian and Savoyard forces was seriously discussed.[30]

Unpleasant events occurred often enough to justify the anxiety of travellers, or to give them a thrilling sense of adventure. In 1592, Wotton wrote that he had planned to visit Milan, but found it too dangerous. Fynes Morison, normally an intrepid traveller, spent only a little time there in 1594 'for the danger of my abode there'.[31] One of Wotton's spies in Milan, Roland Woodward, was arrested by the Inquisition in 1606, and another, Charles Bushy, in 1607.[32] In 1608, Coryat had an unpleasant experience when he was visiting the Castello and was mistaken for a Dutchman.[33] In 1610, when Viscount Cranborne, the son of the Earl of Salisbury, was passing through Milan, a member of his entourage was arrested for carrying a pistol.[34] In 1613, the Earl of Arundel left the city in a hurry because the gov-ernor of Milan had not treated him with the courtesy customary to someone of his rank.[35]

After 1640, a political thaw was in progress, and the state

[29] Bromley (1692), 52.
[30] Brown (1864), vol. 11, no. 213; vol. 12, no. 786; vol. 14, no. 665.
[31] Moryson (1617), 171.
[32] Wotton (1907), 327, 399.
[33] Coryat (1611), 102.
[34] Brown (1864), vol. 12, no. 125.
[35] Hervey (1921), 76.

papers refer much less to Milan. All the same, it took time for travellers to adapt themselves to the new climate, and in any case the Inquisition remained a presence in the city. In 1646, Evelyn noted that the English were known to visit Milan but rarely, 'for fear of the Inquisition', while some of his fellow-travellers '(in dread of the Inquisition, severer here than in any place of all Spain) thought of throwing away some Protestant (by them called Heretical) books and papers'. Evelyn himself was bold enough to enter the palace of the governor, 'tempted by the glorious tapestries and pictures', but left hurriedly when he was taken for a spy.[36]

Despite the dangers, Milan made a positive impression on most of our travellers, and the reasons for this tell us something about English cities as well as about the manner in which cities were perceived at this time. Morison, for example, noted that 'the streets are broad.' Coryat mentioned the population (300,000, certainly an exaggeration) and the importance of handicrafts (a point also made by Veryard nearly a century later).[37] Ray also recorded the figure of 300,000, 'but I believe they who report it, speak by guess and at random.' What impressed him was the cheapness of 'all provisions for the belly'. Veryard too noted the plenty of provisions, while Raymond thought it 'worth a day's journey only to see the market of Milan'. Bromley also noted the population ('300,000 souls') and also the 'many gardens'.[38] Evelyn thought it 'one of the princeliest cities in Europe' and was impressed by the 'stately wall' and the number of 'rich coaches' in the streets. Raymond noted the 'more than common breadth' of those streets, and Burnet 'the surprising riches of the churches and convents'. Berkeley commented on the size of the city ('above 500 thousand', a wild overestimate), and on the fact that 'there is no man can go armed with as much as a poiniard or knife in this town.'[39] Raymond and Addison were impressed by the 'Colonna infame' (later made famous by the novelist Alessandro Manzoni), the pillar erected in dishonourable memory of a barber accused of spreading the plague of 1630.

As recommended in the treatises on the art of travel, including

---

[36] Evelyn (1955), vol. 2, 491, 494, 507.
[37] Veryard (1701), 116.
[38] Bromley (1692), 64.
[39] Sloane 682, f. 11 verso (British Library, Dept of MSS).

Bacon's essay on the subject, churches, fortifications, hospitals and libraries occupy most of the space in British accounts of Milan.

The sheer number of churches in the city impressed more than one visitor, 'near 100' according to Evelyn, '200' according to Bromley, and '238' according to Ray, while Raymond asserted that 'the great number of churches' was one reason for the nickname 'Milan the Great'. Almost everyone who visited Milan had something to say about the cathedral or Duomo, a medieval structure to which important additions were made in the early seventeenth century. What is interesting to note is the variety of reactions to the Gothic architecture, which was not condemned as universally as one might have imagined. Coryat, for instance, found the cathedral 'exceedingly glorious and beautiful'. Raymond called it 'the most like ours' of the churches he saw in Italy, possibly expressing homesickness but also giving us a valuable hint of the cultural distance between some British observers and the architecture of the baroque. In similar fashion, Lassels described the Duomo as built 'like our old cathedrals with aisles and huge pillars'.[40] Evelyn praised the marble portico and the exterior of the Duomo with '4000 statues all of white marble', while he found the cupola 'unfortunate in nothing but the Gothic design' (he was, incidentally, the first recorded Englishman to use the term 'Gothic' to refer to architecture).[41] Ray considered the cathedral, next to St Peter's, 'the greatest, most sumptuous and stately pile of building in Italy'.[42] Pseudo-Bromley thought it 'one of the handsomest and largest churches I had seen'. Acton was still more enthusiastic. 'The Duomo or cathedral church is the finest fabric in Milan, and if one had a month to spend there, one might see it every day and yet find something to please one's curiosity, that one had not seen or at least taken notice of before.'[43] Veryard thought it 'a stately pile of old Gothish work'. The only dissentient voices were those of Burnet and Addison. For Burnet, 'The Dome hath nothing to commend it of architecture, it being built in the rude Gothic manner.' As for Addison, he records his disappointment on entering 'the great church that I

[40] Lassels (1654), 164.
[41] Evelyn (1955), vol. 2, 493; cf. Frankl (1960), 356ff.
[42] Ray (1673), 243.
[43] Acton (1691), 73.

had heard so much of', a 'vast Gothic pile' of marble, but the interior 'smutted with dust and the smoke of lamps'.[44]

After the churches, the fortifications. Not the city walls, though they too were considered impressive, but the Castello Sforzesco, not (as for tourists today) as a monument of the Renaissance, but as a functioning fortress and a reminder of Spanish power. Some visitors did not try to enter. Morison decided not to visit the Castello 'lest I should rashly expose myself to great danger'. Mundy 'passed by the Castle, accounted one of the strongest in Christendom'. Ray used a similar formula, 'esteemed one of the principal fortresses of Europe'. So did Evelyn, who commented that 'for its strength, works, and munition of all kinds, the whole world shows none like it.' Coryat called it 'the fairest without any comparison that ever I saw'; 'it seemeth rather a town than a citadel.' For Lassels it was 'one of the best in Europe'. Raymond called it 'the fairest, the strongest fortification or citadel in Europe', adding that 'they are very cautelous in letting strangers to see it.' Bromley managed with 'some difficulty' to enter the Castello, although his party was 'strictly examined' because they were suspected of being French in the age of Louis XIV's conflicts with Spain. Acton described the Castello in loving technical detail. 'It is a very regular Hexagon with half moons; it is esteemed one of the completest pieces of fortification in all Italy, and of great strength, upon every one of the bastions is planted twelve pieces of cannon.' Addison, on the other hand, dismissed it in a sentence. 'The citadel of Milan is thought a strong fort in Italy.'

After the fortifications, the hospital. Coryat called it 'very magnificent' and noted that it could relieve four thousand people. Evelyn thought it 'of a vast compass' and 'in earnest a royal fabric', a formula which was echoed again and again, making one suspect that it was used by professional guides. For Raymond, it was 'fitter to be the court of some kings than to keep almsmen in'. Lassels called it 'the rare hospital surpassing in beauty the best king's house I have yet seen', adding with his usual humour that 'it would almost make a man wish to be sick a while therein.' For Ray, it was 'more like a stately cloister or Prince's Palace than a hospital'. For Burnet, it was 'a royal building', for Bromley 'very stately', its apartments 'very commodious'.

[44] Addison (1705), 367.

Pseudo-Bromley found it 'so large that ... I concluded at my first entrance I was in the palace of some prince.' Acton considered it 'well worth taking notice of', though Addison did not notice it at all.

Views of the Ambrosiana

Cabinets of curiosities were among the sights recommended to intending travellers. Milan was the site of one of the most famous of such cabinets, the museum of Canon Manfredo Settala.[45] It attracted the attention of Evelyn, Acton (who most admired what he called 'three large Unicorns horns'), and especially Ray, who was also impressed by the 'rhinoceros horns' as well as the flies in amber, 'pictures made of feathers by the Indians', and machines 'counterfeiting a perpetual motion'.

However, Settala's museum was overshadowed by the great new library of Milan, founded by Federigo Borromeo and named in honour of Carlo Borromeo's hero, St Ambrose. It already attracted the attention of Coryat in 1608, when it was 'not fully finished, so that there is not one book in it'. As in the case of the rest of the city, or indeed the rest of Italy, travellers tended to make the same kind of comment about the library, whether or not they had consulted the description published by Pietro Paolo Boscha, *De origine et statu bibliothecae ambrosianae* (1672). For this reason it is convenient to summarize their remarks topic by topic.

In the first place – and for the majority of visitors this was indeed the most important aspect of the Ambrosiana – the building and the decoration. Evelyn noted that a 'vast sum' had been spent on the construction. Ray and Skippon called it 'a handsome building' and 'a fair building' respectively. Burnet thought it 'a very noble room'. Almost equally impressive were the 'curiosities' (Evelyn), 'curious pictures' (Skippon) or 'many choice pieces' (Veryard) in the picture gallery attached to the library. The 'portraits of divers learned men' in the reading room also attracted attention, though not always favourably. Lassels, for instance, described the series as 'a thing of more cost than profit, seeing with that cost many more books might have been bought' (a few

[45] Impey and Macgregor (1985).

years earlier he had been more complimentary).[46] Burnet jumped
to the conclusion that 'their libraries ... all Italy over are scan-
dalous things, the room is often fine and richly adorned, but the
books are few, ill bound and worse chosen.' Bromley, more
empirically, complained of the lack of books in the libraries of
Venice, Mantua and Naples. Whether or not he had been reading
his predecessors, Addison made a similar comment, which he
turned into a general critique of Italian culture, 'the Italian
Genius' as he called it. 'I saw the Ambrosiana Library, where, to
show the Italian Genius, they have spent more money on Pictures
than on Books ... Books are indeed the least part of the
Furniture that one ordinarily goes to see in an Italian Library,
which they generally set off with Pictures, Statues and other
ornaments.' The comment (like Ray's thirty years earlier, quoted
above) is a relatively early example of the northern European
propensity to see Italy, and the south in general, as a land of
façades.

We come at last to impressions of the books and manuscripts.
The figure of 40,000 items, mentioned in a guidebook of 1628,
was echoed by visitors for the rest of the century (despite more
than seventy years of new accessions), until pseudo-Bromley
updated it to 50,500. Travellers were equally fond of repeating
the story that a king of England, sometimes identified as James I,
had offered a vast sum for the Leonardo manuscript, a story
which can be traced back to a notice on the library wall.

The collection was condemned by Burnet because it 'is too full
of School-men and Canonists, which are the chief studies of Italy,
and it hath too few books of a more solid and useful learning.'
Skippon noted the detail of the 'wire lattices' in front of the
books, 'which the library-keeper opens as there is occasion'. As a
Protestant, he found two Catholic features of the library exotic
enough to be worthy of note. In the first place, the notice excom-
municating anyone who removed books from the library, a document he found so remarkable that he transcribed it in his text. In
the second place, ecclesiastical censorship. 'We looked into
Gesnerus his works, printed at Frankfurt, and observed on the
top of the title page, *Damnati Authoris, etc*, was written; and all
those notes which Gesner calls superstitious and magical were
blotted out.'

[46] Lassels (1670); Lassels (1654), 164; Veryard (1701), 115.

A more positive feature of the Ambrosiana also surprised British and other foreign visitors. Ray noted that the library was 'free for all persons, as well strangers as citizens, to enter into and make use of'. Skippon added the vivid detail that books will be delivered to 'any one that will study here, who must then sit down in a chair on one side of the room'. Lassels waxed enthusiastic. 'The Bibliotheca Ambrosiana is one of the best libraries in Italy, because it is not so coy as the others, which scarce let themselves be seen; whereas this opens its doors publicly to all comers and goers, and suffers them to read what book they please.' Even the grudging Burnet produced a sentence of pure praise. 'One part of the disposition of the room was pleasant, there is a great number of chairs placed all round it at a competent distance from one another, and to every chair there belongs a desk with an escritoire that hath pen, inks and paper in it, so that every man finds tools here for such extracts as he would make.' It is clear that our travellers did not expect a major library to be truly accessible. In Oxford, foreigners could not take notes on books in the Bodleian Library unless they were supervised by a graduate of the university. In London, the famous Reading Room of the British Museum, complete with desks and pens, did not open until the middle of the nineteenth century. For once, the upside-down world proved to have its advantages.

7

Public and Private Spheres in Late Renaissance Genoa

U rban historians and urban sociologists used to concentrate their attention on the economy of cities, their social structure and their politics, but in the last generation they have become increasingly concerned with what has been termed 'the city as artefact', including the history of urban space. What he calls 'the fall of public man', and its complementary opposite, the increasing value attributed to private life, have been studied by the American sociologist Richard Sennett in spatial terms. Sennett describes the social and political 'theatre' of Paris and London and its setting, the public squares, from which trading and popular entertainment were banned from the late seventeenth to the early eighteenth century, and other places, from theatres to parks, where strangers might meet. In the nineteenth century, he argues, the rise of the bourgeoisie led to a withdrawal into domestic space and private affairs.[1] His book is a fascinating one, but its central argument can be challenged. How, for example, is it related to the famous thesis of Jürgen Habermas about the rise of the 'public sphere' in the same cities and the same period? Habermas too looks at spaces, the public spaces of coffee-houses and the semi-public spaces of clubs.[2] Again, if the argument is supposed to apply to Western society in general, Sennett's chronology is somewhat problematic, as the example of Renaissance serves to demonstrate. Studies of Florence and

[1] Sennett (1977).
[2] Habermas (1962); cf. Brewer (1995), 341–5.

Venice have linked the history of public life to that of public space, especially the space of the piazza. In Florence, government buildings were supposed to be treated as 'sacred places', and gambling, drinking and whoring in the vicinity was forbidden. In this way the Florentines constructed what has been called 'worshipful space'.[3]

In Venice, Piazza San Marco was at once the sacred centre and the civic centre. The church was the Doge's chapel, while his palace was the setting for meetings of the senate and the great council. The theatrical appearance of Piazza San Marco and the adjoining piazzetta has often been noted, especially as viewed from the balcony of the Doge's Palace, with the Doge himself in his 'box' overlooking events. The piazza was redesigned in the early sixteenth century, by a leading architect, Jacopo Sansovino, at the initiative of Doge Andrea Gritti. Shops and stalls were cleared away from Piazza San Marco, a library built and a loggetta added to the base of the Campanile. As important as the buildings themselves was the reconstruction of the public space which they enclosed. One of the purposes of this reconstruction was to create a more appropriate setting for public rituals, rituals which were of particular importance in what has been called the 'republic of processions'.[4]

The implication of these studies of Florence and Venice is that the heyday of 'public man' was the fifteenth century in the first case and the sixteenth century in the second, the 'fall' occurring with the end of the Florentine republic in 1530 and with the less dramatic, more gradual decline of Venice in the seventeenth century. The case of Genoa is rather different. Here it might be suggested that public man did not fall because he never rose; or to use the language current in Renaissance studies, because the 'civic humanism' so important in the history of Florence and Venice was lacking.[5] The point of this chapter is to argue that there was a civic humanist movement in Genoa, although it arrived relatively late and was never very strong. The writings of these civic humanists have something important to tell us about perceptions of the public sphere and of public space in the late Renaissance.

Genoa is the Cinderella of Italian Renaissance studies, gener-

---

[3] Trexler (1980), 47–54.
[4] Tafuri (1969); Howard (1975), 13ff.; Muir (1981), ch. 5.
[5] On the idea of civic humanism, Baron (1955).

ally neglected. Up to a point this neglect is almost justified, in the sense that in the early Renaissance and even in the High Renaissance, the Genoese did not make the contribution one might have expected from a northern Italian city of this size (about 85,000 people).[6] In a study of Italy in the fifteenth and early sixteenth centuries I have discussed the local origins of 600 Italian artists, writers and scholars. Tuscany, with 10 per cent of the total population, provided 26 per cent of this 'creative elite', but Liguria, with 5 per cent of the population, provided only 1 per cent. The only Genoese humanist of this period reasonably well known today is Bartolommeo Fazio. We remember Federico and Ottaviano Fregoso only because Castiglione gave them speaking parts in his *Courtier*. Even the patronage of art and humanism seems to have lacked the importance it possessed in Milan, let alone Venice or Florence.

Historians, notably Roberto Lopez, himself Genoese by birth, have offered various explanations for the lack of Genoese participation in the Renaissance.[7] To my mind one of the most convincing is the lack of civic patronage, linked in turn to lack of civic or public spirit. Compared with Florence and Venice the Genoese state was weak, unable to tame the magnates. Genoa was a classic case of 'private affluence and public squalor', to quote John Kenneth Galbraith's famous phrase describing the United States in the 1950s – still more true today.[8] As Galbraith was doubtless aware, he was repeating the ancient historian Sallust's verdict on Rome. Sallust's words were *publice egestas, privatim opulentia*. An anonymous sixteenth-century dialogue on Genoese affairs made a similar point in its discussion of the physical spaces of the city, the foreigner admiring the 'superb palaces' and the 'charming gardens', while the native points out that the streets by contrast are 'narrow and twisted'.[9]

The point was that in Renaissance Genoa the magnates still ruled. The great families or clans (*alberghi*) had private armies and private prisons.[10] As in Florence, the members of a particular family tended to live in the same quarter of the city, and they sometimes 'privatized' some of its public spaces. Piazza San

[6] Heers (1961).
[7] Lopez (1952).
[8] Galbraith (1958), 211.
[9] 'Genovese e Romano' (attributed to Leonardo Lomellini, Paris, Bibliothèque Nationale, MSS ital. 751, f. 2).
[10] Heers (1961).

Matteo, for example, was effectively the territory of the Doria clan. As late as 1565 Piazza San Luca was in dispute between the Spinola and the Grimaldi, each clan claiming the right to celebrate St John's Eve with a bonfire in the square.[11]

The patricians' sense that public spaces were really their territory is vividly illustrated in the journal kept by one of them, Giulio Pallavicino, between 1583 and 1589. At one point he describes how an aristocratic youth club of which he was a member, the Giovani di San Siro, commandeered the Strada Nuova and organized tournaments in fancy dress. On a more everyday occasion, Pallavicino records the reaction of a patrician who was bumped by a man with a mule passing in the street. 'You didn't notice me [Tu non mi vedi],' he complained (one can imagine his tone). 'Neither did you [E voi non vi vedete],' came the cheeky answer. The patrician ordered his servant to beat up the muleteer (*dargli delle bastonate*). In similar fashion, Pallavicino himself felt on another occasion that his personal space had been invaded by a commoner (*un certo forfante*). His reaction too was the apparently formulaic complaint *non mi vedi*. When the other did not reply or at least not audibly, Pallavicino gave him *un buon schiaffo*. When the man responded, he received a stab in the back, *una pugnalata nelli schiene*.[12] One is reminded of colonial cities in which whites expected blacks to step into the road to let them pass. The point is not that this virtual claim to own the city was unique to the patricians of Genoa, for there are parallels in Venice, Rome and elsewhere. However, this territorial imperative was even stronger or at least better documented in Genoa.

The grasp on the city of the patricians, or more exactly of a minority of patricians, tightened in the course of the sixteenth century. The crucial date is 1528, when Andrea Doria, who had served François I, changed sides and made a pact with Charles V. As his supporters put it, Doria 'liberated' Genoa, to rule it for more than thirty years. The century following 1528 was the century of what might be called the 'Spanish connection', in which Genoese patricians established themselves in Seville, supplied galleys to the Spanish navy, and above all lent money to the Spanish Habsburgs. Genoa had been a satellite of Milan and of France. Now it had become a satellite of Spain. One might speak of the

---

[11] Grendi (1987), 85.
[12] Pallavicino (1975), 6, 73.

Genoese 'military-financial complex' in the sense that the same families (Grimaldi, Pallavicino, Spinola, etc.) were involved in both the military and the financial operations. The military success of Ambrogio Spinola, who commanded the Spanish army in the Low Countries in the early seventeenth century, was due in part to the fact that he paid his troops regularly, and he was able to do so by spending his own money.

The years after 1528 ('28', as the Genoese called it) were marked by cultural changes as well as economic and political ones. The Venetian Renaissance is sometimes described as 'retarded', but the Genoese entered the field still later. Conspicuous consumption on art and architecture began in the age of the Spanish connection. The commune built a palace for Andrea Doria on Piazza San Matteo, while Andrea built himself a magnificent villa at Fassolo.[13] The decoration of the Palazzo Doria by Raphael's pupil Perino del Vaga was praised by no less a critic than Michelangelo.

However, the true turning-point came in the 1550s, with the construction of Strada Nuova, a street of palaces belonging to the great financial dynasties.[14] According to the Englishman Richard Lassels, the Strada Nuova 'surpasseth in beauty and building all the streets of Europe that ever I saw anywhere, and if it did but hold out at the same rate a little longer it might be called the queen street of the world.'[15] The street is now known as Via Garibaldi but the palaces still exist, appropriately enough owned by financial organizations like the Banca d'America e d'Italia. The same families built splendid villas for themselves outside the city.[16] As for painting, it was in the 1550s that the first important Renaissance artist who was Genoese by birth began his work: Luca Cambiaso, a follower of Giulio Romano. A concern was shown for vernacular literature. The poet Torquato Tasso was invited to lecture in Genoa, and local patricians published poems, particularly in the circle of the academy of the Addormentati, first recorded around 1563.

There was also a rise of political literature (in print and manuscript), from 1559, when the humanist lawyer Oberto Foglietta published his *Repubblica di Genova*, to the early 1620s, when

[13] Grendi (1987), 139–72.
[14] Poleggi (1968).
[15] Lassels (1654), 156.
[16] Poleggi (1969).

Ansaldo Cebà published his plays. This literature deserves a larger place in the history of political thought than it has so far been given outside Genoa.[17] Political thought is too often identified with political 'theory' in the strict sense of the term. For a 'total history' of political thought historians need to spread their nets more widely.

Generally speaking, what is published is the most important, but it might be argued that in late Renaissance Genoa things were the other way round. What was published was usually (though not always) anodyne. On the other hand, criticisms of the government circulated in manuscript, sometimes in multiple copies, a kind of *samizdat*. The works were usually anonymous. Some took the form of humanist dialogues in the manner of Lucian, with titles such as 'The Dream' or the 'Dialogues of Charon'.[18] Others took the form of *Relationi*, the genre pioneered by the Venetian ambassadors but widely imitated elsewhere, sometimes by satirists describing their own cities as if from outside.[19] One, the *Discordie*, is a work of history reminiscent of Sallust's *Conspiracy of Catiline*, stressing the evils of faction and offering a sophisticated analysis in terms of *interessi* and *contrapeso*.[20]

The language of more than one text is reminiscent of Machiavelli, applying his ideas to the analysis of Genoa and its factions, and one dialogue mentions him by name.[21] One of the few printed texts is in verse, a series of sonnets in dialect, describing the Roman Republic, 'Quell' antiga Repubrica Romanna', but obviously thinking of the present. Some of these texts were printed in the nineteenth and twentieth centuries, but others remain in manuscript in Genoese archives and libraries. They deserve a more detailed analysis from the point of view of historians of political thought than they have received so far. In any case, they form the basis for this chapter.

[17] Costantini (1978), ch. 7; cf. Savelli (1981), 40ff., on the *Sogno*.
[18] 'Dialoghi di Caronte', Archivo Storico del Comune di Genova (henceforward ASCG), MS 164; 'Sogno', ASCG, fondo Brignole Sale, 104 A21.
[19] Goffredo Lomellino, 'Relatione della repubblica di Genova' (1575), ASCG, MS 120; 'Relazione dello stato politico ed economico della serenissima repubblica di Genova' (1597), Genoa, University Library, MS B. VI. 23; [Giacomo Mancini], 'Relazione di Genova' (1626), Florence, Biblioteca Nazionale, fondo G. Capponi, vol. 81, no. 4.
[20] Lercari (1579).
[21] Lercari (1579); [Mancini], 'Relazione di Genova'; 'Dialoghi di Caronte', f. 9 verso.

This political literature contrasts with what was produced in the sister republic of Venice, a series of eulogies of the system which historians now describe as 'the myth of Venice'.[22] There was no 'myth of Genoa', but the opposite, an anti-myth. The Genoese patricians were constantly criticizing their political system. In this political literature there were three main themes.

The first theme was the conflict between the 'old' noble families and the new, the *vecchi* and the *nuovi*. It was the *vecchi* who were becoming rich from banking and who were building palaces in the Strada Nuova. But there were only about 700 male *vecchi* by the middle of the century, compared to some 1,400 *nuovi*. The *vecchi* believed that there should be parity between the two groups, as was decreed in 1547. The *nuovi* continued to argue that there should be equal access to office on an individual basis. Two rival concepts of equality, one might say. The conflict was aggravated by the fact that the old nobles, female as well as male, excluded the new from social intercourse (*conversazioni famigliari*). As in Naples, the nobles had the custom of meeting regularly in certain loggias or porticos to discuss politics and other subjects. The action of the *vecchi* forced the *nuovi* to create their own meeting place in another part of the city.[23]

The conflict between old and new boiled up in 1575, when the young men of the *nuovi* organized a carnival tournament in Piazza Ponticello, a 'popular' quarter, thus expressing in one dramatic gesture their claim to parity with the *vecchi* and their link to the *popolari*. The *vecchi* reacted with scorn and satire, referring to the recent trading origins of their rivals. This acting out of social hostilities in the piazza is reminiscent of the urban carnival staged five years later, in Romans (a small town in Dauphiné), and made famous a few years ago by Emmanuel Le Roy Ladurie.[24]

In the case of Genoa, there was nearly a civil war. Barricades were erected in the streets and the *vecchi* called their rural vassals to arms. All the same, they were forced to concede the official abolition of the distinction between old and new.[25] The humanist Oberto Foglietta, who had been exiled for criticizing the *vecchi* in

[22] Gaeta (1961); Haitsma Mulier (1980).
[23] Lercari (1579), 16; cf. Lomellino, 'Relatione', 130–1; 'Relazione dello stato politico'.
[24] Le Roy Ladurie (1979).
[25] Costantini (1978), 101–22; Savelli (1981), ch. 1.

print (in a book published in Rome in 1559), and for daring to suggest that more *popolari* should be allowed into the patriciate, was not only allowed to return but also appointed official historian of the city.[26]

The second major political theme was the fear of Spain, connected to the first theme because the *vecchi* were more involved with Spain than the *nuovi*. Indeed, in '75 (as the Genoese called it) there was a rumour that the *vecchi* wanted to hand the city over to Spain.[27] The Spaniards hated the economic dominance of the Genoese, commemorated in Quevedo's bitter poem *Don Dinero*.

> Nace en las Indias honrada
> Donde el mundo le acompaña,
> Vien a morir en España
> Y es en Génoa enterrada.

For their part, the Genoese, or some of them, feared the political dominance of the Spaniards. They were afraid that the Spanish Empire might swallow them up. The threat gave some of them what has been described as a 'siege mentality'.[28] A dialogue of *c.*1574 presents the Duke of Alba in conversation with Philip II about the possibility of taking over Genoa. Alba warns the king of the difficulties, and suggests that it would be cheaper to make use of Genoa while allowing it independence. Philip on the other hand argues that a takeover would be easy because the Genoese are more concerned with private than with public affairs, loving *il ben proprio* more than *libertà*.[29] Spanish mediation was important in the peace of 1576. In the 1580s there was another dispute with Spain because the Spaniards refused to give the republic the title of Serenissima. The opponents of Spain saw themselves as 'lovers of liberty'.[30]

The third major theme in this literature, and the one at the centre of this contribution, is that of civic spirit. I want to suggest that the threat from Spain (present from 1528 but apparently most acute from the 1570s to the 1620s) awakened the civic

---

[26] Foglietta (1559); cf. Costantini (1978), 66ff.
[27] [Mancini], 'Relazione di Genova', ch. 10.
[28] Spinola (1981), 43; cf. ibid., 87, 98, 100, 114, 189.
[29] 'Dialogo', Florence, Biblioteca Nazionale, fondo Capponi, 109.c.6.
[30] Pallavicino (1975), 158, 192.

consciousness or civic patriotism of some Genoese patricians in much the same way that, according to Hans Baron, the threat from Milan had encouraged the rise of Florentine 'civic humanism' nearly 200 years earlier. Indeed, the phrase 'civic humanism' itself seems appropriate in at least two cases, since the thought of Ansaldo Cebà and his friend Andrea Spinola was nourished by the classics, notably (as one might expect by the early seventeenth century) Seneca and Tacitus.[31]

Unlike Florence according to Baron, however, the rise of civic patriotism appears to have been a reaction not only to a political threat but also to an economic one, the rise of luxury. What was perceived as the rise of *fasto, splendore, grandezza, lusso* – or as we might say, following Veblen, 'conspicuous consumption' – became a serious preoccupation in Genoa from the middle of the sixteenth century onwards (in Florence, Guicciardini had already shown a similar preoccupation in his *Discorso di Logrogno* early in the century).[32] The magnificence of certain individuals was criticized as a threat to civic liberty, notably in the play by Paolo Foglietta (Oberto's brother), *Il Barro*. Among the individuals criticized by name at this time was Doge Gianbattista Lercari, for instance, whose quasi-regal manner gave offence, and the Prince of Salerno, who was nicknamed *il monarca*. A text of 1575 (attributed to Gioffredo Lomellino, a noble who made an epitome of one of the moral works of Seneca) notes that 'splendour has increased, and expensive buildings, clothes and luxurious foods have been introduced into Genoa,' and relates this to a withdrawal from public affairs by the *vecchi*, who preferred *la grandezza privata* to the public good.[33] A text of 1579 claims that the *vecchi*, richer than ever before, had been abandoning their civic lifestyle (*modi civili*), 'building sumptuous palaces with royal ornaments and living in the houses with unprecedented splendour and grandeur, much in excess of civic moderation [*la modestia civile*]'. A dialogue of 1583 refers to the 'proud palaces, that look more like the habitations of princes than of private individuals'.[34]

There is a hint that this trend exemplified not only the moral corruption which follows enrichment but was an attempt on the

[31] Burke (1991).
[32] Pocock (1975), 135–6.
[33] Lomellino, 'Relazione', 173–6.
[34] Lercari (1579), 17; Paschetti (1583), 6.

part of the old families to differentiate themselves from the new
nobles. In similar fashion, it was said that the old families called
themselves *vecchi* and used double-barrelled names 'to reveal the
difference' (*far palese la differenza*) between themselves and the
nuovi. These people seem to have known their Bourdieu as well
as their Veblen.[35]

The most elaborate and thoughtful expressions of civic values
in this period of crisis came in the early seventeenth century.
They were the work of two friends, both minor patricians and
both members of the academy of the Addormentati. Ansaldo
Cebà (*c.*1565–1623) has a secure though small place in histories
of Italian literature. He studied with Sperone Speroni in Padua,
was a friend of the poet Gabriele Chiabrera, and himself wrote
an epic, *La reina Esther* (1615), and a number of plays. *Esther*
concentrates on the theme of liberation, and its aim (according to
the preface) was to kindle the love of great enterprises in the
hearts of readers. The tragedy *Alcippo* (1622) is equally political,
concerned as it is with a noble Spartan who is accused of 'royal
pride' (like Doge Lercari) and of hostility to the free city, though
his defenders describe him as a man of modest habits. In a letter
to his friend Gioffredo Lomellino, Cebà argues that the family of
a senator should live with more modesty than a lesser noble, and
that the senator himself should be a champion of liberty and
strive for constancy of mind in times of adversity.[36] Even more
important for the purposes of this chapter is Cebà's treatise *Il cittadino di repubblica* (1617).[37] Much of this treatise is conventional or anodyne enough, but not all of it. Written for young
men in a free city, and making regular reference to Plutarch,
Sallust and Seneca, *Il cittadino* recommends its readers to study
Tacitus, and to be suspicious of both authority and luxury.[38]
What is needed, according to Cebà, is 'civic discipline' (*disciplina
civile*), to be encouraged by meditating on the continence of
Scipio (who figures in the same author's *Silandra*) and the self-
denial of Cato the Censor.[39] Similar attitudes to the control of the
passions are expressed in his *Esther*.

Andrea Spinola (1562–1631), on the other hand, did not

[35] Lercari (1579), 17; [Mancini], 'Relazione di Genova', ch. 8.
[36] Cebà (1623), 49ff.
[37] Cebà (1617). On him, Costantini et al. (1976), 75–114.
[38] Cebà (1617), 35.
[39] Cebà (1617), 69.

publish his reflections and was virtually forgotten even in Genoa until a few years ago. Although a Spinola, he was comfortably off rather than rich.[40] He made himself a spokesman for the interests of the second-class patricians, and was once reprimanded, in 1616, for speaking too freely, and once imprisoned, three years later, for criticizing his colleagues in office. Spinola's nickname was *il filosofo*. He wrote down his thoughts in a text variously known as his *Capricci*, his *Dizionario*, or his *Ricordi politici*, consisting of thoughts arranged in alphabetical order on such themes as 'Corruption', 'Discipline' and 'Equality'. The text was a kind of political commonplace book.[41]

This text shows that Spinola was a civic humanist whose points of reference included Juvenal, Sallust, Seneca and Tacitus.[42] What Spinola opposed was corruption, luxury and tyranny. For example, he criticized the 'ridiculous ceremonial' associated with 'despots' such as the King of Spain, and now appropriated by Genoese doges and even ordinary citizens.[43] He was also against the acceptance of places in Spanish military orders (*habiti e croci*), which made free citizens into slaves. Spinola also criticized the magnificence of recent funerals (if they were really necessary, he remarks, the poor could not afford to die).[44] He rejected the word 'palace' and the habit of living in grand houses on the grounds that this lifestyle gave children over-ambitious ideas (*opinioni vane*).[45] He regarded the new fashion for carriages as a 'mad' form of luxury.[46] Just as he criticized private luxury, he condemned 'public poverty'.[47]

What Spinola passionately supported was republican liberty and equality ('l'egualità civile') and the tradition of a simple, thrifty life ('l'antico severità del vivere parco'). 'Equality' is a term which echoes through his writings.[48] The models he held up

---

[40] Bitossi, (1976) 158n.
[41] The MSS quoted here are ASCG, fondo Brignole Sale, 106 B3 and 106 B11–12 (henceforth B3 and B11–12). On the author, Fenzi (1966); Bitossi (1976).
[42] On Juvenal, B11–12, s.v. 'Educatione'; on Sallust, Spinola (1981), 102, 187; on Seneca, ibid., 102, 201, 204, 248, 256, 265, 292; on Tacitus, ibid., 79, 84–6, 101–2, 121, 139, 165, 167, 195, 204, 259, 260.
[43] B11–12, s.v. 'Cerimoniale'.
[44] B11–12, s.v. 'Essequie private'.
[45] B11–12, s.v. 'Palazzi di cittadini'.
[46] B11–12, s.v. 'Carrozze'.
[47] On luxury, Spinola (1981), 97, 100, 187, 252ff.; on public poverty, 97.
[48] Bitossi (1976), 98–9, 102, 187; B11–12, s.v. 'Egualità civile'.

to his fellow Genoese were ancient Rome, ancient Sparta and modern Switzerland, which might be rough but which preserved the customs of free men ('con qual vivere loro rozzo e parco hanno costumi proprii d'uomini liberi').[49] He even left money to the Swiss cantons.[50] In order to keep republican values alive, he recommended public lectures on ethics and politics.[51] Like Foglietta sixty years before, Spinola wanted more commoners admitted into the nobility. Unlike Pallavicino (above, p. 114), he considered that the nobles should show courtesy to commoners, returning their greetings for example.[52]

Metaphorically speaking, one might say that Spinola wanted to enlarge public space (or if you prefer, the public sphere) at the expense of the private. However, he also expressed views on public space in the literal sense of the term. For example, he complained about the lack of respect for public buildings. He suggested that the watchmen should police the Loggia di Banchi (the building where the merchants met, restructured in the late sixteenth century), in order to prevent youths sleeping there or playing football there. In other words Spinola had a sense of the sacrality of public buildings of the kind which the American historian Richard Trexler has noted in the case of Florence.[53]

More positively, Spinola suggested spending money on street cleaning, since it was indecorous as well as insanitary to allow pigs to search for food in the centre of the city.[54] Money should also be spent on the Palazzo publico, which Spinola refused to call the Doge's Palace, gilding the ceiling, laying a marble pavement and decorating the walls with pictures. This magnificence, he explained, is not vanity. 'Such decorations serve to maintain the *maestà publica*.'[55] He also recommended the erection of a marble statue in the Piazza della Signoria in honour of the local hero, Christopher Columbus.[56] Spinola was an admirer of Venice, 'the most prudent regime there has ever been in the world.'[57] There was of course a similar trend in Venice at much

[49] On Sparta, Spinola (1981), 79, 111, 232; on the Swiss, 83, 149
[50] Bitossi (1976), 151.
[51] B11–12, s.v. 'Scuole pubbliche'.
[52] B3, f. 63 verso: B11–12, s.v. 'Cavarsi di beretta'.
[53] Trexler (1980), 51–2.
[54] B11–12, s.v. 'Strade pubbliche'.
[55] B11–12, s.v. 'Palazzo pubblico'.
[56] B11–12, s.v. 'Statue'.
[57] Spinola (1981), 81, 83, 111, 122, 129, 165, 214; B11–12, s.v. 'Venetia'.

the same time, which came to a head in the movement of Renier
Zen, a leading noble who became the spokesman of the poor
nobles.[58] A movement which did not last.

In similar fashion, the appeal of Cebà and Spinola to traditional republican values went unheeded in Genoa. It is impossible
to say how many people shared their opinions. The sixteenth-
century texts quoted above show that they did not stand completely alone, and the circulation of Spinola's reflections in
manuscript suggests sympathy for his ideas, but on the other
hand the two friends were unable to make much impression on
the system. In the next generation the greatest literary and intellectual figure was a patrician of quite another stamp, Anton
Giulio Brignole Sale, yet another member of the Addormentati,
who wrote against Tacitus, built a magnificent palace and had
himself painted on horseback by Van Dyck before joining the
Jesuits. English visitors were impressed by the 'Kingly magnificence' of the Strada Nuova and the 'Kingly luxury' of the
Genoese.[59] This luxury led Joseph Addison, who visited the city
at the beginning of the eighteenth century, to the Sallustian conclusion that 'as the state of Genoa is very poor, though several of
its members are extremely rich, so one may observe infinitely
more splendour and magnificence in particular persons' houses,
than in those that belong to the public.'[60]

The traditional dominance of the private sphere – *publice egestas, privatim opulentia* – was too strong to break. Indeed, a
seventeenth-century Genoese writer, inverting Spinola and antici-
pating Bernard Mandeville, argued that private vices were public
benefits: 'che è danno e vizio del privato risulta in qualche
maniera in grandezza e gloria del pubblico.'[61] It is no surprise to
find that the mid seventeenth-century Dutch businessman and
political writer Pieter de la Court, in his *Politike Weegschaal*
(1661), described Genoa as 'marvellous and noteworthy' ('ver-
wonderens en aanmerkenswaardig'), an even better model for the
Dutch Republic than Venice.[62]

---

[58] Cozzi (1958), 243–88.
[59] Moryson (1617), 167; Raymond (1648), 13.
[60] Addison (1705), 363.
[61] Casoni, 'Costumi', ASCG fondo Brignole Sale, 110 E14, f. 2 recto.
[62] Quoted in Haitsma Mulier (1980), 153.

8

Learned Culture and Popular Culture in Renaissance Italy

The study of the Italian Renaissance continues to flourish. The history of popular culture continues to expand. Recent studies of popular culture have argued, reasonably enough, that it is more fruitful to study interactions between learned culture and popular culture than to attempt to define what separates them.[1] All the same, studies of the Italian Renaissance have little to say about popular culture, and studies of Italian popular culture even less to say about the Renaissance.[2] To consider whether the gap should be filled and how it might be filled is the purpose of this chapter.

It is understandable that the two cultures should have been studied separately, since a number of barriers excluded ordinary people from the world of Renaissance art and literature. In the first place, there was the barrier of language. Much of high culture was Latin culture, but the vast majority of the population did not study Latin. Ordinary people spoke their regional dialect, and outside Tuscany only the upper classes knew the reformed Tuscan which was on its way to becoming standard literary Italian. In the second place, there was the barrier of literacy. Reading and writing were skills possessed by only a minority of the population, even if that minority was a large one in the case

[1] Kaplan (1984); Chartier (1987).
[2] Burke (1972), 29–31, and Burke (1978), 271–2; cf. Cohn (1988).

of urban males. In the third place, there was the economic barrier preventing ordinary people from buying books or paintings.

However, all these obstacles could be surmounted. According to a recent history of Italian education in this period, 'almost all the vernacular schools taught the rudiments of Latin grammar.'[3] The dialect of Tuscans, especially Florentines, gave them access to the literary language. Inhabitants of large towns such as Venice, Florence, Rome and Milan had relatively easy access to schools, and also to works of art displayed in public places – frescoes in churches, statues on the piazza, and so on.

Historians of Italian culture of this period have therefore to deal with a two-way process. On one side, there is the spread of the forms and ideas of the Renaissance from the elites to the people, their social as well as their geographical diffusion. For convenience – using a simple spatial metaphor – we may call this a movement 'downward'. On the other side, there is movement 'upward', in which Italian artists and writers drew on the heritage of popular culture.

This essay will therefore be divided into two parts. All the same, it has a common theme. On both sides of the interaction, we must look not only for appropriation but also for reception and assimilation. Ariosto, for example, transformed the traditional romances of chivalry he read into something very different in tone and spirit. On the other side, Menocchio the miller, a long-forgotten figure restored to history by Carlo Ginzburg, read the *Golden Legend*, the *Travels* attributed to Sir John Mandeville, Boccaccio's *Decameron* and so on, but what he found in these texts was rather different from what was seen by the inquisitors who interrogated him.[4]

The Popularization of the Renaissance

In Italy in the sixteenth and seventeenth centuries, some ordinary people were familiar with a part of the classical tradition. For example, works by Cicero, Ovid and Virgil were translated into the vernacular at this time. The story about the Roman matron Lucretia and her suicide following her rape by King Tarquin appears to have been quite well known. A version quoting 'Livy

[3] Grendler (1988), 50.
[4] Ginzburg (1976), sections 12–14.

of Padua' as its source (though it probably drew more directly on Boccaccio) was turned into an Italian ballad which was printed in Venice by Agostino Bindoni, whose family of printers specialized in cheap popular texts.

A relatively clear-cut example of movement downwards is that of the popularization of Ariosto's *Orlando Furioso*. The poem was of course written by a noble for nobles, and in its published form it was quite expensive. However, the 'laments' of characters from the poem such as Bradamante, Isabella, Rodomonte, Ruggiero and so on, as well as other verse paraphrases, supplements and summaries, were available in chap-book form in the sixteenth century. Some of these texts were anonymous, but one – an attempt to compress the 'beauties' of the poem into sixteen pages – was the work of the Bolognese poet Giulio Cesare Croce, a well-known mediator between learned and popular culture.[5]

It cannot be assumed that these paraphrases and summaries were intended for ordinary people alone. The library of Henri III of France contained a book entitled *Bellezze del Furioso*, almost certainly selections from Ariosto. However, Ariosto's popular appeal was noted by some contemporary observers. According to the poet Bernardo Tasso, the *Furioso* was read by craftsmen and children. According to the Venetian publisher Comin dal Trino, it appealed to common people (*il volgo*).[6] Unusually for the sixteenth century, this modern text was taught in some schools alongside the Latin classics.[7] There is also evidence from the archives, mainly from heresy trials, for interest in Ariosto on the part of ordinary people. In Venice a swordsmith's apprentice, a silk merchant and a prostitute all confessed to reading *Orlando Furioso*. In Calvin's Geneva an Italian once found himself in trouble because he had described the book as his 'Bible'.[8]

Montaigne's journal of his visit to Italy offers us further evidence of Ariosto's penetration of popular culture. At a spa near Lucca, for example, he met a poor peasant woman named Divizia, who could not read or write but had often heard Ariosto read aloud in her father's house, thanks to which she had become a poet herself. Near Florence, and elsewhere in Italy, Montaigne

[5] Camporesi (1976).
[6] Quoted Javitch (1991).
[7] Grendler (1988), 298.
[8] Mackenney (1987), 184; Martin (1987); Ruggiero (1993); Monter (1969), 66.

tells us that he was surprised to meet peasants and shepherdesses who knew Ariosto by heart. In the eighteenth century, visitors to Naples sometimes described the professional storytellers who read, or more exactly performed Ariosto's poem in the streets and squares of the city, with the text at hand to assist their memory if it failed.[9]

The poems of Torquato Tasso also seem to have entered popular culture. His epic *Gerusalemme liberata* was translated into a number of dialects – Bolognese in 1628, Bergamask in 1670, Neapolitan in 1689, Venetian in 1693, and so on. Joseph Addison's *Remarks on Several Parts of Italy* (1705) noted the custom 'of the common people of this country, of singing stanzas out of Tasso', a point which would be repeated by Rousseau and Goethe in the case of the Venetian gondoliers.

One would of course like to know much more about these incidents – how faithfully the peasants, storytellers and gondoliers remembered the texts, and, still more important, what the epics of Ariosto and Tasso meant to them. My own hypothesis would be that ordinary people read or heard *Orlando Furioso* and *Gerusalemme liberata* as examples of romances of chivalry – or as they called them, 'books of battles' (*libri di battagie*) – which were widely available in chap-book form in sixteenth-century Italy and were sometimes used in elementary schools to encourage boys to learn to read. Menocchio the miller also enjoyed this kind of literature.[10]

In the case of the visual arts, the relation between learned and popular is considerably more complicated, because the 'high' art of the Italian Renaissance was generally produced by men with the training and status of craftsmen. They produced religious paintings without the opportunity to study theology, and scenes from classical mythology without being able to read Latin, let alone Greek. It follows that works like Botticelli's *Primavera*, or Titian's *Sacred and Profane Love*, which appear to refer to Neoplatonic ideas, must have been the outcome of a complex process of mediation between learned and popular culture, in which the participants included not only artists and patrons but also humanists, such as Angelo Poliziano and Marsilio Ficino, and popularizers, such as the Venetian professional writers or *poligrafi*.[11]

[9] Moore (1781), letter 60; Blunt (1823), 290.
[10] Grendler (1988); cf. Lucchi (1982); Ginzburg (1976), section 14.
[11] Panofsky (1939), 129–69; Ginzburg (1978).

Paintings of this kind, secular in subject-matter, were not widely seen during the Renaissance. They belonged to the 'private' rather than the 'public' circuit.[12] It was, however, possible for a wider public to see graphic versions of some of them, notably the engravings after Raphael by Marcantonio Raimondi. The work of art had already entered the age of mechanical reproduction. Like printing, engraving was a great popularizer, at least in the sense that it allowed many more people to see images, and probably more kinds of people as well.

Ceramics offered another means of diffusing images more widely, since the raw material was cheap. The majolica plates and jugs produced in Faenza, Urbino, Deruta and elsewhere were frequently decorated with scenes from classical mythology and ancient history. Some were based on the Raimondi engravings after Raphael. Some of these ceramics were made for wealthy patrons, but others were simple drug-pots for the shops of apothecaries.[13] The painted terracotta images produced by the Della Robbia family workshop in Florence might be regarded as the poor man's sculptures. The workshop produced some large expensive altarpieces for churches, but also small images for wayside shrines or private individuals. It would be an exaggeration to speak of 'mass-production' but signs of hasty work can be found and it is not uncommon for a particular image (an Adoration, say, or a Madonna and Child) to survive in eight, nine, ten, or even twenty almost identical copies.[14]

The problem is of course to discover how people who were not members of a cultural elite perceived these objects, and especially whether or not they were interested in the styles as well as the stories. In the case of Florence, at least, there is evidence of a sophisticated popular visual culture. Some ordinary people, craftsmen and shopkeepers, were not only familiar with the names of the leading artists of their city, past and present, but they were not afraid to offer opinions – often critical opinions – about the value of particular works. Some of the evidence for this statement comes from Vasari's *Lives of the Artists* (1550), which from time to time discusses popular reactions to particular works of art or artists. Particularly interesting in this respect is Vasari's discussion of Florentine responses to Perugino, beginning with

[12] Ginzburg (1978) 79, adapting Burke (1972), 144, 158.
[13] Rackham (1952).
[14] Marquand (1922), nos 122–42, 157–67, 302–9, 312–20.

enthusiasm and ending with satire. Vasari's testimony to popular interest in aesthetics may be supplemented by that of Antonfrancesco Grazzini, a man of the shopkeeper class (probably an apothecary), whose poems, or more exactly songs (*madrigalesse*), sometimes mention works of art. Two of these songs comment critically on Vasari's decision to paint the cupola of the cathedral of Florence, declaring 'the fault was George's' ('Giorgin fece il peccato') and that it showed 'little sense and less judgement' ('poco senno e men giudizio').

Popular Inspiration in the Renaissance

It is time to turn from the popularization of the Renaissance to the importance of 'low' elements in 'high' culture. The presiding genius over this section of the chapter is of course Mikhail Bakhtin, whose *World of Rabelais* (written in the 1930s, but not published until 1965) argued that the author of *Gargantua and Pantagruel* drew heavily on the 'culture of folk humour', in particular the grotesque and the carnivalesque.[15] This work, which is a *tour de force* of the historical imagination, has been taken as a model for recent studies of Breughel, Shakespeare and other artists and writers of the Renaissance.

The World of Rabelais has also been criticized by Renaissance specialists. On the assumption that Bakhtin claims that *Gargantua and Pantagruel* belongs wholly to popular culture, critics have pointed out that Rabelais was a learned man and that his work would not have been fully comprehensible to ordinary people.[16] Unfortunately, Bakhtin's account of the relation between 'high' and 'low' culture was neither precise nor explicit. At times the contrast or opposition with which he is concerned seems to be that between the culture of two social groups, the elite and the people. At other times the two opposed cultures are defined in functional terms as the 'official' and the 'unofficial'. These distinctions may overlap but they do not coincide. The students of Montpellier, for example, whose festivities Bakhtin describes, belonged to a social elite, but participated in unofficial culture.

Another important distinction which remains blurred in

[15] Bakhtin (1965).
[16] Screech (1979).

Bakhtin's work is that between appropriating (and transforming) elements from popular culture (which Rabelais certainly does) and participating fully in that culture. I have argued elsewhere that sixteenth-century European elites were 'bicultural'. They had a learned culture from which ordinary people were excluded, but they also participated in what we now call 'popular' culture.[17] Would these elites have participated in the same way as people for whom popular culture was all the culture they had? Or did they associate popular culture with particular times and places of relaxation? The concept of 'participation' is itself somewhat elusive. Despite these ambiguities, and the need to draw more careful distinctions, Bakhtin's study both could and should inspire future research on the various cultures and subcultures of Renaissance Italy, encouraging us to ask exactly what artists and writers took from popular traditions, as well as what they did with what they appropriated.

There have been relatively few studies of this kind. Before Bakhtin, Domenico Guerri had already examined what he called 'the popular current in the Renaissance', but he virtually limited himself to the subject of jokes and comic verses in Florence.[18] The art historian Eugenio Battisti published a wide-ranging study of what he called the 'Anti-Renaissance', a fascinating collection of essays on medieval, mannerist, grotesque, occult and other themes in art and literature. However, Battisti tried to pack too much into his category of 'anti-Renaissance'. His chapters range from self-conscious rejections of classicism to medieval survivals which might be better described as 'non-Renaissance'.[19]

In the case of art, one might begin the study of the interaction between high and low with certain grotesque or comic sculptures, already mentioned in the chapter on humour. It might be unwise to assume that whatever is comic is necessarily popular, but it is worth remembering that Aristotle – as interpreted by Italian humanists – argued that comedy was concerned with 'low' people. Take for example the statue by the sculptor Valerio Cioli representing Grand Duke Cosimo de' Medici's favourite dwarf, nicknamed 'Morgante' after the giant in Pulci's poem of that name. The statue was placed in the Boboli gardens, a place of

[17] Burke (1978), 24–9.
[18] Guerri (1931).
[19] Battisti (1962).

relaxation which has been described as a kind of sixteenth-century 'fun house'.[20] In similar fashion the famous gardens of Bomarzo, created for the Roman aristocrat Vicino Orsini, might be described as a kind of sixteenth-century Disneyland. The huge stone monsters, the leaning tower, and the hell mouth all play on a popular taste for the grotesque, whatever layers of learned meaning have been superimposed on it.[21]

The Commedia dell'Arte also deserves study from the point of view of this essay, with special reference to the fascinating and perplexing problem of the relation between the characters or masks of this apparently popular art form – the boastful soldier, the foolish old man, the cunning servant – and those of ancient Greek and Roman drama. Did the extemporizers owe their knowledge of these masks to the humanists? Or did the classical masks survive 'underground' in popular culture, to emerge in the sixteenth century, and inspire 'high' Renaissance drama?

The paragraphs which follow concentrate on literature, and especially on four writers: Boccaccio, Folengo, Ariosto and Aretino (at the expense of Burchiello, Berni, Pulci, Ruzante, Calmo and other examples of mediators between the two cultures). These four writers will be discussed in chronological order, which also happens to be a logical order, an order of increasing complexity in the relation between learned and popular culture. The increase in complexity over time is probably no accident, but the result of a process which may be described as the 'withdrawal' of elites from participation in popular culture.[22]

The obvious place to start is of course Boccaccio's *Decameron*. As in the case of Rabelais, Boccaccio is remembered today for his 'vulgarity', so that it needs to be emphasized that he too was a learned man, a university teacher who wrote treatises in Latin and lectured on Dante. His Tuscan was 'canonized' in the sixteenth century (along with Dante's and Petrarch's) as a model of pure Italian. All the same, it is clear that many of the stories in the *Decameron* were taken from popular oral tradition, from what nineteenth-century scholars called 'folktales', and also that they illustrate some of Bakhtin's favourite themes.

The place of the carnivalesque in Boccaccio's work is clear

[20] Barolsky (1978), 153ff.; Heikamp (1969).
[21] Battisti (1962), 125ff.; Bredekamp (1985); Lazzaro (1990).
[22] Burke (1978), 270–81.

enough, above all in the story of Frate Alberto (day 4, story 2), which ends with a ritualized hunt of the 'wild man' on Piazza San Marco in Venice.[23] A number of the stories include episodes of what Bakhtin calls 'grotesque realism' or 'degradation'. This would, for example, be a plausible way of reading the first story in the collection, the tale of the wicked notary who managed to trick posterity into venerating him as a saint. Tricks recur in Boccaccio's *novelle*, as they do in those of other storytellers of the Renaissance (such as Sacchetti, Masuccio Salernitano, Bandello, and Grazzini), who draw on the popular tradition of the *beffa* described above (chapter 5). For example, Bruno and Buffalmaco persuade the painter Calandrino, who is portrayed as a simpleton, to look for a magic stone which is supposed to make whoever carries it invisible, or they steal his pig and then 'prove' to him that he stole it himself.

The Benedictine monk Teofilo Folengo also drew on the tradition of the *beffa* in the twelfth section of his poem *Baldus*, describing a sea voyage with the owner of a flock of sheep, in which the trickster buys the ram and immediately throws it into the sea, where it is inevitably followed by the rest of the flock. Rabelais later appropriated this episode for his own purposes (in his *Fourth Book*, chapter 6). However, *Baldus*, published in 1517 under the pseudonym 'Merlin Cocaio', is essentially an example of the grotesque, a mock romance of chivalry narrated in a mock epic style. The poem tells the story of a young nobleman, a descendant of the paladin Rinaldo, who is raised among peasants but has his head as full of romances as Don Quixote's would be later in the century. Baldus, together with two companions, a giant called Fracassus and a trickster called Cingar, becomes involved in a series of comic adventures which draw on popular traditions. Bakhtin himself drew attention to the episode in which someone is resurrected from the dead by a drenching in urine.[24]

The subject of Folengo's poem is a hybrid, at once bucolic and chivalric, and the style, appropriately enough, is also hybrid. The language is a form of Latin which often behaves as if it were Italian or dialect – a mixture of two or three codes, or better, a product of their interaction.[25] In a battle scene, for example, the

[23] Mazzotti (1986).
[24] Bakhtin (1965), 150; cf. Bonora and Chiesa (1979).
[25] Cf. Borsellino (1973), 89.

rhetoric of the 'high' style, appropriate for epic encounters, is constantly pulled down to earth by the use of crudely Latinized technical terms such as *alebardae* (halberds), *banderae* (banners), *lanzae* (lances), *partesanae* (partisans), *picchiae* (pikes), *stendardi* (standards) and so on, or by words imitating the sound of drums and trumpets:

> Stendardique volant, banderae; timpana pon pon
> continuo chioccant; sonitantque tarantara trombae.

The epic begins with an invocation not to the muses, but to plump country girls, fattened on polenta and macaroni (or gnocchi). Hence the style is now known as 'macaronic' Latin. Folengo was the greatest master of this language but he was not its inventor. It was a literary elaboration of the language of notaries, who wrote it for convenience, and of students, who spoke it for fun.[26]

The first example, that of Boccaccio, shows a learned man drawing on a popular tradition in which he participated. The second, that of Folengo, is more complex, since it shows a learned man making a self-conscious synthesis of learned and popular traditions, or at least playing with the tensions between them.

The example of Ariosto is still more complicated. Like the *Baldus*, *Orlando Furioso* is a romance of chivalry, or a mock romance of chivalry – it is difficult to choose between these alternatives because Ariosto deliberately hovers on the edge of parody. The romance of chivalry was originally a high-status genre: stories about nobles, written for nobles, and in some cases (including that of Ariosto himself) written by nobles. However, as we have seen, this genre was also part of Italian popular culture in the sixteenth century. It took the form of printed chapbooks and also of oral performances by wandering singers of tales, or *cantimbanchi*, who sang or recited the stories on the piazza, asking for money at the end of each instalment, thus leaving the audience in suspense till they had made their contribution. The printed versions and the oral versions influenced each other.

Like other men of letters, Ariosto enjoyed these oral performances and his poem owes something to them.[27] For example, although he wrote to be read, the author took over some of the

26 Paoli (1959).
27 Bronzini (1966).

popular formulas telling the audience to listen – 'as I shall continue the story in the next canto' ('come io vi seguirò ne l'altro canto'), and so on. Ariosto thus exemplifies a complex process of reappropriation, that of an educated man borrowing and transforming popular themes which had earlier been borrowed from high culture. When the *Furioso* was itself popularized, as we have seen it was, we are confronted with a case of double reappropriation. Circularities of this kind are not unknown today. For example, a novel by the Brazilian writer Jorge Amado, *Tereza Batista* (1972), draws on a chap-book by Rodolfo Coelho Cavalcanti (these booklets were and perhaps still are circulating in the northeast of Brazil, at least in the areas most remote from towns and television). Cavalcanti drew in turn on the traditional theme of the *donzela guerreira* or warrior maiden which goes back to the romances of chivalry – and of course to Ariosto's heroine Bradamante (cf. chapter 9 below).[28]

The last example to be discussed here is that of Pietro Aretino. Aretino made his reputation in Rome as a composer of biting pasquinades.[29] The *pasquinata* was a genre on the frontier between learned and popular culture. The practice of attaching satiric verses to the mutilated classical statue on Piazza del Pasquino in Rome goes back to the later fifteenth century, and at that time the verses were in humanist Latin. In the early sixteenth century, it became common to write the verses in a vernacular which everyone could understand. Aretino went on to write *Il Marescalco*, the carnival comedy built around a *beffa* described in chapter 5 (above, p. 83).

However, the best example of the mixture or interaction of learned and popular elements in Aretino's work is surely his *Ragionamenti*, dialogues in which an old prostitute instructs a young one in the skills of the profession. The dialogues offer a series of scenes from low life in early sixteenth-century Rome, apparently faithful to the colloquial language and the slang of that social milieu. At the same time, humanist readers would have been aware that the dialogues borrow from and allude to a classical Greek text, Lucian's *Dialogues of the Courtesans*. The dialogues also may be read as a parody of Renaissance treatises on good manners, and especially of Castiglione's famous *Book of the Courtier*.

[28] Slater (1982), 146.
[29] Larivaille (1980), 47ff.

Here as elsewhere Aretino exploits the similarities between the terms *cortegiano*, 'courtier', and *cortegiana*, 'courtesan'.

Aretino was the son of a craftsman, he grew up in the world of popular culture, and to the end of his life he appreciated street singers. He was a friend of Andrea, one of the court fools to Pope Leo X. Like the painters already discussed, he lacked the opportunity for a conventional humanist education in Latin and Greek (it was presumably a more learned friend who drew Lucian to his attention). He came to high culture as an outsider and he rejected some of it as artificial and affected, notably the conventions for the Petrarchan love sonnet and the rules for spoken Italian laid down by Castiglione's friend Pietro Bembo (rules which are mocked in the *Ragionamenti*). Like his friend the artist Giulio Romano, Aretino liked to break rules. In this sense he was a self-conscious 'mannerist' or 'anti-classicist'.[30] Low culture, the culture in which he grew up, was his instrument to subvert high culture, or at least those parts of it which he disliked. One might say that he drew on the non-Renaissance for the purposes of an anti-Renaissance.

Cultural historians are surely right to shift, as they have been doing, from concern with popular culture in itself to a study of the long process of interaction between learned and popular elements. If we focus on the interaction between high and low, however, we need to recognize the variety or polymorphism of this process. The examples cited in this chapter do not exhaust the range of possibilities, but they may at least be sufficient to suggest the remarkable range of possible relationships between high and low, the uses of popular culture for Renaissance writers, the uses of the Renaissance for ordinary people, and finally, the importance of the 'circular tour' of images and themes, a circular tour in which what returns is never the same as what set out.

[30] Larivaille (1980); Borsellino (1973), 16–40.

9

Chivalry in the New World

❧

The message of this chapter can be summed up in a sentence, almost a headline. Charlemagne is not dead: he is living in Latin America, or he was until comparatively recently. The New World came late to chivalry, since it was obviously impossible for its inhabitants to learn about this European value system and the romances which expressed it until 1492, and it may be thought that the behaviour of Cortés and Pizarro in Mexico and Peru did nothing to make the value system more intelligible to the Aztecs or the Incas. On the other hand, once the tradition had been transplanted, it was in the New World, or parts of it, that the romances of chivalry retained their appeal longest, notably in the north-east of Brazil.

At the time of the discovery of America, or to use a somewhat less ethnocentric expression, at the beginning of a series of encounters between the cultures of Europe and the cultures of America, the Renaissance movement had long been under way. However, as we have seen (above, chapter 8), the enthusiasm for classical antiquity did not drive out the love of romances of chivalry. In both the literal and the metaphorical sense these romances formed an important part of the baggage of the *conquistadores*.

In Spain in the Middle Ages, romances of chivalry were a popular oral and literary genre. Muslims as well as Christians composed, recited and read them, and a considerable number of these stories, including the usual giants, enchanted palaces, swords with names and female warriors, survive in Spanish written in the Arabic script.[1] As in other parts of Renaissance Europe, a number of Spanish humanists rejected the romances of chivalry as 'foolish' or 'silly books', generations before the more affectionate mockery of Cervantes. In 1524, Juan Luis Vives condemned *Amadís*, *Lancelot* and *Pierre de Provence*, and five years later, Antonio de Guevara condemned *Amadís*.[2] Similar criticisms were made later in the century by the humanists Pedro Mexia and Benito Arias Montano and the preacher Luis de Granada. Whatever Don Quixote may have been doing, Cervantes himself was not tilting at windmills. In Spain in the first half of the sixteenth century, new romances of chivalry were published 'at an average rate of almost one a year', while the total number of editions of such romances totalled over 150.[3] The authors included at least one woman, the noble lady Beatriz Bernal of Valladolid, who published two romances in 1545, *Don Cristalion* and *Lepomene*.[4]

One at least of these romances is still taken seriously by literary critics, and was recently translated into English: the fifteenth-century Catalan romance *Tirant lo Blanc*. Even the book-burners in *Don Quixote* agreed to save it because it was, as the priest said, 'the best book of its kind in the world', a judgement shared by one of today's leading Latin American writers, Mário Vargas Llosa. Even more successful in the sixteenth century were two cycles of romances in Castilian. There was *Palmerín de Oliva*, which began publication in 1511, and there was *Amadís de Gaula*, first published about the year 1508. *Amadís* was not only much reprinted but followed by a series of continuations by some half-a-dozen authors, dealing with the adventures of the son of Amadís, the grandson of Amadís, and so on, heroes with names like Esplandián, Lisuarte and Amadís of Greece. By 1546 the cycle had been extended to twelve books. These adventure stories had a wide appeal in Renaissance Italy, in France, in England and elsewhere.

In Spain the *aficionados* of these romances included Emperor Charles V, the diplomat Diego Hurtado de Mendoza, and the

---

[1] Galmés de Fuentes (1967).
[2] Leonard (1949), 68–9; cf. Ife (1985).
[3] Thomas (1920), 147; Chevalier (1976), 67.
[4] Bennassar (1967), 519.

reformer Juan de Valdés.[5] Among the more famous examples of documented reader response are the testimonies of two Counter-Reformation saints who happen to have left us accounts of their lives. In his autobiography, Ignatius Loyola tells us that he was 'much given to reading the worldly and false books known as romances of chivalry' ('muy dado a leer libros mundanos y falsos que suelen llamar de cabellerías') and that before he was ordained priest, he kept vigil before the altar of Our Lady of Monsarrat because 'his head was full of ... Amadís of Gaul and similar books' ('tenía todo el entendimiento lleno de ... Amadís de Gaula y de semejantes libros').

Similarly, Teresa of Avila remarks in her memoirs that her mother was 'a fan of romances of chivalry' ('aficionada a libros de caballerías') and that she shared this enthusiasm in her youth, information which makes Beatriz Bernal's decision to write in this apparently male genre easier to understand. Research on the history of reading based on the study of library inventories confirms the impression of widespread enthusiasm for these books on the part of sixteenth-century Spaniards, merchants as well as nobles.[6] The romances were shortened and published in the form of verse chap-books or *pliegos sueltos*, which suggests that they had become part of popular culture.[7]

Like the Spaniards, Portuguese readers of the sixteenth century loved romances of chivalry, including the famous *Amadís*, which may have been originally composed in Portugal around the year 1350. Books 7, 9 and 10 of the continuation were printed in Lisbon in the sixteenth century.[8] The humanist João de Barros was not only a famous historian of the exploits of the Portuguese in Asia, but also the author of a romance, *Clarimundo* (1520), which enjoyed considerable success. The Palmerín cycle was continued by Portuguese writers such as Francisco de Morães and Diogo Fernández. When the poet Luis de Camões introduced his epic *The Lusiads* (1572) by contrasting his narrative with the 'fantastic' or 'fabulous' deeds of Roland and Roger, he could assume that his readers were familiar with these romances. One publisher of the Amadís and Palmerín cycles was Marcos Borges, who had been appointed royal printer in 1566. The king on the

[5] Leonard (1949), 19–21.
[6] Bennassar (1967), 511–19; cf. Chevalier (1976), ch. 1; Berger (1987).
[7] Norton and Wilson (1969).
[8] Anselmo (1926), nos 789, 815, 364.

throne at the time was Sebastian, who was killed at the battle of Alcazarkebir in 1578 after invading North Africa to conquer and convert the 'Moors'. Whether or not the king was a particular enthusiast for romances of chivalry, Sebastian certainly tried to behave like one of the heroes of these romances, while after his death he would be assimilated to these heroes, as we shall see.

Given this continuing interest in the genre in Spain and Portugal, it is scarcely surprising to find references to romances of chivalry early in the history of the conquest and settlement of the New World. Whether Columbus read them or not we cannot be sure, but a number of these romances could be found in the library of his son Fernando.[9] References in the letters of Cortés imply that he too was familiar with this literature.[10] By 1531 the government was worried enough by the spread of this enthusiasm to order the House of Trade at Seville to prohibit the export to the Indies of 'vain' romances such as *Amadís*.[11]

One of the most interesting pieces of evidence comes from the history of the conquest of Mexico written by Bernal Díaz del Castillo. When Díaz is describing the first sight of the Aztec capital, the city in the lake, he writes that 'we said that it was like the enchanted things related in the book of Amadís because of the huge towers, temples, and buildings rising from the water.' As in the case of the travellers discussed in chapter 6, we find life imitating art, or more exactly experience influenced by fiction. Díaz also made the revealing assumption that a reference to *Amadís* would make this exotic land seem more familiar to his readers. His aim was 'to translate ... the utterly strange into what we might call the familiarly strange'.[12]

Another interesting early piece of evidence about chivalry in the New World is a name: California. By the middle of the sixteenth century, it was already being used about the Pacific Coast of North America. However, the name was first used of a fictional island. In the romance *Esplandián*, a continuation of the Amadís story first published in 1510, we learn of a group of warlike women ruled by a certain Queen Calafia, 'mistress of the great island of California, celebrated for its great abundance of gold and jewels', an island on which men are forbidden to set

[9] Huntington (1905).
[10] Leonard (1949), 50.
[11] Sánchez (1958), 246–7.
[12] Sánchez (1958); Gilman (1960–3); Hulme (1994), 170.

foot. The queen challenges both Amadís and his son Esplandián to single combat, is vanquished, and becomes a Christian. The application of the name California to part of America suggests that other people besides Bernal Díaz and his comrades perceived the New World through spectacles coloured by romances of chivalry.

A similar point could be made about the vast region of Amazonia, which began to be explored by the Spaniards in the early 1540s. The expedition led by Francisco de Orellana is said to have given the River Amazon its present name after a fight with the local Indians in which women took active part. According to the Dominican friar Gaspar de Carvajal, who took part in this expedition, the women warriors were tall and pale, they were armed with bows and arrows, and they lived in villages of their own, subject to a female ruler called Coroni.[13]

Traditional myths or stereotypes of the so-called 'monstrous races' were thus revitalized and projected onto the New World.[14] Although the myth of the Amazons went back to classical times, as humanists well knew, it had been revived in fifteenth-century Italy. It was at this time that viragos begin to play an important role in Italian romances and that we find the topos of the maiden who will only accept as a husband a man who vanquishes her in battle, like Galiziella in the Aspramonte of Andrea da Barberino, an Amazon from the 'kingdom of women' (*regno feminino*). The figure of Marfisa in Matteo Boiardo's *Orlando Innamorato* (1483), of Bradamante in Ludovico Ariosto's still more famous *Orlando Furioso* (1516) and of Clorinda in Tasso's *Gerusalemme liberata* (1581) are the most memorable examples of this tradition.[15] It may at least be suggested – and it has indeed been suggested – that the Renaissance revival of interest in the classical tradition of the Amazons was encouraged by Columbus's report of Amazons in the Indies.[16] For Carvajal and Díaz alike, the New World seemed to be the place where European romances of chivalry came true.

The emigrants from Spain to Mexico and Peru took these romances of chivalry with them, or had them supplied by booksellers, as has been shown by the American scholar Irving

[13] Carvajal (1955), 97, 105; cf. Sánchez (1958), 250–4.
[14] Friedman (1981), 9, 170–1, 197–207.
[15] Rajna (1872), 49–52; Tomalin (1982), 82ff.
[16] Leonard (1949), 53.

Leonard, who studied records of book shipments preserved in the archives of the House of Trade at Seville.[17] Thanks to his research, it is now known that in Mexico City in 1540, the printer Juan Cromberger had no fewer than 446 copies of *Amadís* in stock in his shop.[18] In Lima in 1583, Amadís was 'still among the favourites'.[19] In Tucumán in 1597, a provincial synod condemned the spread of 'immoral books and romances of chivalry'.[20] In 1600, 10,000 copies of the romance *Pierres y Magalona* entered Mexico.[21] Among the New World enthusiasts for these romances was the 'Inca Garcilaso', a Peruvian nobleman and historian who emigrated to Spain.[22]

At this point we are faced with a gap in the evidence. In the case of Brazil, there appear to be no sixteenth-century references to romances of chivalry. Indeed, a history of the press in Brazil remarks on the absence of books of any kind from inventories as late as the seventeenth century, in striking contrast with the Spanish viceroyalties of Mexico and Peru.[23] Books might be imported, but they were not allowed to be printed in Brazil until the early nineteenth century. All the same, it is in Brazil that we find the richest documentation for chivalry in the New World in the late nineteenth and early twentieth centuries. Charlemagne and his paladins occupied a significant place in the popular imagination.

About the year 1840, an American Protestant missionary, the Reverend Daniel Kidder, was visiting the small town of Maceió, in the north-east of Brazil, on the coast between Salvador and Recife. He entered a shop and found the shop assistant reading at the counter. 'His book', Kidder remarked, apparently with some astonishment, 'was a life of Carlos Magno.'[24] The missionary should not have been surprised, for the interest in stories about Charlemagne was in no way unusual for the region and the period.

The *História de Carlos Magno* which the shop assistant was reading is the key text in the Brazilian reception of the romances

[17] Leonard (1933).
[18] Leonard (1949), 98.
[19] Leonard (1949), 223.
[20] Leonard (1949), 88.
[21] Marín (1911), 36.
[22] Durand (1948), 263.
[23] Sodré (1966), 12.
[24] Kidder (1845), vol. 2, 96.

of chivalry. It was still being read in the twentieth century, when the avant-garde writer Oswald de Andrade recorded his enthusiasm for the book, an enthusiasm which he shared with anarchists and labour leaders.[25] Research on the history of this text goes some way towards filling the gap mentioned above. In the National Library of Lisbon there is a chap-book of 1794 with a similar title, *Historia nova do imperador Carlos Magno e dos doze pares de França*. It has been shown that this text was derived from a Spanish romance of 1525, which drew in turn on a French romance of 1486. The gap between Portugal in 1794 and Brazil in the 1870s has to be filled by conjecture, but it is plausible enough to suggest that the Portuguese chap-book was exported to Brazil, which as noted above relied more heavily on Europe for books than the Spanish American colonies did.

In Brazil itself, chap-books, which used to be called *folhetos* and are now best known as 'stories on a string', *literatura de cordel*, began to be printed only in the later nineteenth century. These texts are still produced in considerable numbers today. As in the case of early modern European chap-books, they were and are well adapted to a situation of restricted literacy. They are generally in verse, normally what are known as *sextilhas* (six-line stanzas with seven syllables to the line). They were (and are) generally printed on small presses and distributed in the first instance by the composers or *cantadores* themselves, who gave oral performances accompanied by music in marketplaces on market days and then sold the texts to the listeners. The text may be regarded as a kind of souvenir of the performance, or the performance as a kind of commercial for the text. It does not matter too much whether the buyers can read or not, for it is generally possible for them to find someone else who will read or chant the text to them.[26]

The repertoire of these *cantadores* was and remains varied, but an important group of late nineteenth- and early twentieth-century *folhetos* was derived from the romances of chivalry and dealt with the exploits of Roland, the treason of Ganelon, and so on.[27] For example, the first major writer of *folhetos*, Leandro Gomes de Barros, who died in 1918, was well known for his

[25] Meyer (1993), 147–59.
[26] Arantes (1982); Slater (1982).
[27] Ferreira (1979); Peloso (1984), 62ff.

Batalha de Oliveiros com Ferrabrás. The story of Fierabras is a medieval French verse epic which was adapted into other languages such as Provençal, Spanish, English, German and Italian. Like the Spanish *conquistadores*, the poets of north-eastern Brazil appear at times to see the world through the spectacles of romances of chivalry. The famous bandit Lampião, for example, who was finally killed by the police in 1938, was described in contemporary ballads as 'worse than Robert the Devil' ('pior do que Roberto do Diabo'), a reference to a medieval French romance which was still circulating in Brazil at that point in time.[28]

Even today, a few *folhetos* dealing with subjects from romances of chivalry can still be found, as well as modern works which exploit this tradition. Jorge Amado, whose novels were sometimes inspired by the *cordel*, has created several modern Amazons with knives in their skirts, such as Rosa Palmeirão and Tereza Batista. The great classic of modern Brazilian literature, *Grande Sertão* (1956), by João Guimarães Rosa, may also be interpreted as a New World transformation of the romance of chivalry, by an author familiar from childhood with the *História de Carlos Magno*.[29] *Grande Sertão* deals with the adventures of Riobaldo and Diadorim, a pair of *jagunços*, that is, honourable men of violence who live in the backlands. The two comrades are as close as Roland and Oliver, or perhaps closer, but it is only at the end of the story, when Diadorim is killed in a shoot-out, that we learn that she was a beautiful woman in disguise, a warrior maiden (like Bradamante in Ariosto's *Orlando Furioso*), who had taken to the backlands to avenge the death of her father. An Amazon not so far from Amazonia.[30] The relation of Guimarães Rosa to popular culture was not unlike that of Ariosto. A diplomat, polymath and polyglot who was well acquainted with European literature, he had earlier practised as a doctor in the backlands of Minas Gerais. It is said that when his patients could not afford to pay him, he asked them to tell him a story instead. He was certainly an assiduous student of the local folklore, which appears in his own stories, coexisting and interacting, as in the case of Diadorim, with themes from European high culture.

[28] Peloso (1984), 75.
[29] Meyer (1993), 147–59.
[30] Rosa (1956); Meyer (1993), 147–59.

This classic novel was recently made into a film. Hence the remark at the beginning of the chapter that Charlemagne is still living in Latin America, and the decision of a recent Italian student of the *cordel* to call his book 'The Middle Ages in the Backlands'.[31]

Why have the Middle Ages survived so long in this region? There is of course a sense in which we can say that the romance of chivalry still forms part of Western culture. Children and adults still read adventure stories of different kinds, and some of these genres owe a good deal to the traditions of the medieval romance. It is commonplace to say that stories and films about cowboys are transformations of stories about knights, armed struggles between good and evil with the heroes using six-shooters in the place of swords and the villains wearing sombreros (or in Mexican films, stetsons) instead of turbans. The Amazon or virago has also survived as in the case of Annie in *Annie Get your Gun* (1946) or her lesser-known American predecessors such as Hurricane Nell. Science-fiction offers another type of transformation, drawing some of its material (not to mention plot structures such as the quest) from the magical world of medieval romance.

How do we account for the persistence of these themes? The answers which have been given to this question are very different. On one side we have the ideas of the Canadian critic Northrop Frye about the universal appeal of the basic plot of the romance, the importance of the quest and so on, a brilliantly developed literary analysis which assumes what it ought to prove, the universality of the appeal of this type of adventure story.[32] It may be worth remarking in passing that Frye does not discuss the adventure stories of China or Japan, from the *Water Margin* to *The Forty-Seven Ronin*, and it may be doubted whether these stories, despite their superficial similarities to 'eastern westerns' would altogether fit his categories. For example, the collective heroes of the two stories just cited are very different from the 'Lone Ranger' tradition of Western individualism.

This contrast between East and West supports explanations of the persistence of motifs which are framed in terms of cultural traditions and of social conditions which favour the persistence

[31] Peloso (1984).
[32] Frye (1959), 186ff.

of these traditions. Let us investigate this possibility in the case of the romance of chivalry.

The case of Brazil is not a unique one. In Sicily, a popular puppet theatre featuring Rinaldo and other heroes from romances of chivalry was still flourishing in the early twentieth century, even if it is the tourist industry which keeps it alive today.[33] The tales of Charlemagne and his paladins were the favourite boyhood reading of the famous bandit Salvatore Giuliano, who was killed in 1950.[34] In France, the stories were still being reprinted in cheap format in the middle of the nineteenth century, and it is said that during the First World War, some Breton soldiers passed their time in the trenches reading the medieval romance *The Four Sons of Aymon*. Vargas Llosa's admiration for *Tirant lo Blanc* has already been mentioned.[35] All the same, the continuing importance of the romance of chivalry in the culture of rural Brazil, at least in the north-east, still cries out for explanation.

In parts of Brazil, such as Minas Gerais, Bahia, Pernambuco and Ceará, certain features of the popular culture of early modern Europe remain very much alive. The most obvious example is carnival – not just the big commercialized carnival of Rio, as much for the tourists and the television cameras as for the locals, but the smaller, more traditional, participatory, violent carnivals of Olinda, Salvador, Maranhão and elsewhere (below, chapter 10). Again, *Irmandades* or religious confraternities together with their church-ales or *quermesses* still flourish in the small towns of Minas Gerais. The survival of the chap-books, and in particular of the romances of chivalry, is not an isolated phenomenon.

But how does one explain these survivals? To speak of 'archaism' is to describe, not to explain. To note other cases (such as the Appalachia studied by the musicologist Cecil Sharp) in which colonies or ex-colonies are more faithful to the cultural traditions of the mother country than the metropolis itself is helpful but not sufficiently precise.[36] If we accept the suggestion that a culture's heroes tell something about its basic values, a suggestion which has been developed in an interesting way in the case of Brazil by the anthropologist Roberto Da Matta, the

[33] Lanza (1931).
[34] Maxwell (1956), 34.
[35] Llosa (1969).
[36] Sharp (1907).

problem appears even more central, without of course coming any nearer to a solution.[37]

If we are trying to explain the survival of the romance of chivalry in Brazil, it is of course crucial to establish – if we can – what these stories mean to the participants. We need to take into account the responses of the readers. As it may well be imagined, this task is not an easy one.[38] It is at least possible, however, to focus on one relatively well-documented episode in twentieth-century Brazilian history in which the reading of romances of chivalry played a part. This is the popular revolt of 1912–15, the so-called 'war of Contestado'. It was a revolt of the periphery against the centralizing state, similar in this respect to the more famous revolt of the holy man Antonio Conselheiro in 1896–7, who founded the holy city of Canudos in the backlands of Bahia, in north-eastern Brazil. This revolt has inspired a classic of Brazilian literature, Euclides da Cunha's 'The backlands' (*Os Sertões*, 1902), and, more recently, a novel by Mário Vargas Llosa, *The War of the End of the World* (1980).[39] The Contestado rebellion, in the backlands of Paraná and Santa Caterina, in southern Brazil was also led by holy men, including the monk José Maria, who read to his followers from the *História de Carlos Magno*, the same text which the American missionary Kidder found in the shop in Maceió. The rebels included a small group of skilled fighters who were known as 'the twelve peers of France'.[40]

This rebellion gives us some kind of context in which to place Charlemagne. This is a context of what Eric Hobsbawm has called 'primitive' rebellions against the modern secular state, with its taxes, its censuses and so on.[41] The Brazilian rebellions were viewed by participants as a holy war against this infidel, diabolical state centred in distant Rio de Janeiro. The rebels appealed to 'Dom Sebastião', the sixteenth-century king of Portugal already mentioned, a figure who seems to have been amalgamated with St Sebastian and was expected to return, like King Arthur, in this case to free Brazil from the yoke of the Republic. The

[37] Da Matta (1978).
[38] Meyer (1993), 147–59.
[39] Cunha (1902); Levine (1992).
[40] Monteiro (1974); Diacon (1991), 2, 116, 137, 152.
[41] Hobsbawm (1959).

disobedience of Roland, who ignored the orders of Charlemagne to retreat and lost his life fighting the Moors, seems to have legitimated a revolt against a modern state.[42]

This political interpretation is a plausible one, but it needs to be placed in a wider cultural context. Like the North American cowboy and the South American *gaucho*, the Brazilian *jagunço* may be viewed as a descendant of the medieval knight, especially the knight-errant, thanks to his nomadic way of life, to his concern with honour and not least to his horsemanship, a skill displayed in dramatic form in the rodeos which still take place in Brazil as well as in the USA. As an English medievalist once remarked, 'it is impossible to be chivalrous without a horse.'[43] Like medieval La Mancha, Don Quixote's stamping-ground, and Extremadura, the native region of so many *conquistadores*, north-eastern Brazil was a frontier area, a relatively empty territory of cattle-raising and violence, out of reach of the short arm of the law.[44] In such a region, stories of individualized heroic deeds would find a public ready to listen to them.

In other words, the frontier environment is important to the romance of chivalry as well as to related literary genres such as the ballad and the oral epic.[45] The backlands of north-east Brazil were a frontier society. The New World of the sixteenth century was a frontier society. Come to that, the Iberian peninsula of the late Middle Ages was a frontier society, lacking a central authority and engaged in a constant struggle of Christians against Muslims.[46] In all these places, the ethic of independence prevailed and defiance of a distant authority made good sense. In each region the romance tradition was adapted to local circumstances, but it was because there was already some degree of 'fit' between the tradition and the circumstances that chivalry appealed to local writers, singers, listeners and readers. Transplanting is only possible in the right soil.

[42] Cunha (1902), 136, 164; Monteiro (1974), 109ff.
[43] Denholm-Young, quoted White (1962), 38.
[44] Bishko (1963).
[45] Entwistle (1939); Lord (1960).
[46] Bishko (1963); cf. MacKay (1977), 36ff.

10

The Translation of Culture: Carnival in Two or Three Worlds

For anyone living in Brazil today it is difficult to avoid hear-
ing carnival songs or seeing carnival images all year long,
especially from New Year onwards. As Shrove Tuesday
approaches the newspapers carry more carnival news, and
there is more and more speculation on the relative chances of
different 'samba schools' winning the competition, long before
the spectators enter the Passarela do Samba in Rio or in São
Paulo and the great show begins. Carnival is presented as a
Brazilian speciality and is viewed as such not only by Riotur, the
tourist board of Rio da Janeiro, but also by many ordinary
Brazilians.

Carnival is not only a theme of novels and of films about
Brazil such as Marcel Carné's *Orfeu Negro* (1958), but also a
recurrent theme in Brazilian culture itself. The screenplay of
Orfeu Negro was the work of the poet Vinicius de Morães,
adapting his play *Orfeu da Conceição*, while the music for the
film was written by Luis Bonfa and Antonio Carlos Jobim, better
known as 'Tom'. Other literary examples include Manuel
Bandeira's *Carnaval* (1919), Mario da Andrade's *Carnaval
Carioca* (1923), and Jorge Amado's first novel *O Pais do
Carnaval* (1932). Some of the best songs by Chico Buarque,
Gilberto Gil and other leading composers were originally written
for particular carnivals. For representations of Carnival in

popular culture one has only to look at series such as *Carnaval Duchen* (Rádio e TV Record); *Meu Carnaval não era assim* (TV Tupi); or *Carnaval do passado* (TV Rio).

Carnival is also the theme of a number of recent studies in Brazilian anthropology, sociology and history, most of them by Brazilians themselves. Of these the most famous is Roberto Da Matta's *Carnavais, malandros e heróis* (1978), not so much a study of Carnival for itself as a study of Brazil and of what the author calls 'the Brazilian dilemma'. Da Matta uses Carnival as a means to analyse the conflict between equality and hierarchy in Brazil, along the lines of Clifford Geertz's famous study of the Balinese cock-fight.[1]

Da Matta's study is a brilliant and original one, but (like that of Geertz) it may be criticized as too Durkheimian in the sense that it assumes the unity of the phenomenon, ignoring regional variation and the different meanings of the event for different social groups. Carnival may be a moment of emotional union or *communitas*, and even a truce in the class war. All the same, it does not necessarily have the same meaning for all participants – young working-class men with a need for 'release' (*desabafo*), middle-class middle-aged women who want to join the 'people', tourists who see the festival as a symbol of Brazil, and so on.[2]

Da Matta's interpretation has been supplemented by a number of in-depth studies of the Rio Escolas de Samba by his pupils, notably Maria Julia Goldwasser (1975) on the famous Estação Primeira de Mangueira.[3] One of Brazil's leading sociologists, Maria Isaura Pereira de Queiroz, recently published a history of the Brazilian carnival from colonial times to the present. Maria Isaura's conclusions, and more especially her views of nineteenth-century Rio, have recently been criticized (like Da Matta's) as too unitary.[4] This chapter is not constructed on the assumption that Carnival has a single shared meaning, but it will be limited to a single main theme, the inverse of Da Matta's. The theme, discussed in general terms in chapter 12 below, is that of cultural interaction between different groups – elites and subordinate classes, blacks and whites, men and women. Other aspects of

[1] Geertz (1973), 412–53.
[2] Cf. Turner (1983).
[3] Goldwasser (1975); Leopoldi (1978); Cavalcanti (1994).
[4] Queiroz (1992); Soihet (1993); Pereira (1994).

Carnival, notably its relation to sex and violence, will not be pursued here.[5]

The View from Europe

A European visiting Brazil in February or March may well feel that the Brazilians have annexed Carnival. After all, they did not invent it. Like other European institutions, the carnival, with all its ambiguities and ambivalence, was transported or 'translated' (in the original sense of that term) to the New World. At least to that part of it which was colonized by Catholics from the Mediterranean. It is thanks to French, Spanish and Portuguese immigrants that Carnival became important in the life of New Orleans, Port of Spain and Havana as well as in Rio, Salvador and Olinda.

Anyone familiar with European carnivals will feel at home in many ways when observing or indeed participating in carnivals in the New World. The parallels are impressive. The throwing of eggshells or wax balls full of water, much practised in nineteenth-century Rio, for example, derived from the tradition of the Portuguese *entrudo*, a tradition with many parallels in France, Spain and Italy, whether the missiles were eggs or oranges.[6] The wearing of fancy dress and masks was a traditional European custom, and even some of the favourite American costumes, such as the hussars and harlequins of Rio and the Pierrots and Punchinellos of Trinidad, followed European models. The *desfile* of the Escolas de Samba in Rio today is reminiscent of the parades and allegorical floats which could already be seen in fifteenth-century Florence and Nuremberg.

Again, the Escolas de Samba and their middle-class predecessors, such as the 'Democratics', 'Lieutenants of the Devil' and 'Fenians' in nineteenth-century Rio, are reminiscent of the Abbeys of Youth and other European festive societies. What the Fenians (founded in 1858) meant in Rio a few years later is a fascinating but elusive question. Apart from adding an exotic Irish touch to the festivities, they were probably chosen for their republicanism. This political ideal appealed to a substantial

[5] Parker (1991), ch. 6; Linger (1992).
[6] Graham (1988), 68; Baroja (1965), 57ff.

number of Brazilians before the Republic was founded in 1889, and political references are traditional in Brazilian carnivals. In Rio in 1903, for instance, there were criticisms of the stamp duty. In 1964, after the generals had taken power, the successful samba 'Tristeza' began 'Please go away' ('por favor vá embora'). In this case too there are European parallels, similar political themes ranging from protests against the stamp duty in Madrid in 1637 to the recent Italian carnivals mocking the corruption of the former prime minister, Benito Craxi.

In the case of Brazil's relation to Europe, we need to consider not only unconscious tradition but also conscious imitation. Brazilians of the middle classes in particular were and indeed still are much attracted by foreign cultural models. The carnivals of Venice, Rome and Nice in particular were exemplary in nineteenth-century Brazil. They were quoted in the press as models of 'civilized' Carnival in attempts to suppress the *entrudo* and to replace it with something more rational, hygienic, moral, and 'European'. To a European historian, the situation is likely to seem somewhat ironic. The Brazilian elite viewed the European carnival as non-violent, a 'good' or civilized carnival in contrast to the 'bad' or uncivilized Brazilian carnival. The European carnival may have become relatively restrained by this time, but in the early modern period violence had been commonplace. An English visitor to Venice at the end of the sixteenth century recorded that 'there were on Shrove-Sunday at night seventeen slain, and very many wounded.'[7]

The Peculiarities of the Americans

This New World carnival is much more than a European import. Like so many items of European culture, it has been transformed in the course of its sojourn in the Americas, transposed or 'translated' in the sense of being adapted to the local conditions. These transformations are most important or at least most easily noticeable in three domains – the place of women, of dancing and of African culture.

In the first place, the importance and the active role of women in the carnivals of the Americas contrasts with traditional European customs, in which a woman's place was generally on the balcony, observing (and sometimes throwing missiles at) the men below, rather than in the street, participating fully. Despite the practice of cross-dressing or the many references to reversal, the patriarchal world was not turned completely upside down at this time.

Indeed, the emphasis on drink and violence in the traditional European carnivals, as well as the composition of the carnival societies (dominated by young adult males), suggest that the events should be interpreted as – among other things – rituals for the affirmation of masculinity. There were other popular festivals in which women were 'on top', symbolically dominating men, like the Spanish feast of Santa Agueda described by the late Don Julio Caro Baroja, but this was not a major theme of the European carnival.[8]

In the New World, on the other hand, despite the transplantation of patriarchalism – described by Latin American writers from Gilberto Freyre to Gabriel García Marquez – women have long been more visible and more active in carnival. Thus an English officer in Trinidad in 1826 noted that 'a party of ladies, having converted themselves into a party of brigands, assailed me in my quarters.'[9] In Brazil, female participation in the *entrudo* was considered worthy of note by foreign visitors such as Thomas Lindley (1805), Henry Koster (1816), John Mawe (1822), Robert Walsh (1830), and Ferdinand Denis (1837).

Today, whether the role of women is passive or active, whether their function is to be viewed by men or to enact their own fantasies (or both), it is impossible to imagine a Brazilian carnival without an overwhelming female presence, including the *destaques*, symbolic figures on the floats; the *pastoras*, 'shepherdesses' dancing in front of or behind the floats; the *baianas*, middle-aged women in the traditional costume of Bahía; and finally the *porta-bandeira* or standard-bearer, whose dance with her male partner the *mestre-sala* counts for several points in the competition between samba schools in Rio. Carnival schools, clubs and 'blocks' usually have a female wing and a female as well as a male directorate.[10]

Linked to the more active role of women, the importance of

[8] Baroja (1965), 371–81; cf. Davis (1975), esp. 138ff.
[9] Quoted in Pearse (1955–6), 180.
[10] Simson (1991–2).

dancing makes the New World carnivals distinctive. Dance was not completely absent in Europe. Sword-dancing in particular occurred in traditional European carnivals. All the same, the dance did not have the same importance there as in Brazil (say) or in Trinidad, where the *calinda* or stick-dance has been a central part of the festivities from the early nineteenth century at the latest, or in New Orleans, which impressed a French visitor in 1802 because 'they dance everywhere.'[11]

The examples just cited are of male dances, but mixed dancing has also been important in the carnivals of the Americas since the nineteenth century. In early nineteenth-century Trinidad, men and women of the planter class danced the *belair*, the *bamboula* and the *ghouba*. The classic instance of mixed dancing is that of Brazil, in the age of the polka, dominant from 1850 to 1900, the age of the *maxixe*, from the 1870s to the 1910s, and the age of the samba, dominant from 1916 or thereabouts to our own time. In Rio, dancing was and is a most important part of the *desfile*, the carnival parade, which itself became a central part of the festivities from the mid-nineteenth century onwards. Not only the 'infantry' accompanying the floats, but many of the women displayed on the floats themselves dance the samba, despite the risk of falling.

Besides dancing in the streets, the Brazilian carnival has long included balls in private houses, clubs, hotels (starting with the Hotel Itália in Rio in 1840), and theatres (such as the Teatro São Pedro in Rio in 1844, or the Teatro São João in Salvador in the 1860s).[12] In other parts of Latin America, dancing has also been an important element in Carnival: in Buenos Aires, for example, and in Havana, where masked balls took place in the Tacón theatre from 1838 onwards.[13]

The View from Africa

Linked in turn to the dance is the place of African elements in carnival as in other Latin American festivities. To begin with these other festivities. The celebration of the feast of Corpus

---

[11] Hill (1972), 11; Kinser (1990), 22.
[12] Alencar (1965).
[13] Amuchástegui (1988), 158ff.; Ortiz (1954), 204.

Christi in colonial Brazil, in the province of Minas Gerais, for instance, included allegorical floats and dances by blacks with flags, drums and songs – all elements to be found later in Brazilian carnivals. The tradition of the *maracatu, cucumbi, congada* or 'kings of the Congo', the enthronement of black kings and queens in splendid costume on the feast of Our Lady of the Rosary, again in Minas Gerais, was also transferred to Carnival.[14]

The transition from the brotherhoods who organized such festivals to the later carnival societies and samba schools was an easy one.[15] Brotherhoods themselves probably attracted blacks in Minas, Bahía and elsewhere because they offered a substitute family for slaves uprooted from their homeland, and a form of social organization with parallels in West Africa, notably the secret societies. In similar fashion, when twentieth-century missionaries to Mozambique formed scout groups (*Patrulhas*), their success seems to have owed something to local traditions of sociability.[16]

The Africa from which slaves were transported to the New World was of course a cluster of cultures some of which were already interacting with the West and with Christianity. Take the case of the Congo, for example. Local rulers saw advantages in working with the missionaries and using the new doctrines and rituals to legitimate their power. Confraternities were founded. Christian festivals such as the feast of St James were celebrated not only by processions but by traditional African dances and combined with other festivals like the commemoration of the accession of Afonso, King of the Congo. While the missionaries believed that they had converted the Africans to Christianity, it is extremely likely, to say the least, that the people of the Congo saw themselves as incorporating exotic Western rituals into the local religion. The synthesis or syncretism between Christianity and African traditions so often noted in the cases of Brazil and Cuba had already begun in Africa itself.[17] Behind these rituals it is occasionally possible to glimpse elements of African tradition,

---

[14] Real (1967), xv; Meyer (1993), 161–74.
[15] Cf. Da Matta (1978).
[16] Mandelbaum (1989), 173.
[17] Thornton (1983); Hilton (1985), 50ff., 95ff.; Gray (1991), 13ff., 42ff.; MacGaffey (1986), 191–216; MacGaffey (1994), 254–9; cf. Balandier (1965), 39, 259, 264; Prins (1980).

such as the Nigerian festival of the queen, *Damurixá*.[18] Carnival itself did not exist in Africa, and to this day it has only taken root in a few regions (notably Cabo Verde and Réunion), but what Westerners might call the 'carnivalesque' was common.

Wherever and however they originated, Afro-American elements spread through the Brazilian carnival. In Rio in 1881, the allegorical float of the Democráticos, a white carnival society of high status, represented an African prince, Obá. If we try to escape what might be called the 'Riocentrism' of the majority of studies of Brazilian carnival and look at Olinda, Recife or Salvador, the survival or reconstruction of African traditions is even more obvious, long before the late twentieth-century movement of 're-Africanization' linked to black consciousness and black power. In Recife, for instance, a group of *maracatus*, led by a queen and vice-queen, is recorded to have participated in the carnival of 1872.[19]

The dance, whether religious or secular, was and may still be a more important art form in Africa than anywhere else. In East Africa, for example, there was the tradition of the *ngoma*, a dance which often took the form of a 'parade' or 'march past' by members of different dance associations, associations in which women played a prominent part. In late nineteenth-century Mombasa, these parades included floats reminiscent of 'the carnivals at Nice or at New Orleans', according to one British official.[20]

In West Africa, more relevant to the Americas since the majority of slaves came from that region, the dance was often closely associated with religious practices. The association between dance and religion was closer than in Europe, where there has been a long tradition of official hostility to dances in church or even on the occasion of religious festivals.[21] Among the Tallensi of West Africa, on the other hand, the anthropologist who knew them best reported that 'the dancing-ground is sacred.'[22] The dance was a ritual provoking loss of consciousness and the possession of the dancers by spirits or gods, as in the case of the Yoruba in Dahomey and Nigeria.

[18] Manuel Querino, quoted Risério (1981), 49.
[19] Real (1967), xvi-xvii; Fry (1988), 232–63; Risério (1981), 13, 17.
[20] Ranger (1975), 34, 167ff.
[21] Backman (1952).
[22] Fortes (1987), 51.

Possession, or 'spirit mediumship' as it is sometimes called, should not be regarded as a form of hysteria. As anthropologists have emphasized, it should be analysed as ritual or even as theatre. The possessed impersonate their particular spirit in much the same way as Carnival revellers enact the behaviour appropriate to their costume, their *fantasia*. Some of these spirits behave in a carnivalesque way: the *caboclo* spirits in *candomblé*, for example, male spirits who take over females and make their human vehicles smoke, drink and use bad language.[23] Drumming was central to these possession rituals. The drums were considered the voices of the gods, each god being associated with a distinctive rhythm.[24] Possession cults of this kind continue among blacks in the Americas, from the *vodun* of Haiti and the *santería* of Cuba to the *candomblé* of Brazil (which has particularly close links to Yoruba traditions), or its equivalent in Maranhão, the *tambor de mina*, the name emphasizing the beat of the drum.[25]

The central argument of this chapter is that these religious practices have made an important contribution to Afro-American carnivals. The place of drums in these carnivals is central in the cases of the *baterías* of Rio and the 'steel bands' of Trinidad (which replaced the traditional drums in the 1930s). The dances of the *candomblé* are sometimes compared with the carnival samba not only by observers but also by participants.[26] In Brazil, other religious practices were incorporated in Carnival via the *afoxé*, a word which means not only a musical instrument (a gourd rattle) and a dance performed by blacks, but also a *maracatu* or a procession of adepts of *candomblé*. The Brazilian composer and singer Gilberto Gil tells the story that when he was parading in the carnival of Salvador with the rest of his *afoxé* group, he once saw a middle-aged woman cross herself, apparently thinking that what she was watching was a religious procession.[27]

In the religious rituals described above, women have traditionally played an important part. The Hausa Bori possession cults, for example, were and are controlled by women. The so-called 'mother of the saint' (*mãe de santo, ialorixa*) remains the central

[23] Wafer (1991), 55–6.
[24] Leiris (1958); Verger (1969), 50–66.
[25] Mars (1946); Bastide (1958); Drewal (1989).
[26] Wafer (1991), 73–4; Omari (1994), 136.
[27] Bastide (1958), 248; Real (1967), 57; Risério (1981), 12, 52, 55–6.

figure in *candomblé*.[28] In Recife, the queens who lead the *maracatus* in the carnival are *mães de santo*.[29] To reinforce the hypothesis of the connection between African religion and American Carnival, it may be added that in Salvador, female spirits called *tobosa* ('girls') 'descended' at Carnival, in other words took possession of worshippers.[30] To speculate for a moment, I should like to suggest that the *baianas* so prominent in the carnival of Rio and other cities today, dignified ladies whirling in their long white dresses, are a secular version of the *mães do santo*. Indeed, the excitement and exaltation of Carnival, the 'vibrations' as the Brazilians call them, are a secular form of religious ecstasy.

Masks reveal other links between Africa and the Americas. They have an important role to play not only in Carnival but also in West African secret societies, such as the Poro of Liberia.[31] In Trinidad, one of the traditional carnival masks, the 'Moco Jumbie', has been traced back to religious practices in West Africa.[32] In Cuba, as in the Saturnalia of ancient Rome, the temporary liberty of slaves was central to the festival, which is said to have owed something to the African tradition of the Ekuaeansu. The blacks took to the streets of La Habana dressed as *congos* (again), *lucumíes*, *ararás* and *mandingas*.[33]

In Brazil in particular, Afro-American popular traditions are currently being studied with more attention than before by historians. At the same time they are receiving more emphasis in the carnivals themselves as part of the black consciousness movement. For example, *afoxé* groups such as the 'sons of Gandhi' (founded in 1949 but revived in the 1970s) play an important role in the carnival of Salvador.[34] In 1995, the Salvador carnival focused on Zumbi, leader of the rebel slave community of Palmares, in order to mark the tercentenary of his death.

Research on African elements in Carnival, like other aspects of black popular culture in colonial and nineteenth-century Brazil, has scarcely begun.[35] All the same, the elements mentioned above may be sufficient to launch the hypothesis that New World

[28] Landes (1947), 71ff., 142ff.
[29] Real (1967), 67.
[30] Bastide (1958), 194. On Umbanda and Carnival, Da Matta (1978), 136.
[31] Harley (1950); cf. Sieber (1962).
[32] Hill (1972), 12.
[33] Ortiz (1954), 210–11.
[34] Risério (1981), 52ff.
[35] Meyer (1993), 175–226; Soihet (1993).

carnivals are 'overdetermined', in the sense that they have emerged out of the encounter between two festive traditions, the European and the African. There is 'syncretism' in the precise sense of the temporary coexistence and interaction of elements from different cultures, just as there is 'anti-syncretism' in the sense of attempts to purify Carnival, first of its African elements (in the later nineteenth century), and more recently of its European ones.[36] There may also have been Amerindian elements in this compound, but if so it is difficult to identify them now (the use of Indian *fantasías* by blacks and whites is another matter).[37]

It looks as if there is some kind of cultural magnetism involved, an attraction between similar elements in the African and European traditions, just as there is a kind of circularity or reciprocal influence between elite and popular traditions.[38] For example, the mock combat appears to derive both from the dances associated with the cult of the Yoruba warrior-god Ogun and from the Iberian tradition of representing conflicts between 'Moors and Christians' in popular religious dramas or *autos*.[39] In 1816, the English visitor Henry Koster witnessed a Brazilian *entrudo* which included the 'christening of the king of the Moors' and a mock battle between Moors and Christians. The tradition of the *cucumbi* or 'kings of the Congo' owes something to the European tradition known in France as the *reinage*, in which men and women dressed as kings and queens ride to church in a cavalcade.[40] It may also follow African traditions. Again, carnival masks are related to two cultural traditions, the European and the African. The festivals thus exemplify what the Cuban sociologist and folklorist Fernando Ortiz, himself an enthusiast for carnival, called 'transculturation' (below, p. 208), in other words the reciprocal interaction between two cultures, as opposed to 'acculturation', in which the influence is supposed to be one-way.[41]

---

[36] Pye (1993); Stewart (1994).
[37] Real (1967), 84ff.
[38] Soihet (1993).
[39] Drewal (1989), 225; Baroja (1965), 174.
[40] Real (1967), 58; Hanlon (1993), 155.
[41] Ortiz (1952).

The Trajectories of Carnival

The trajectory of carnivals in the New World over the last two hundred years or so runs parallel to that of European carnivals between the sixteenth and the nineteenth centuries.[42] There have been four main stages in this process; participation, reform, withdrawal, and rediscovery. It must of course be remembered that the sources for the history of Carnival generally offer a vision 'from above', in which some popular activities are scarcely visible, but so far as the upper classes at least are concerned this model has its uses.

The stage of participation may be illustrated from Trinidad in the early nineteenth century, when (according to an English observer) 'high and low, rich and poor, learned and unlearned, all found masking suits for the carnival.' Another example from mid nineteenth-century Petrópolis, where the Brazilian court retired for the summer, is the Emperor Pedro II's enjoyment of the traditional *entrudo*, water-throwing and all.

The stage of reform was reached in Trinidad in the later nineteenth century, when some members of the ruling class went so far as to demand the complete abolition of Carnival.[43] In Brazil, from the 1830s onwards, criticisms of Carnival were regularly expressed. In 1844, Father Lopes Gama, the famous Recife journalist, noted the inconsistency between the 'madness' of the *entrudo* and the claim of Brazilians to participate in the progress of civilization.[44] By the late nineteenth century there was a campaign to replace the 'grosseiro e pernicioso entrudo' (as the *Jornal de Notícias* of Salvador called it in 1884) with something more 'rational', 'hygienic' and 'civilized' on the European model (as was remarked above, the Brazilian elite was apparently unaware of the importance of sex and violence in the European carnival tradition). These attempts at reform probably reached their climax in Rio in the age of prefect Francisco Pereira Passos, around 1900, when the carnival parades were transferred from Rua do Ouvidor in the heart of the city to avenues on the periphery where they could be controlled more easily. This attempt

[42] Burke (1978), 178ff., 207ff., 270ff., 281ff.; Queiroz (1978); cf. Pereira (1994), introduction.
[43] Pearse (1955–6), 187.
[44] Quoted in Real (1967), xii–xiii.

coincided with a public health campaign and a reconstruction of the city which provoked resistance and even riots.[45]

The language of 'civilization' versus 'barbarism' expressed masked white fears of the growing 'Africanization' of Carnival, fears expressed openly in letters to the Salvador newspaper the *Jornal de Notícias* in the first years of the twentieth century. For it was in the 1890s that black carnival clubs such as the Pândegos de Africa were founded in that city.[46] How successful the reform campaign was it is difficult to say. Maria Isaura Pereira de Queiroz has written of 'the domestication of an urban mass' in the carnival of Rio, but her concern with the central events of the festival needs to be balanced against the evidence for a more traditional and informal carnival in other parts of the city.[47]

That the reform was less than complete is suggested by the third stage, in other words the withdrawal from public participation on the part of the elites, who now organized their own festivities indoors, a 'closed carnival' replacing the old open one. In Trinidad, it was as early as the emancipation of the slaves in 1833 that the white elite 'withdrew from public participation' in Carnival, while the blacks 'appropriated' it, or at least became more visible, using the festivities to commemorate their emancipation and to mock the whites.[48] In Brazil both emancipation and withdrawal occurred half a century later. In Rio, in the words of the *Gazeta de Notícias* in 1890, 'the elegant carnival withdrew into ball-rooms, abandoning the streets to the poor devils.'[49] By contrast, in New Orleans the white clubs or 'krewes' have not withdrawn and continue to dominate the carnival. The parallel black groups like the Zulu Aid and Pleasure Club which once mocked the official festivities have now been incorporated into them.[50]

Brazil, like other parts of the New World, is now living through the fourth stage of the process, that of the rediscovery of popular culture, in particular Afro-American culture, on the part of the elites, including the 're-Africanization' of Carnival. There

[45] Pereira (1994), 39ff.
[46] Quoted in Fry et al. (1988), 236, 253–4.
[47] Queiroz (1992), 71–116; Zaluar (1978).
[48] Pearse (1955–6); Hill (1972), 23, 40, 43, 100.
[49] Quoted in Pereira (1994), 202.
[50] Contrast Edmondson (1955–6), 233–45, and Kinser (1990); cf. Da Matta (1978), 124–30.

has also been (at least in Recife) a return to the street on the part of the middle class, which had withdrawn to the closed world of clubs and hotels.[51] Needless to say, this fourth stage is linked to the commercialization of a festival which has become big business and in which television and record companies as well as tourist agencies (not to mention owners of gambling establishments and drug dealers) have become deeply involved.[52] In this respect as in others, modern Rio is the heir of nineteenth-century Nice and eighteenth-century Venice.

What makes American carnivals so different from European ones is essentially the African element. To return to Da Matta's idea of Carnival as a microcosm of Brazil, we might say that the festival both displays and dramatizes the interaction between different ethnic groups and subcultures.

---

[51] Real (1967), 158–9.
[52] Cavalcanti (1994).

I I

Strengths and Weaknesses of the History of Mentalities

❧

The history of mentalities is not easy to define to everyone's satisfaction. Carlo Ginzburg and the late Richard Cobb were and are often seen as leading practitioners of this approach, despite their denials that the history of mentalities was what they are doing. Even in France, where the tradition is the most self-conscious and the most continuous, the approach has undergone modifications in the fifty years which separate Marc Bloch from (say) Jacques Le Goff.

For the purposes of this essay the approach will be defined in terms of three distinctive features. In the first place, a stress on collective attitudes rather than individual ones, and the thought of ordinary people as well as that of formally educated elites. Secondly, an emphasis not so much on conscious thoughts or elaborated theories as on unspoken or unconscious assumptions, on perception, on the workings of 'everyday thought' or 'practical reason'. And finally, a concern with the 'structure' of beliefs as well as their content, in other words with categories, with metaphors and symbols, with how people think as well as what they think. In other words, to assert the existence of a difference in mentalities between two groups is to make a much stronger statement than merely asserting a difference in attitudes.[1]

[1] Critical surveys include Vovelle (1982); Gismondi (1985).

In all these respects the history of mentalities differs from other approaches to intellectual history, such as the American 'history of ideas', the traditional German *Geistesgeschichte*, and even the newer German *Begriffsgeschichte*.[2] It might be described as a historical anthropology of ideas. From Émile Durkheim onwards, sociologists and social anthropologists have been concerned with what they variously call the 'collective representations', 'modes of thought' or 'cognitive systems' of other cultures.[3] Durkheim's follower Lucien Lévy-Bruhl helped put the term 'mentality' into circulation with his study *La mentalité primitive* (1922), which argued that primitive peoples thought in a 'pre-logical' or 'mystical' way.

However, the problems raised by the study of mentalities are too important for even two disciplines to deal with, and they have been discussed in many more, including philosophy, psychology, economics, literature, the history of art, and the history of science (although participants in these debates have not always been aware of all the interdisciplinary ramifications).

For example, the so-called 'sociology of knowledge', represented by the essays of Karl Mannheim, for example, was independent of, but similar to, the work of the Durkheimians. In the 1920s, Mannheim studied what he called 'world-views', 'mental habits' or 'styles of thought', with their distinctive logics. His most famous example was the contrast between two opposite styles of thought in the early nineteenth century, associated with German conservative historicists and French liberal universalists.[4]

In the history of science, Abel Rey found 'les beaux ouvrages de M. Lévy-Bruhl' an inspiration for his work on scientific thought in antiquity.[5] Rey collaborated with Lucien Febvre and thus contributed to the development of the French 'mentalities' tradition. Again, there are similarities to the mentalities approach in the focus on 'epistemological obstacles' in the work of Gaston Bachelard (Rey's successor at the Sorbonne), and on 'epistemological breaks' in the work of his pupil Georges Canguilhem, who was in turn one of the teachers of Michel Foucault.[6]

Even closer to the mentalities approach was the work of the

[2] Koselleck (1972).
[3] Durkheim (1912); Evans-Pritchard (1937, 1940).
[4] Mannheim (1927), esp. 35–7, 191.
[5] Rey (1930), 434–5, 456–9.
[6] Bachelard (1947); Canguilhem (1955); Foucault (1961, 1966).

Polish microbiologist Ludwik Fleck (written in the 1930s, rediscovered in the 1970s) on 'thought communities' and what he
called (like Mannheim) their distinctive 'styles' of thought.[7] The
parallel with anthropology is clear, and the idea of an 'anthropology of science' or an 'anthropology of knowledge' is now
in circulation.[8] The point is to investigate 'changing pre-
suppositions, expectations, questions, methods, arguments, justi-
fications' rather than to focus attention on ideas in the narrow
sense.[9]

As we have seen (above, p. 14), an interest in these problems
goes back at least as far as the eighteenth century. Phrases such
as 'mode of thought', *manière de penser*, *Denkungsart* and so on
came into use, usually in the context of an encounter between
two cultures distant in space or time, the modern Western
European using these phrases to express a sense of distance from
'savages', the Middle Ages, and so on.

A systematic historical approach is rather more recent. It has
of course been associated with the French journal *Annales* since
the days of its founders Lucien Febvre and Marc Bloch, who
were much concerned with what they variously called 'historical
psychology' (*psychologie historique*), 'collective mentalities'
(*mentalités collectives*), 'conceptual apparatus' (*outillage mental*),
or, in the phrase they borrowed from Durkheim, 'collective representations' (*représentations collectives*). However, Bloch and
Febvre were not alone in their concern. Marcel Granet the sinolo-
gist and Georges Lefebvre the historian of the French Revolution
were already writing this kind of history in the 1930s.[10]

What they were doing was not even a French monopoly, for it
shaded into the cultural history practised by Johan Huizinga
(below, p. 184), whose *Waning of the Middle Ages*, first published in 1919, was concerned with collective attitudes, with the
history of feelings, and, most important, with what the author
called 'forms of thought' (*gedachtensvormen*), such as personification and symbolism. In this last respect Huizinga moved away
from Jacob Burckhardt and towards the social psychologist
Wilhelm Wundt, with whom he had once studied at Leipzig.

This chapter attempts an assessment of both the strengths and

[7] Fleck (1935); cf. Crombie (1994).
[8] Elkanah (1981); Vickers (1984).
[9] Crombie (1994), vol. 1, 7.
[10] Granet (1934); Lefebvre (1932).

the weaknesses of the history of mentalities, as practised in France in particular from the days of Bloch and Febvre to those of Duby, Le Goff, Vovelle and Le Roy Ladurie. In the last few years the term has been going out of fashion, to be replaced by 'representations' or 'the collective imagination' (*l'imaginaire social*).[11] In practice, however, the difference between the old history of mentalities and the new history of representations is not great enough for these reflections to have lost their relevance.

The first point to make about the history of mentalities is that something is needed to occupy the conceptual space between the history of ideas and social history, in order to avoid having to choose between an intellectual history with the society left out and a social history with the thought left out. The 'social history of ideas' practised by a historian of the Enlightenment, Peter Gay, was a step in this direction, but it remained on the intellectual side of the frontier. The 'social history of ideas' practised by a more recent historian of the Enlightenment, Robert Darnton, goes further; indeed Darnton uses the phrase more or less as a synonym for the history of mentalities.[12] One of the main points of this approach is to take more seriously than before the place of ideas in everyday social life. It is precisely for this reason that the Swedish historian Eva Österberg recently described her work as concerned with 'mentalities and other realities'.[13]

Consider the following recurrent problems in cultural history. Why is it that individuals from different cultures often find communication difficult? Why does one individual or group find absurd precisely what another takes for granted? How is it possible to be able to translate every word in a text from an alien (or even a half-alien) culture, yet to have difficulty in understanding the text? Because – so one is able to say if one adopts this approach to the past – there is a difference in mentality, in other words different assumptions, different perceptions, and a different 'logic' – at least in the philosophically loose sense of different criteria for justifying assertions – reason, authority, experience and so on. No wonder that a historian of the Middle Ages and an anthropologist have tried, independently, to revive the ideas of the French psychologist Jean Piaget in order to analyse

---

[11] Chartier (1988); Baczko (1984).
[12] Gay (1959), preface; Darnton (1990).
[13] Österberg (1991).

differences in mentality, following him in distinguishing 'pre-operatory' from 'operatory' thought and linking the latter to formal schooling.[14]

A classic example of the kind of problem for whose solution we need the concept of mentality – or something roughly like it – is that of the medieval ordeal, an example which has exercised educated Europeans from Montesquieu onwards. Trial by ordeal is easy enough to condemn in the name of reason, but it is difficult to explain historically without recourse to what Montesquieu called 'la manière de penser de nos pères' (in other words, mentality). A number of recent studies of the ordeal have adopted precisely this approach.[15] Again, in fields as far apart as economic history and the history of science, other scholars have found it impossible to solve their problems without invoking a concept like that of mentality, as opposed to a timeless rationality which usually turns out to have been defined ethnocentrically.

In the case of the economy, the Polish historian Witold Kula, in a brilliant account of the workings of the 'feudal system' in seventeenth- and eighteenth-century Poland, has demonstrated that it cannot be understood without taking into account the attitudes, values or mode of thought of the magnates who gained most from it.[16] Again, Edward Thompson's famous article on what he called the 'moral economy' of the English crowd suggested that food riots should be seen not as a simple response to hunger but as an expression of collective moral assumptions, a suggestion which was soon taken up and utilized in the study of rebellions in societies as distant as South East Asia.[17] There are obvious similarities between this approach to economic history and that of 'economic anthropology', which also stresses alternative rationalities, emphasizing, for example, the social function of what used to be called 'conspicuous waste' as a means of acquiring prestige and power.

In the history of science, too, recurrent attempts have been made to turn 'rationality' from an assumption into a problem, to abandon the simplistic distinction between the irrational 'magic' associated with the 'other' and the rational science associated

[14] Hallpike (1979), 12–40; Radding (1978).
[15] Brown (1975); cf. Morris (1975) and Radding (1979). Contrast Bartlett (1986).
[16] Kula (1962).
[17] Thompson (1971); Scott (1976); cf. Thompson (1991).

with 'us'. Hence the interest in collective 'styles of thought' already mentioned, invoked in order to supplement explanations of scientific innovation in terms of internal necessity or the achievement of individual geniuses.[18]

To defend, as well as describe, the approach it may be useful to cite four concrete examples from the early modern period where it seems particularly difficult to give a plausible account of certain beliefs without a concept like the idea of mentality or mode of thought.

(1) The idea of 'correspondences' between the seven planets, the seven metals, the seven days of the week, and so on.[19] Correspondences are neither identities nor similarities but seem to be somewhere in between, a middle category which seems to have parallels in other cultures, notably the Bororo (a tribe living in the Amazon region), who claimed to be macaws, and the Nuer, for whom 'a twin is a bird.'[20] The Bororo example was taken up by Lévy-Bruhl, who described the relationship between men and macaws in terms of 'mystical participation', a characteristic, so he suggested, of 'pre-logical' thought or 'primitive mentality'.

(2) The idea of the 'great chain', ladder or 'scale' of being, according to which it is better to live than to exist, better to feel than to live, better to think than to feel; in other words, better to be a tree than a stone, a horse than a tree, a human being than a horse.[21] The problem is that 'the complex system of analogies up and down the chain cannot be taken entirely literally, nor can it be understood as a mere convention, a useful and pleasing metaphor.'[22] The fact that this projection of the social hierarchy on to the cosmos has now come to seem quaint indicates a major change in Western mentality since the sixteenth century.

(3) Hence, to take a third example, the modern reader is likely to be somewhat puzzled by the following statement of Cardinal Bérulle's: 'L'état de l'enfance, état le plus vil et le plus abject de la nature humaine, après celui de la mort' ('The state of childhood,

[18] Crombie (1994).
[19] Tillyard (1943); cf. Foucault (1966), ch. 1.
[20] Evans-Pritchard (1956), 128f.; Crocker (1977).
[21] Lovejoy (1936).
[22] Walzer (1965), 156.

the most vile and abject state of human nature, after that of death').[23] The oddness is not – or not only – a function of the content of Bérulle's beliefs, of the fact that childishness has become more acceptable to adults than it seems to have been in the seventeenth century. It is the hierarchical arrangement, the structure of his beliefs, that we are likely to find most alien. It has also come to seem rather odd to describe death as an *état*. Yet personifications of abstractions were common enough in the medieval and early modern periods. Johan Huizinga, whose interest in personification has been mentioned already, once discussed a statement by St Francis to the effect that he was married to Lady Poverty. Huizinga suggested that this statement should not be taken either literally or metaphorically. Its logical status was somewhere in between.[24]

(4) Huizinga's suggestion may be helpful in interpreting a final example, which comes from the rebellion of the so-called 'red bonnets' in Brittany in 1675. The rebels expressed their demands in a document known as the 'peasant code'. One of its clauses runs as follows: 'It is forbidden to give refuge to the *gabelle* and her children, to give them anything to eat or anything they need; but on the contrary everyone is ordered to fire on her as one would on a mad dog' ('Il est défendu ... de donner retraite à la gabelle et à ses enfants, et de leur fournir ni à manger ni aucune commodité; mais au contraire, il est enjoint de tirer sur elle comme sur un chien enragé').[25] This 'gabelle' was of course the salt tax.

Some historians believe that the code is a forgery, precisely – one suspects – because they find this clause a stumbling block to credibility, although there is supporting evidence for the personification of the *gabelle*.[26] It is a scandal for historians who do not believe in differences in mentality. What could the rebels have meant? Whether or not the Breton peasants had a more archaic mentality than that of peasants elsewhere in France is a question I do not feel competent to answer. It is true that they employed

[23] Quoted in Snyders (1964), 194.
[24] Huizinga (1938), 162ff.
[25] Garlan and Nières (1975), 102.
[26] Le Braz (1922), 136ff.

personifications of death and plague as well as of the *gabelle*.[27] However, similar personifications can be found elsewhere in Europe. Even the notorious clause about giving the *gabelle* food differs only in degree of elaboration from the cry of some fif-teenth-century Tuscans, 'Death to the tax' ('Muoia il catasto'); and this is a special case of a more common Italian slogan, 'Death to bad government' ('Muoia il malgoverno'). Is the injunc-tion to be taken literally or metaphorically? Perhaps it is another statement which will not fit our own cultural categories of 'literal' and 'metaphorical', and so indicates an alien mentality.[28]

Faced with examples like these, historians need a concept like that of 'mentality' in order to avoid two opposite dangers. The first danger is that of dismissing the Breton peasants or Cardinal Bérulle as irrational or as unworthy of serious historical consideration. If a specific seventeenth-century attitude strikes us as odd, we have to remember that it was part of a belief system in which the different parts supported one another, making the central propositions vir-tually unfalsifiable. The second danger is that of sweeping the examples under the carpet, of assuming that seventeenth-century Frenchmen must 'really' have thought in the same way as we do, and so succumbing to what might be called 'premature empathy', an intellectual illness which was diagnosed some sixty years ago by Lévy-Bruhl (though Vico and Rousseau had been aware of it long before). Lévy-Bruhl offered his analysis precisely in order to replace the idea 'of substituting ourselves imaginatively for the primitives we are studying, and making them think as we would do if we were in their place', a diagnosis which has passed into British social anthropology under the name of the 'If I were a horse' problem.[29] The point is that to understand the behaviour of people in other cultures it is not sufficient to imagine oneself in their shoes, in their situation; it is also necessary to imagine their definition of the situ-ation, to see it through their eyes. A similar point was made by Lucien Febvre in an essay which discussed the problem of what he called 'psychological anachronism'.[30]

The great strength of the idea of mentality is to make it pos-sible to steer a course which avoids the two opposite hazards. If

[27] Croix (1981), 1067ff.
[28] Lloyd (1990).
[29] Lévy-Bruhl (1927), 15.
[30] Febvre (1938).

we replace it with some alternative concept, it seems reasonable to require the substitute to deal in a satisfactory way with examples of the kind which have just been discussed.

There is, of course, a case for replacing an approach which suffers from weaknesses and has had serious criticisms levelled against it. One objection, which is not infrequently heard in Britain, ought not to be taken too seriously; it is that the French treat mentalities as impersonal forces. In Britain it is obvious that there are no such forces, but only men thinking, as Herbert Butterfield put it. Or as Vivian Galbraith used to say, with provocative sexism, in his Oxford lectures in the 1950s, 'History is just chaps.' To the French, however (if I dare attempt an act of empathy with them), it is equally obvious that the term *mentalité* is not being used to describe a thing or a force, but rather to characterize the relation between beliefs, which is what makes them into a system. The beliefs are 'collective' only in the sense of being shared by individuals, not in the sense of standing outside them. The contrast between the British intellectual tradition of methodological individualism and the French tradition of holism is so strong, and goes back such a long way, that one is tempted to call the difference itself one between two different mentalities.

I shall be equally laconic, though not, I hope, cavalier, in response to the rather similar objection that historians of mentalities underestimate what human beings have in common. There is a sense (or level) at which human nature is always the same, but another level at which it is not. It is difficult to discuss differences in mentalities (or differences between cultures) without exaggerating their importance. I shall try to refer to differences in worldviews without implying that different groups see the world in *completely* different ways.

There are, however, at least four more serious objections to the mentalities approach to intellectual history. They are usually presented in exaggerated form, but each contains a kernel of serious criticism.

(1) In the first place, to look for broad differences in mentalities encourages historians to treat attitudes they find alien as if they were homogeneous, to overestimate the degree of intellectual consensus in a given society in the past.[31] This is of course one of

[31] Gismondi (1985).

the classic objections to the concept of *Zeitgeist*, and to the traditional cultural history organized around it (*Geistesgeschichte*), and the objection is only partially answered by saying that Hegel (for example) did not treat seventeenth-century thought as homogeneous, but contrasted Francis Bacon (for instance) with his contemporary Jacob Boehme. Bloch and Febvre (like Huizinga) are not so far from traditional *Geistesgeschichte* as their use of the new term 'mentality' might make one think. To write, as they did on occasion, of 'the medieval Frenchman' or 'the sixteenth-century Frenchman' as if there were no important variations in attitude among the inhabitants of France in this period (male and female, rich and poor, literate and illiterate, and so on) is seriously misleading.

There is no reason why a mentality should not be imputed to a social class or other group rather than to a whole society, but this tactic leads to similar problems on a lesser scale. From outside it may seem reasonable enough to talk of, say, the 'legal mentality' in seventeenth-century England, yet it cannot be assumed that all lawyers had the same attitudes. We have to allow for individual variation. Hence Carlo Ginzburg's famous study of Menocchio the heretical miller from a village in Friuli, who compared the cosmos to a cheese with worms in it, was designed to undermine the history of mentalities (though the author also employed his hero as a spokesman, however eccentric, for traditional peasant culture, so that mentalities, thrown out of the door, came back in again through the window).[32] Homogenization of beliefs is not a necessary part of the approach. It is possible to follow Jacques Le Goff and use the term 'mentality' to describe only the beliefs which a given individual shares with a number of contemporaries, limiting the approach to the investigation of common assumptions rather than extending it to the whole of intellectual history.[33] In practice, however, homogenization remains a danger.

(2) Linked to the problem of variation is the problem of change, or variation over time. It is, in the words of a critic from within the French tradition, Roger Chartier, 'the problem on which all history of mentalities stumbles, that of the reasons for and

[32] Ginzburg (1976).
[33] Le Goff (1974).

modalities of the passage from one system to another'.[34] The sharper the contrast between one mentality and another ('traditional' and 'modern', for example), the harder it is to explain how change ever took place. The crucial idea here would seem to be that of a 'system' of beliefs, a circle of thought in which each part at once supports and is supported by the rest, making the whole system impervious to falsification (a 'closed system' in the words of the philosopher Karl Popper).[35]

A particularly clear example of circularity was studied by Marc Bloch in his book about the belief that the rulers of France and England had the power to cure skin disease by touching the sufferer and pronouncing the formula, 'The king touches you, God heals you.' Bloch pointed out that the same sufferers sometimes returned to be touched by the king on another occasion, behaviour which shows both that the ritual had not worked and that its failure to work had not destroyed the faith of the patient in the remedy.[36] Another vivid example is the parallel account given by Evans-Pritchard of the Zande belief in poison oracles. 'In this web of belief,' he wrote, 'every strand depends upon every other strand, and a Zande cannot get out of its meshes because it is the only world he knows.'[37] This notion of a system of beliefs is at once a help and a hindrance to historians. If we do not use it we cannot explain how ideas persist over the generations in the face of awkward empirical evidence, but if we do use it we make it difficult for ourselves to understand change.

To put the point another way, it is all too easy to reify mentalities, to perceive them – in Fernand Braudel's famous metaphor – as 'prisons' from which individuals cannot escape.[38] It is worth stressing that this danger, acute in practice, is not one to which historians of mentalities must inevitably succumb. In the case of Italy, for instance, it is fascinating to see the gradual rise between the thirteenth and seventeenth centuries of what has been called the 'numerate mentality', revealed in practices like the spread and elaboration of censuses as well as in private account-books.[39] For an example of a change in the mentality of a group of

[34] Chartier (1988), 19–52.
[35] Popper (1934).
[36] Bloch (1924).
[37] Evans-Pritchard (1937), 194.
[38] Vovelle (1982); cf. Gismondi (1985), 211ff.
[39] Burckhardt (1860); Murray (1978), 180ff.

intellectuals over the relatively short term, one might point to the so-called 'scientific revolution' of the middle of the seventeenth century, notably to the so-called 'mechanization of the world picture' in which the shift from a view of the world as animate to a view of the cosmos as a vast machine was associated with a major change in ideas or assumptions about causality.[40] At much the same time, and among some of the same groups of people, there was a perceptible shift (even if it was less rapid and profound than used to be thought) from justifying statements by quoting authorities to justifying them by experience.[41] Again, the anthropologists Ernest Gellner and Robin Horton, elaborating ideas from Evans-Pritchard and Popper, have sketched out a general picture of change in modes of thought, emphasizing the importance of competition between theories and of awareness of alternatives to a given intellectual system.[42] In short, despite the force of this objection to the practice of past historians of mentalities, it can be and has been answered.

(3) Another serious objection to the history of mentalities is that it treats belief systems as autonomous. In other words, it is concerned with the relationship of beliefs with one another, to the exclusion of the relationship between beliefs and society. The objection must not be exaggerated. Neither Bloch's *Royal Touch* nor his colleague Febvre's *Problem of Unbelief* (which emphasized the impossibility of thinking all kinds of thought at all times) treated belief systems as completely independent of society. There remains a major difference in emphasis between two approaches to the history of thought. Historians of ideologies see thought as shaped (if not determined) by social forces, and they emphasize the cunning (conscious or unconscious) by which a particular view of the world is presented as natural, indeed the only possible one. Historians of mentalities by contrast see belief systems as relatively innocent and autonomous. The two approaches overlap but they do not coincide.[43]

(4) A still more serious objection to the mentalities approach is that it is built on evolutionism and more specifically, on the

[40] Dijksterhuis (1950); Blumenberg (1960).
[41] Dear (1985).
[42] Gellner (1974), ch. 8; Horton (1967, 1982).
[43] Vovelle (1982).

contrast between logical and pre-logical thought made by Lucien Lévy-Bruhl, foundations which have been undermined by later research. The importance of Lévy-Bruhl in the intellectual history of the early twentieth century still awaits adequate assessment. His critique of simple notions of empathy was a valuable one, and his own notion of 'pre-logical' thought was more subtle than some of his critics have realized.[44] He influenced thinkers as diverse as Ernst Cassirer, Jane Harrison, Johan Huizinga, and Ludwik Fleck. As remarked above, it was Lévy-Bruhl who launched the term *mentalité* in French in the 1920s. (In England, the word 'mentality' had been used as early as 1913, ironically enough by the anthropologist Bronislaw Malinowski in a letter to J. G. Frazer criticizing Durkheim's notion of 'the collective consciousness').[45] However, at the end of his life, Lévy-Bruhl abandoned his famous distinction between the 'pre-logical' and 'logical' mentalities. In any case, anthropologists as different as Evans-Pritchard and Lévi-Strauss have agreed to reject it, together with the evolutionist schema of which it formed a part.[46]

All the same, a rather simple contrast along roughly Lévy-Bruhlian lines, between two mentalities, can be found not only in the work of Febvre (and to a lesser extent in that of Bloch, always the most cautious of the two), but also in some of their successors, such as Jean Delumeau and Robert Muchembled. The last two historians have been criticized for attempting to explain peasant religion in early modern Europe almost entirely in negative terms, in terms of failure, anxiety and the constraints of a harsh environment. After all, it does seem rather implausible (as Wittgenstein once remarked with reference to Frazer) to treat an entire world-view as a mistake.[47] To describe an alien belief system as a failure is a gross form of ethnocentrism. Where do the criteria of success and failure come from if not from the speaker's own culture? Ethnocentrism is encouraged by the description of mentalities as 'traditional' and 'modern' (no less than 'primitive' and 'civilized', 'pre-logical' and 'logical'), since these dichotomies tend to slip into a contrast between Us and Them. The dichotomies elide the differences between (say) Chinese mandarins, Renaissance humanists and Breton peasants, all of

[44] Evans-Pritchard (1965), 78–99.
[45] Ackerman (1987), 267.
[46] Lévy-Bruhl (1949).
[47] Clark (1983), 75–6.

whose beliefs, since they are unlike ours, have to be described as 'traditional'.

All four criticisms of the approach come in different forms, more or less cogent, undermining the work of some historians of mentalities more effectively than others. However, all of them suggest the need to reformulate the approach to meet the objections. The remainder of this chapter will discuss three proposals for reformulation – a greater concern with interests, with categories and with metaphors.

Mentalities and Interests

In the days of Bloch and Febvre, Marxist historians did not have a credible alternative to the history of mentalities, because they dismissed ideas as mere 'superstructure' (or 'ideology' in a reductionist sense), and devoted their attention to economic history. Later Marxists, such as Edward Thompson and Raymond Williams, questioned the notion of 'superstructure', refined the notion of ideology, and revived alternative concepts such as cultural 'hegemony'. In these ways they moved closer to the idea of mentality. Lucien Febvre would have recognized Williams's concern with 'structures of feeling' as akin to his own interest in the history of emotions.[48]

What remains distinctive in the Marxian approach is the concern with interests, a concern which the classic history of mentalities lacked. Looking back on Marc Bloch's great book on the royal touch after more than seventy years, it has come to seem odd that he did not discuss in whose interest it was that the belief in the supernatural powers of kings should continue to exist. The question is a particularly important one for the early modern period, when the monarchy was under attack in the French and English civil wars, and more especially in the late seventeenth century. Charles II and Louis XIV were familiar with the ideas of the 'new science' of their day and they are unlikely to have believed in the virtues of their touch. Nevertheless, they continued the traditional practice, doubtless because they considered it in their interest to do so.

[48] Vovelle (1982).

More generally, historians of mentalities cannot afford to ignore the problems raised by students of ideologies, even if they do not deal with them in the same confident way as (say) the philosopher Louis Althusser. Some scholars who described themselves as historians of mentalities, notably Georges Duby and Michel Vovelle, began to concern themselves with these questions of interests, legitimation, and so on in the 1970s and early 1980s.[49] It is not easy to combine what might be described as the 'innocent' and the 'cynical' views of thought, but a synthesis may be possible along the lines of the study of the unconscious harmonizing of ideas with interests. Conflicts of interest make the unconscious conscious and the implicit explicit, and in this way they lead to change.

Paradigms and Schemata

The second proposal for the reform of the history of mentalities is a greater concern with categories, schemata, formulae, stereotypes or paradigms (the variety of terminology reveals the extent to which similar problems and insights have occurred in different fields and disciplines). In this area we may situate the work of Aby Warburg and Ernst Gombrich on art, of Thomas Kuhn on science, and of Michel Foucault on a variety of topics. The disciplinary and national contrasts between these scholars may make readers pause for a moment, but whatever their other differences, all four demonstrate an interest in categories and 'schemata', not only in the sense of recurrent themes or motifs but also in the structuring of thought.[50] Incidentally, all four scholars have drawn inspiration from one form or another of psychology. Like Bloch and Febvre, Warburg was interested in historical psychology even before his breakdown and subsequent treatment by Ludwig Binswanger. Gombrich and Kuhn acknowledged a debt to Gestalt psychology, while Foucault's studies of psychiatry are well known.

If the great stumbling block for the history of mentalities is, as suggested earlier, 'the reasons for and the modalities of the passage from one system to another', then there is an obvious case

---

[49] Duby (1979); Vovelle (1982).
[50] Warburg (1932); Gombrich (1960b); Kuhn (1962); Foucault (1966).

for taking up Kuhn's notion of an intellectual tradition or 'paradigm' which may absorb or resist change for long periods thanks to relatively minor 'adjustments', but will finally crack and allow a 'Gestalt switch' or intellectual 'revolution'. Kuhn's model of the process of intellectual change is an attractive one precisely because it is dynamic, concerned with a sequence.

The notion of paradigm is of course problematic even in the history of science, where it began. It becomes still more problematic if it is utilized in other intellectual fields.[51] As in the case of 'mentality', a paradigm must not be seen as a prison. It is something individuals use to make sense of their experience, yet at the same time it shapes their thinking. Despite these problems, the notion of paradigm can be and has been utilized with sensitivity, skill and caution – in studies of Renaissance humanism, for example, and of early modern political thought.[52]

Similar kinds of difficulty arise when one tries to work with the parallel notion of 'schema', which has already made its appearance in this book (above, pp. 39–41, 95–7). Schemata are amazingly long-lived on occasion, as Aby Warburg showed in his studies of the classical tradition, and Ernst Curtius (who was inspired by Warburg) in his work on *topoi* or commonplaces in European literature (the image of the world as a book, the *locus amoenus* or 'beautiful place', and so on).[53] All the same, these categories and stereotypes employed by individuals and groups to structure or interpret their experience of a changing world are themselves subject to change over the long term. The problem is to account for these changes. In his *Art and Illusion* (1960), the most creative and the best-known study to use the notion of the schema, Ernst Gombrich suggested that schemata are 'corrected' by artists by checking them against the natural world. However – as a reviewer was quick to point out – if the artist's view of nature is a product of the schemata, it is impossible to break out of the circle.[54] The same point might be made against Thomas Kuhn's view of perceived 'discrepancies' between paradigm and reality as leading to scientific revolutions.

A similar objection might be levelled against the idea of 'episteme', developed by Gaston Bachelard, Georges Canguilhem and

[51] Lakatos and Musgrave (1970); Hollinger (1980).
[52] Seigel (1968); Pocock (1972), 273–91.
[53] Curtius (1948).
[54] Arnheim (1962).

Michel Foucault, or against the idea of mental 'grids' or 'filters' employed by Foucault and some social anthropologists, filters which exclude some messages or aspects of reality while allowing others through.[55] These filters are more general, more abstract and perhaps more flexible than Warburg's 'schemata' but their function too is to assimilate different situations to one another in order to make them easier to understand. In other words, the greater the emphasis on system, the more difficult it is to explain change. One might regard this difficulty as the converse of the success of these models in explaining continuities, traditions and cultural reproduction. The cultural historian seems to be in a situation not unlike that of the physicists who view light as waves for some purposes and as particles for others.

All the same, it may be possible to say something about changes in the schemata. For example, one can focus on the displacement or migration of a given schema or stereotype from one object to another. After the discovery of America, for example, the traditional stereotypes of the 'monstrous races' (people with the heads of dogs, or with their faces in their stomachs and so on) did not disappear. They were relocated in this new world, as in the case of the Amazons (above, p. 140).[56] Again, the early modern stereotype of the witch (associated with sex orgies, the eating of babies, etc.) has been shown to have a long history. In the Middle Ages it was applied by the orthodox to heretics, and in ancient Roman times by pagans to Christians.[57]

To account for changes in the schemata or more generally in mentalities, it is probably necessary to combine external with internal approaches. A so-called 'belief system' may be viewed as a bundle of schemata, which generally support one another but may sometimes be in contradiction. A certain amount of contradiction is not difficult to live with, but once a certain critical threshold is passed, problems arise. Change might therefore be explained in terms of a combination of external 'forces' with 'allies' within the system, traitors within the gates of the fortress.

---

[55] Pike (1954); Foucault (1966); Douglas (1970).
[56] Wittkower (1942), 72–4; Friedman (1981), 197–207.
[57] Cohn (1975).

History of Metaphors

In the last paragraph I was driven to metaphor in the attempt to conceptualize conceptual change. The notions of 'schema' and 'system' may themselves be clarified if we look more closely at language, and especially at metaphor and symbol. Historians, like anthropologists and sociologists, are coming to recognize the importance of language in 'constituting' the reality they study.[58] Linguistics – notably the work of Antoine Meillet – was already influential on Febvre's history of mentalities, but a newer linguistics has something different to offer.

The relation between modes of communication and modes of thought has attracted much attention from both historians and anthropologists in the last generation.[59] Indeed, there is a danger that after many years of neglect, language has now been credited with too much power. Like Braudel's notion of mentalities as 'prisons', Nietzsche's idea of the 'prison-house of language' – developed by the American linguist Benjamin Whorf – is both reductionist and simplistic.[60] At the other extreme, at a time when it has become common to assume that reality is 'constructed' or 'constituted' by individuals and groups, the limits of that power to construct and the limits within which it operates need to be borne in mind. The world is not completely malleable.

However, if we are trying to describe the differences between mentalities, it seems useful to focus on recurrent metaphors, especially those which seem to structure thought. Obvious examples in the history of the West are the metaphor of the world as an organism (a 'body', an 'animal'), and the metaphor of the world as a machine, and the shift from one to the other in the course of the so-called 'scientific revolution' of the seventeenth century. The idea of the 'mechanization of the world picture' in the seventeenth century is a fruitful one which deserves a fuller, richer, wider treatment than it received in the famous book of that title published by the Dutch scholar E. J. Dijksterhuis in 1950. A similar point might be made about the decline of natural symbols like the 'body politic'. In the late Middle Ages, it was argued that a king had two bodies, his natural body, subject to decay

[58] Crick (1976).
[59] Goody (1977); Clanchy (1979); Eisenstein (1979).
[60] Jameson (1972); Whorf (1956).

and death, and his 'body politic', which was immortal. By the seventeenth century, however, this argument was dismissed as mere metaphor. A case might also be made for the decline in the importance, if not in the employment, of personifications like the *gabelle*, discussed above.[61]

The stress on dominant metaphors is especially valuable because it is a means of liberating historians of mentalities from the perils (if not the 'prison') of the binary system, the great divide into traditional and modern. The point is not to suggest that a given period be characterized in terms of one metaphor alone. Seventeenth-century thinkers, for example, were fascinated not only by the image of the machine but by the metaphor of law. They spoke and wrote of the laws of nature and of the 'court' of heaven, complete with its judges, advocates and so on. At times they even enacted the metaphor. The Jansenists, for example, many of whom came from the best legal families of the time, had the habit of leaving written appeals to Christ on altars. 'In 1679 a nun was buried with an *appel* to the Risen Saviour between her hands, and forty days later, since that was the proper legal interval, a *relief d'appel* was lowered into her tomb.'[62]

It is also necessary to ask whether there has been a decline of metaphor, a reaction against metaphor, a gradual shift from a more concrete to a more abstract mode of thought (associated with literacy and numeracy), together with a greater interest in the literal rather than the symbolic interpretation of texts, images and events, a rise of 'literal-mindedness'. Like many other historians, I believe that a shift of this kind took place and would date it – among the elites of Western Europe, at least – to the middle of the seventeenth century. However, what happened might be better redescribed not so much as a decline or abandonment of metaphor as a change in the conception of metaphor, from objective 'correspondence' to mere subjective 'analogy'.[63]

The redescription is necessary to avoid the dangerous illusion that we today think without the help of metaphors.[64] Historians themselves make much more use of metaphors than they generally admit – metaphors of sickness and health, youth and old age,

[61] Kantorowicz (1957); cf. Archambault (1967); Starkey (1977).
[62] Knox (1950), 201.
[63] Hollander (1961), conclusion; Harris (1966); Vickers (1984); cf. Burke (1993, 1997).
[64] Blumenberg (1960); Lakoff and Johnson (1980).

of rivers (the 'flow' of time), of buildings, of theatres, and so on.[65] The power of metaphor is coming to be taken seriously not only by linguists, philosophers and literary critics, but also by social anthropologists, who study its place in social life.[66] Historians of mentalities, who also study thought at the everyday level, have something important to gain by following their example. A case in point is that of the metaphor of purity, as enacted by nobles who refused to contaminate their blood by marrying commoners, dissident Christians who wanted to 'purify' the church, or communities who burned witches or expelled outsiders in campaigns of 'ethnic cleansing'.

It will be noted that of the three points discussed in the last few pages, the last, on metaphors, is concerned with an 'internalist' history of mentalities, in other words with the relation of beliefs to one another. The first, on interests, is concerned with an 'externalist' history, with the relation of beliefs to society. The second point, about categories, is concerned with both. Categories and schemata are ways of structuring thought. They are not neutral, however. They may be associated with interests, with attempts by some groups to control others, as has been suggested by the sociologists who have developed what they call 'labelling theory'. Give a witch a bad name and burn her. It is essential to any reformed or reformulated history of mentalities that it combine the insights of the internalist and externalist approaches.

Despite the renewal of the history of mentalities in the 1970s and 1980s by the appropriation and incorporation of concepts taken from other traditions, there has been a turn against it, even in France. A critique from outside, Geoffrey Lloyd's *Demystifying Mentalities* (1990), was rapidly translated into French and furnished with a more radical title suggesting that the moment had come to 'finish with' the approach, *Pour en finir avec les mentalités*. Today, historians of the *Annales* group, from Jacques Le Goff to Roger Chartier, are more likely to speak either of *représentations* or of *l'imaginaire social*.[67] The first is Durkheim's old term, though it now carries associations with American 'new historicism' and the Californian journal

---

[65] White (1973); Demandt (1978).
[66] Douglas (1970); Sapir and Crocker (1977).
[67] Chartier (1988), esp. ch. 1; cf. Boureau (1989).

Representations. The second is a difficult term to translate, but something like 'collective imagination' may approximate to it. It echoes a series of studies of the imagination by such theorists as Jacques Lacan, Louis Althusser, and Cornelius Castoriadis.

It would be unfair to suggest that current historians of representations or the collective imagination are simply carrying on the old firm under a new sign. Together with the word 'mentality' they have abandoned the misleading idea of 'pre-logical' thought. On the positive side, they show more interest than their predecessors in visual images. All the same, they continue to be preoccupied with the history of everyday thinking. For this reason, whatever term they use to describe their enterprise, they cannot avoid facing some of the same basic problems as their predecessors.

12

Unity and Variety in Cultural History

❧❧❧

Today, we are living through what has been called a 'cultural turn' in the study of humanity and society. 'Cultural studies' now flourish in many educational institutions, especially in the English-speaking world.[1] A number of scholars who would a decade or so ago have described themselves as literary critics, art historians or historians of science, now prefer to define themselves as cultural historians, working on 'visual culture', 'the culture of science', and so on. Political 'scientists' and political historians are exploring 'political culture', while economists and economic historians have turned their attention from production to consumption, and so to culturally shaped desires and needs. Indeed, in contemporary Britain and elsewhere, 'culture' has become an everyday term which ordinary people use when talking about their community or way of life.[2]

All the same, cultural history is not very firmly established, at least in an institutional sense. Come to that, it is not easy to answer the question, What is culture? It seems to be as difficult to define the term as to do without it. As we have seen in chapter 1, many varieties of 'cultural history' have been practised in different parts of the world since the late eighteenth century, when the term was originally coined in Germany (above, p. 2). In the last few years, cultural history has fragmented still further than

---

[1] Hall (1980); Turner (1990); Storey (1996).
[2] Baumann (1996), 4, 34.

before. The discipline of history is splitting into more and more subdisciplines, and most scholars prefer to contribute to the history of 'sectors' such as science, art, literature, education or historiography itself rather than writing about whole cultures. In any case, the nature, or at least the definition of cultural history is increasingly in dispute.

The moment seems a good one for taking stock and attempting to strike a balance. I begin here with a brief account of traditional cultural history, move on to the so-called 'new' cultural history, defined by contrast to the tradition, and end by discussing what is to be done now, whether we should opt for the new, return to the old, or attempt some kind of synthesis. Let me say once and for all that I make no claim to expertise in the whole of this enormous 'field'. Like other historians, I tend to work on a particular period (the sixteenth and seventeenth centuries) and on a particular region (Western Europe, especially Italy), as the case-studies in earlier chapters will have shown. In this final chapter, however, I shall be transgressing these spatial, temporal and disciplinary boundaries in the attempt to view cultural history (despite its internal divisions) as a whole.

Classical Cultural History and its Critics

In the middle of the nineteenth century, when Matthew Arnold was giving his lectures on 'Culture and Anarchy', and Jacob Burckhardt was writing his *Kultur der Renaissance in Italien*, the idea of culture seemed virtually self-explanatory. The situation was not so very different in 1926, when Johan Huizinga delivered his famous lecture, in Utrecht, on 'The Task of Cultural History'.

For all three scholars, 'culture' meant art, literature and ideas, 'sweetness and light' as Arnold described it, or in Huizinga's more prosaic but more precise formulation, 'figures, motifs, themes, symbols, concepts, ideals, styles and sentiments'.[3] The literature, ideas, symbols, sentiments and so on were essentially those to be found in the Western tradition, from the Greeks onwards, among elites with access to formal education. In short, culture was something which some societies had (or more

---

[3] Huizinga (1929); cf. Gilbert (1990), 46–80.

exactly, which some groups in some societies had), while others lacked it.

This is the 'opera house' conception of culture, as it has been labelled by an American anthropologist.[4] It underlies what might be called the 'classic' variety of cultural history, classic in the double sense that it emphasizes the classics, or the canon, of great works and also that it underlies a number of historical classics, notably Jacob Burckhardt's *Renaissance* (1860) and Johan Huizinga's *Waning of the Middle Ages* (1919), the second of these studies being in many ways an attempt both to imitate and to surpass the first. The difference between these works and specialized studies in the history of art, literature, philosophy, music and so on is their generality, their concern with all the arts and their relation to one another and to the 'spirit of the age'.

The two studies by Burckhardt and Huizinga – not to mention other distinguished works by the same authors – are marvellous books by great historians. Both writers had a gift for evoking the past and also for showing connections between different activities. All the same, I shall argue that their approach cannot or should not be the model for cultural history today, because it cannot deal satisfactorily with certain difficulties. Burckhardt and Huizinga themselves, unlike their followers, were at least intermittently aware of these difficulties, but for most of the time the classic approach is what they practised. This classical tradition of cultural history is open to at least five serious objections.

(1) It is suspended in the air, in the sense of ignoring (or at least placing little emphasis on) society – the economic infrastructure, the political and social structure, and so on. Burckhardt himself admitted in later life that his book had paid insufficient attention to the economic foundations of the Renaissance, while Huizinga discussed the late medieval preoccupation with death without relating it to the plagues which ravaged Europe from 1348 onwards. This general criticism was emphasized by the first scholars to criticize the classical model, the Marxists, or more exactly that fraction of the Marxists which took culture seriously.

In the 1940s and 1950s, three Central European refugees in England, Frederick Antal, Francis Klingender and Arnold

---

[4] Wagner (1975), 21.

Hauser, offered an alternative cultural history, a 'social history' of art and literature.[5] In the 1950s and 1960s, the studies of culture and society by Raymond Williams, Edward Thompson and others continued or reconstructed this tradition.[6] Thompson, for instance, objected to the location of popular culture in what he called the 'thin air' of meanings, attitudes and values, and attempted to situate it in 'its proper material abode', 'a working environment of exploitation and resistance to exploitation'.[7]

The alternative cultural history produced within this tradition has had much to say about the relation of what Marx called the cultural 'superstructure' to its economic 'base', though both Thompson and Williams were or became ill at ease with this metaphor.[8] They also showed a concern with what sociologists such as Max Weber have called the 'carriers' of culture. They viewed culture as a system of messages in which it is important to identify 'who says what to whom'. A view, incidentally, which was not and is not confined to Marxists.

In social anthropology, for example, the supporters of what is known as the 'pattern theory' of culture, a morphological approach not unlike that of (say) Huizinga, were criticized by the supporters of a functional theory of culture. One of the leaders of the functional school, Bronislaw Malinowski, took the example of a stick which might be used for digging, punting, walking or fighting. 'In each of these specific uses, the stick is embedded in a different cultural context; that is, put to different uses, surrounded with different ideas, given a different cultural value and as a rule designated by a different name.'[9]

(2) A second major criticism of classic cultural history is that it depends on the postulate of cultural unity or consensus. Some writers within the tradition liked to use the Hegelian term 'spirit of the age', *Zeitgeist*, but even when this phrase was not used the essential assumption remained. Thus Burckhardt wrote of 'the culture of the Renaissance', while Huizinga once advised cultural historians to search for 'the quality that unites all the cultural

[5] Antal (1947); Klingender (1947); Hauser (1951).
[6] Williams (1958, 1961); Thompson (1963).
[7] Thompson (1991), 7.
[8] Williams (1977).
[9] Malinowski (1931); cf. Singer (1968).

products of an age and makes them homogeneous'.[10] In similar fashion Paul Hazard entitled his study of late seventeenth-century intellectuals *The Crisis of the European Mind* (1935), while Perry Miller called his history of academic ideas in or near Harvard *The New England Mind* (1939). Arnold Toynbee took the idea of unity still more literally when he organized his comparative *Study of History* (1934–61) around twenty-six distinct 'civilizations'. The same idea or assumption underlay (indeed, under-pinned) Oswald Spengler's massive volumes on the *Decline of the West* (1918–22).

The problem is that this postulate of cultural unity is extremely difficult to justify. Once again, it was the Marxists who took the lead in criticizing it. Thompson, for instance, remarked that 'the very term "culture", with its cosy invocation of consensus, may serve to distract attention from social and cultural contradictions.'[11] The same argument has been employed against social anthropologists working in the tradition of Émile Durkheim. Ironically enough, similar criticisms have been levelled by Ernst Gombrich against the Marxist historian Arnold Hauser as well as against Burckhardt, Huizinga and the art historian Erwin Panofsky for what he calls their Hegelian assumption of a 'spirit of the age' (above, p. 21), vividly illustrated in Panofsky's elegant essay *Gothic Architecture and Scholasticism* (1951).[12]

The problem is that cultural consensus or homogeneity is very difficult to discover. For example, the movement we call the Renaissance was a movement within elite culture, which is unlikely to have touched the peasant majority of the population. Even within the elite, there were cultural divisions at this time. Traditional Gothic art as well as the new Renaissance style continued to attract patrons. Antal went so far as to claim that the richly detailed and decorative art of Gentile da Fabriano expressed the world-view of the feudal nobility, while the simpler, more realistic art of Masaccio expressed that of the Florentine bourgeoisie. This contrast between two styles and two classes is much too simple, but the point that distinctions existed within the culture of the upper classes in fifteenth-century Florence deserves to be taken seriously.

[10] Huizinga (1929), 76.
[11] Thompson (1991), 6.
[12] Gombrich (1969).

In similar fashion, popular culture in early modern Europe, for instance, not only varied between one region and another but also took different forms in cities and villages, or among women and men. Even the culture of an individual may be far from homogeneous. The upper classes of early modern Europe may be described as 'bicultural' in the sense that they participated fully in popular culture as well as possessing a culture of their own which ordinary people did not share.[13] Again, in nineteenth-century Japan, some upper-class men, at least, began to live what has been called a 'double life', a life both Western and traditional, consuming two kinds of food, wearing two kinds of clothes, reading two kinds of books and so on.[14]

(3) A central notion in classic cultural history, taken over from the church, is that of 'tradition', the basic idea being that of handing over objects, practices and values from generation to generation. The complementary opposite of tradition was the idea of 'reception', the reception of Roman law, for instance, or that of the Renaissance outside Italy. In all these cases, it was widely assumed that what was received was the same as what was given: a cultural 'heritage' or 'legacy' (as in the titles of a once famous series of studies of *The Legacy of Greece*, *The Legacy of Rome*, and so on).

This assumption was undermined by the German Aby Warburg and his followers (pioneers in the 1920s of interdisciplinary 'cultural studies', or *Kulturwissenschaft*) in a series of remarkable monographs on the classical tradition in the Middle Ages and the Renaissance. They noted, for example, how the pagan gods 'survived' into medieval times only at the price of some remarkable transformations: Mercury, for instance, was sometimes represented as an angel, more often as a bishop.[15] Warburg was particularly interested in elements of tradition which he called 'schemata' or 'formulae', whether visual or verbal, which persisted over the centuries although their uses and applications varied.[16] The identification of stereotypes, formulae, commonplaces and recurrent themes in texts, images and performances and the study of their transformation have become an important part of the practice of

[13] Burke (1978), 23–64.
[14] Witte (1928); Seidensticker (1983).
[15] Warburg (1932); Seznec (1940).
[16] Warburg (1932), vol. 1, 3–58, 195–200

cultural history, witness the recent work on memory and travel discussed above (chapters 3 and 6).

Tradition, as a specialist on ancient India has put it, is subject to an inner conflict between the principles transmitted from one generation to another and the changing situations to which they are supposed to be applied.[17] To put the point another way, following the letter of tradition is likely to mean diverging from its spirit. No wonder that – as in the case of the disciples of Confucius (say), or Luther, the followers so often diverge from the founders. The façade of tradition may mask innovation.[18] As we have already seen, this point may be made about historiography itself. Ranke was not a Rankean, or Burckhardt a Burckhardtian, any more than Marx was a Marxist.

The idea of tradition has been subjected to a still more devastating critique by Eric Hobsbawm, who has argued that many practices which we regard as very old were actually invented relatively recently, many of them (in the case of Europe) between 1870 and 1914 in response to social change and to the needs of the increasingly centralized national states.[19] It might be suggested that Hobsbawm's distinction between invented and 'genuine' traditions is too sharp. Some degree of conscious or unconscious adaptation to new circumstances is a constant feature of the transmission of tradition, as Goody's example from West Africa (above, p. 58) illustrates more dramatically than most. All the same, Hobsbawm's challenge to cultural historians requires a response.

Given its ambiguities, one may well ask whether historians would not be better off if they abandoned the idea of tradition altogether. My own view is that it is virtually impossible to write cultural history without it, but that it is high time to abandon what might be called the traditional notion of tradition, modifying it to allow for adaptation as well as adoption, and drawing on the ideas of 'reception' theory, discussed below.

(4) A fourth criticism of classic cultural history is that the idea of culture implicit in this approach is too narrow. In the first place, it equates culture with high culture. In the last generation in

---

[17] Heesterman (1985), 10–25.
[18] Schwartz (1959).
[19] Hobsbawm and Ranger (1983), 263–307.

particular, historians have done a great deal to redress the balance and recover the history of the culture of ordinary people. However, even studies of popular culture often treat culture as a series of 'works', as examples of 'folksong', 'popular art', and so on. Anthropologists, on the other hand, have traditionally used the term 'culture' much more widely, to refer to the attitudes and values of a given society and their expression or embodiment in 'collective representations' (as Durkheim used to say) or 'practices', a term which has become associated with recent social theorists such as Pierre Bourdieu and Michel de Certeau. The ex-literary critics such as Raymond Williams and Richard Hoggart who founded British 'cultural studies' have moved in the same direction, from literary texts to popular texts and from popular texts to ways of life.

(5) The classical tradition of cultural history may also be criticized on the grounds that it is no longer appropriate or adequate for our time. Although the past does not change, history needs to be rewritten from generation to generation in order for that past to continue to be intelligible to a changing present. Classic cultural history was written for as well as about European elites. Today, on the other hand, the appeal of cultural history is wider and more diverse, geographically and socially. In some countries, this increasing appeal is associated with the rise of multidisciplinary courses under the umbrella of 'cultural studies'.

Classic cultural history emphasized a canon of great works within the European tradition, but the cultural historians of the late twentieth century are working in an age of decanonization. The well-publicized critique of the so-called 'canon' of great books in the USA and the ensuing 'culture wars' are only part of a much wider movement which has been labelled 'multiculturalism'.[20] Educated Westerners as well as Third World intellectuals are less and less at ease with the idea of a single 'great tradition' with a monopoly of cultural legitimacy. It is no longer possible for any of us to identify 'culture' with our own traditions.

We are living in an age of widespread discomfort with, if not rejection of, the so-called 'grand narrative' of the development of Western culture – the Greeks, the Romans, the Renaissance, the Discoveries, the Scientific Revolution, the Enlightenment, and so

[20] Bak (1993).

on, a narrative which can be used to legitimate claims to superiority on the part of Western elites.[21] There is equal discomfort with the idea of a literary, intellectual or artistic canon, or at least with the particular selection of texts or images which used to be presented as 'the' Great Books, Classics or Old Masters. Today, the process of 'canonization' and the social and political conflicts underlying it has become an object of study by cultural historians, but more for the light which it throws on the ideas and assumptions of the canonizers than on those of the canonized.[22]

What is to be done? To state my own view on an issue on which consensus seems at best to be somewhat remote, and at worst impossible, we should not abandon the study of the Renaissance and other movements in the 'high' culture of the West, which still have much to offer many people today despite the increasing cultural distance between late twentieth-century ideas and assumptions and those of the original audiences. Indeed, I should like to suggest that courses in 'cultural studies' would be much enriched if they were to make space for movements of this kind alongside contemporary popular culture. However, historians should write about these movements in a way which recognizes the value of other cultural traditions rather than regarding them as barbarism or absence of culture.

Anthropological History

Readers may be wondering whether the moral of the criticisms listed above is to abandon cultural history altogether. Perhaps this is the reason that the cultural studies movement – despite the example of one of its leaders, Raymond Williams – has been so little concerned with history (another reason might be the marginal position of cultural history in Britain). Yet it might well be argued that cultural history has become even more necessary than before in our age of fragmentation, specialization, and relativism. It is perhaps for this reason that scholars in other disciplines, from literary criticism to sociology, have been turning in

---

[21] Lyotard (1979); Bouwsma (1990), 348–65.
[22] Gorak (1991); Javitch (1991).

this direction. We seem to have been experiencing a rediscovery of the importance of symbols in history as well as in what used to be called 'symbolic anthropology'.

Another reaction to the criticisms might be to practise a different kind of cultural history. As we have seen, a number of Marxist historians and critics have attempted to do this. The work of Hauser, Antal, Thompson, Hobsbawm and Williams has already been mentioned, and it would not be difficult to extend the list to include Georg Lukács, Lucien Goldmann, and others. One might describe the work of these individuals as an alternative style of cultural history. Yet there remains something odd about the idea of a Marxist tradition of cultural history. To follow Marx was generally to affirm that culture was simply the 'superstructure', the icing on the cake of history. Marxists interested in the history of culture were in a marginal position which exposed them to attacks from two sides, from fellow-Marxists and from fellow-historians of culture. The reception of Edward Thompson's *The Making of the English Working Class* illustrates this point clearly enough.

A new style of cultural history, whether one calls it a second or a third style, has in fact emerged in the last generation, thanks in large part to ex-Marxists, or at least to scholars who once found some aspects of Marxism attractive. This approach is sometimes known as the 'new cultural history'.[23] Since novelty is a rapidly diminishing asset, it might be wiser to describe the new style in another way. One possibility is to speak of the 'anthropological' variety of history, since many of its practitioners (the present author among them) would confess to having learned much from anthropologists. They have also learned much from literary critics, like the 'new historicists' in the USA, who have adapted their methods of 'close reading' to the study of non-literary texts, such as official documents, and indeed to the study of 'texts' in inverted commas, from rituals to images.[24] Come to that, some anthropologists have learned from literary critics, as well as vice versa. Semiotics, the study of signs of all kinds, from poems and paintings to food and clothes, was the joint project of students of language and literature such as Roman Jakobson and Roland Barthes and anthropologists such as Claude Lévi-Strauss. Their

[23] Hunt (1989); cf. Chartier (1988).
[24] Greenblatt (1988a, 1988b).

concern with 'deep', unchanging structures of meaning diminished their appeal (to put it mildly) to historians, especially at first, but over the last generation or so the contribution of semiotics to the renewal of cultural history (the idea of a room or a meal as a system of signs, the awareness of oppositions and inversions, and so on) has become increasingly visible.

Despite the complex origins of the movement, 'anthropological history' may be a convenient label for it. It is clear enough that such history – like every style of history – is a child of our time, in this case a time of cultural clashes, multiculturalism and so on. For this very reason it has something to contribute to the study of the present as well as the past, viewing recent trends from the perspective of the long term.

Aby Warburg and Johan Huizinga already took an interest in anthropology at the beginning of the century, but today its influence among historians is much more pervasive than it was in their day. A substantial group of scholars now view the past as a foreign country, and like the anthropologists they see their task as one of interpreting the language of 'their' cultures, both literally and metaphorically. It was the British anthropologist Edward Evans-Pritchard who conceived of his discipline as a kind of translation from concepts of the culture being studied into those of the student's culture.[25] To employ the now famous distinction made by the anthropologist-linguist Kenneth Pike, it is necessary to move backwards and forwards between the 'emic' vocabulary of the natives of a culture, the insiders, and the 'etic' concepts of the outsiders who study them.

Cultural history is also a cultural translation from the language of the past into that of the present, from the concepts of contemporaries into those of historians and their readers. Its aim is to make the 'otherness' of the past both visible and intelligible.[26] This is not to say that historians should treat the past as completely alien. The dangers of treating another culture in this way have been made abundantly clear in the debate on 'orientalism', in other words the Western view (or views) of the East (or easts).[27]

Rather than thinking in terms of a binary opposition between Self and Other, as participants in cultural encounters have so

[25] Beidelman (1971); Lowenthal (1985); Pálsson (1993).
[26] Darnton (1984), 4; Pallares-Burke (1996).
[27] Said (1978).

often done, it may be more illuminating to try to think in terms of degrees of cultural distance. We could try to acquire a double vision, to see people in the past as unlike ourselves (in order to avoid the anachronistic imputation of our values to them), but at the same time as like us in their fundamental humanity.

The differences between the current anthropological model of cultural history and its predecessors, classical and Marxist, might be summed up in four points.

(1) In the first place, the traditional contrast between societies with culture and societies without culture has been abandoned. The decline of the Roman Empire, for instance, should not be viewed as the defeat of 'culture' by 'barbarism', but as a clash of cultures. Ostrogoths, Visigoths, Vandals and other groups had their own cultures (values, traditions, practices, representations, and so on). However paradoxical the phrase may seem, there was a 'civilization of the barbarians'. The assumption built into this third model is a cultural relativism as alien to the Marxists as it would have been to Burckhardt and Huizinga. Like anthropologists, the new cultural historians speak of 'cultures' in the plural. They do not assume that all cultures are equal in every respect, but they refrain from value judgements about the superiority of some over others, judgements which are inevitably made from the viewpoint of the historian's own culture and act as so many obstacles to understanding.

(2) In the second place, culture has been redefined along Malinowskian lines as comprising 'inherited artefacts, goods, technical processes, ideas, habits and values', or along Geertzian lines as 'the symbolic dimensions of social action'.[28] In other words, the meaning of the term has been extended to embrace a much wider range of activities than before – not only art but material culture, not only the written but the oral, not only drama but ritual, not only philosophy but the mentalities of ordinary people. Everyday life or 'everyday culture' is central to this approach, especially the 'rules' or conventions underlying everyday life, what Bourdieu calls the 'theory of practice' and the semiologist Jury Lotman, the 'poetics of everyday behaviour'.[29]

---

[28] Malinowski (1931), 621; Geertz (1973), 30.
[29] Bourdieu (1972); Lotman (1984); Frykman and Löfgren (1996).

Of course the process of learning how to be a medieval monk or a Renaissance noblewoman or a nineteenth-century peasant involved more than internalizing rules. As Bourdieu suggests, the learning process includes a more flexible pattern of responses to situations which – like the scholastic philosophers – he calls 'habitus'.[30] It might therefore be more accurate to use the term 'principle' rather than 'rule'.

In this wide sense, culture is now invoked in order to understand economic or political changes which had previously been analysed in a narrower, internal manner. For example, a historian of the decline of British economic performance between 1850 and 1980 explained it by 'the decline of the industrial spirit', linked to the gentrification of industrialists and ultimately to a revolution (or as the author calls it, a 'counter-revolution') in values.[31] For their part, political historians are making increasing use of the idea of 'political culture' to refer to attitudes, values and practices transmitted as part of the process of 'socializing' childen and taken for granted thereafter.

A striking example of a shift in this direction is the late F. S. L. Lyons, a political historian who entitled his last book *Culture and Anarchy in Ireland 1890–1939*. The point of the wry reference to Matthew Arnold was Lyons's conviction that Irish politics in that period could only be understood by taking into account 'the fact that at least four cultures have for the last three centuries been jostling each other in the island'. The dominant English culture coexisted and clashed with the Gaelic, Ulster Protestant, and Anglo-Irish cultures.[32]

(3) In the third place, the idea of 'tradition', central to the old cultural history, has been joined by a cluster of alternatives. One is the concept of cultural 'reproduction' launched in the 1970s by the French social theorists Louis Althusser and Pierre Bourdieu.[33] One advantage of this concept is to suggest that traditions do not continue automatically, out of inertia. On the contrary, as the history of education reminds us, it takes a great deal of effort to hand them down from generation to generation. The disadvantage of the term is that the idea of 'reproduction' suggests an

[30] Bourdieu (1972), 78–87.
[31] Wiener (1981).
[32] Lyons (1979).
[33] Althusser (1971); Bourdieu and Passeron (1970).

exact or even a mechanical copy, a suggestion which the history of education is far from confirming.[34] The idea of reproduction, like the idea of tradition, needs a counterpoise, such as the idea of reception.

The so-called 'reception theorists', among whom I include the Jesuit historian-anthropologist Michel de Certeau, have replaced the traditional assumption of passive reception by the new assumption of creative adaptation. They argue that 'the essential characteristic of cultural transmission is that whatever is transmitted changes.'[35] Adapting the doctrine of some Fathers of the church, who recommended Christians to 'despoil' pagan culture in the same way that the Israelites despoiled the treasures of the Egyptians, these theorists emphasize not handing down but 'appropriation'. Like the medieval scholastic philosophers, they argue that 'whatever is received is received according to the manner of the receiver' ('Quidquid recipitur, ad modum recipientis recipitur').[36] Their position implies a criticism of semiotics, or more exactly a historicization of semiotics, since it denies the possibility of finding fixed meanings in cultural artefacts.

In short, the stress has shifted from the giver to the receiver, on the grounds that what is received is always different from what was originally transmitted because receivers, consciously or unconsciously, interpret and adapt the ideas, customs, images and so on offered to them. The cultural history of Japan, for instance, offers many examples of what used to be called 'imitation', first of China and more recently of the West. This imitation is often so creative that a more accurate term for it might be 'cultural translation'. Thus Ch'an Buddhism was translated into Zen, and the Western novel domesticated by Natsume Soseki, who claimed to have written one of his stories 'in the manner of a haiku'.

The idea of reception may be linked to that of the schema, defined as a mental structure rather than in Warburg's sense of a visual or verbal topos. A schema can shape attitudes to the new, as in the case of the British travellers studied in chapter 6 above. The schema in this sense is sometimes described as a 'grid', a screen or a filter, which lets in some new elements but excludes

[34] Williams (1981), 181–205.
[35] Dresden (1975), 119ff.
[36] Jauss (1974); Certeau (1980); cf. Ricoeur (1981), 182–93.

others, thus ensuring that the messages which are received are different in some respects from the messages originally sent.[37]

(4) The fourth and last point is the reversal of the assumptions about the relation between culture and society implicit in the Marxist critique of classic cultural history. Cultural historians, like cultural theorists, have been reacting against the idea of the 'superstructure'. Many of them believe that culture is capable of resisting social pressures or even that it shapes social reality. Hence the increasing interest in the history of 'representations', and especially the story of the 'construction', 'invention' or 'constitution' of what used to be considered social 'facts' such as social class, nation, or gender. A number of recent books have the word 'invent' in their title, whether they deal with the invention of Argentina, Scotland, the people, or – as we have seen – of tradition.[38]

Associated with the interest in invention is the history of the collective imagination, *l'imaginaire social*, a new emphasis if not a new topic which crystallized in France partly in reponse to Michel Foucault's celebrated criticism of historians for what he called an 'impoverished' idea of the real which excluded what was imagined. This approach was effectively launched by two studies of the Middle Ages which appeared at much the same time, one concerned with this world and the other with the next, Georges Duby's *The Three Orders* (1979) and Jacques Le Goff's *Birth of Purgatory* (1981). The history of the imagination developed out of the history of collective mentalities, discussed in chapter 11 above. However, its practitioners pay more attention to visual sources, and also to the influence of traditional schemata on perception.

Historians were already producing studies of perception in the 1950s: images of the New World, for example, as a 'virgin land' or of Brazil as an earthly paradise, or the South Pacific as the home of noble or ignoble savages.[39] Indeed, Burckhardt and Huizinga were already aware that perception had a history. Burckhardt wrote of the rise of the view of the state as a 'work of

[37] Foucault (1971), 11; Ginzburg (1976).
[38] Hobsbawm and Ranger (1983); Morgan (1988); Pittock (1991); Shumway (1991).
[39] Smith (1950); Buarque de Holanda (1959); Smith (1960).

art', in other words as the result of planning, while Huizinga was interested in the influence of the romances of chivalry on the perception of social and political reality.[40] In their days, however, studies of this kind were viewed as marginal to the preoccupations of historians.

Today, on the other hand, what was once marginal has become central, and a number of traditional topics have been restudied from this viewpoint. Benedict Anderson, for instance, has rewritten the history of national consciousness in terms of what he calls 'imagined communities', noting the influence of fiction, as in the case of the Filipino José Rizal and his novel *Noli me tangere* (1887).[41] The continuing debate over the significance of the French Revolution is now particularly concerned with its place in the French 'political imagination'.[42] The history of witchcraft and demonology has also been studied as the history of the collective imagination, from the myth of the 'sabbath' to the projection of secret fears and desires onto individual scapegoats.[43] In short, the frontier between 'culture' and 'society' has been redrawn, and the empire of culture and of individual freedom has expanded.

Problems

How successful is the new cultural history? In my opinion, the approaches described above have been necessary ones. They are not simply a new fashion but responses to palpable weaknesses in earlier paradigms. This is not to say that all cultural historians should follow these approaches – it is surely better for a variety of styles of history to coexist than for one to gain a monopoly. In any case, reactions against the conventional wisdom have sometimes been pushed too far. For example, the current stress on the construction or invention of culture exaggerates human liberty as much as the older view of culture as the 'reflection' of society diminished that liberty. Invention is never free from constraints. One groups's invention or dream may be another group's prison. There are indeed revolutionary moments when the freedom to

[40] Burckhardt (1860), ch. 1; Huizinga (1919).
[41] Anderson (1983), 26–9.
[42] Furet (1984).
[43] Cohn (1975); Ginzburg (1990); Muchembled (1990); Clark (1996).

invent is at its maximum and everything seems possible, but these moments are followed by cultural 'crystallization'.

As so often happens in the history of disciplines, not to mention life in general, the attempt to solve some problems has raised others which are at least equally intractable. In order to highlight the continuing difficulties, it may be helpful to point to some of the weak points of two well-known recent examples of these new approaches. These books are among the most brilliant works of cultural history published in the last two or three decades. It is for this reason, as in the cases of Burckhardt and Huizinga, that their weaknesses are worth exploring.

In *The Embarrassment of Riches* (1987), a study of the Dutch Republic in the seventeenth century, Simon Schama invokes the names of Émile Durkheim, Maurice Halbwachs and Mary Douglas, and like these anthropologists he focuses on social values and their embodiment in everyday life. The Dutch Republic was a new nation, and Schama is concerned with the formation – if not the invention – of a new identity, expressed in the Dutch sense of themselves as a second Israel, a chosen people who had freed themselves from the yoke of the Spanish Pharaoh. He goes on to suggest that everyday life was influenced, or even shaped by this new identity. According to Schama, this is what accounts for the unusually sharp sense of privacy and domesticity in Holland, as well as for the cleanliness of Dutch houses, remarked upon by so many foreign travellers. They were showing the world, and especially the southern or Spanish Netherlanders, that they were different. For the first time, the obsessive cleanliness of Dutch housewives is presented as a part of Dutch history rather than remarked upon, as in the past, by historians on the way to more serious topics.

The weakness of this book, which it shares with the work of Burckhardt and Huizinga as well as with the Durkheimian anthropological tradition, is its emphasis on cultural unity. Schama dismisses views that regard culture as 'the outcrop of social class'. Unlike so many of the new cultural historians, he has not passed through a phase of sympathy with Marxism. He concentrates on what the Dutch had in common and has little to say about cultural contrasts or conflicts between regions or between religious or social groups. He interprets the obsession with cleanliness as a sign of Dutchness rather than as an attempt by middle-class townswomen to distinguish themselves from peasants or from their poorer urban neighbours. And yet, as recent work by a team of Dutch historians makes abundantly clear, contrasts and conflicts between rich and poor, urban and rural, and, not least, Catholic and Protestant were important in the history of the so-called 'United Provinces' in the seventeenth century.[44] The presence of an 'Orange' party in both cultures is not the only similarity between the northern Netherlanders in the seventeenth century and the northern Irish in the twentieth.

Carl Schorske's equally celebrated book is concerned with Vienna at the end of the nineteenth century, the Vienna of Arthur Schnitzler, Otto Wagner, Karl Lueger, Sigmund Freud, Gustav Klimt, Hugo von Hofmannsthal and Arnold Schoenberg. His many insights into the work of all these men, into the different arts they practised, and into their social milieu will have to be ignored here in order to concentrate attention on a single general problem, the tension between unity and variety. Schorske is well aware of the importance of subcultures in the polyglot imperial capital he chose to study. Indeed, he emphasizes the segregation of different groups of intellectuals and the fragmentation of culture, 'with each field proclaiming independence of the whole, each part in turn falling into parts'.[45] In similar fashion, his own study is divided into seven essays on different aspects of the culture of *fin de siècle* Vienna – literature, architecture, politics, psychoanalysis, painting, and music.

Fragmentation was doubtless a deliberate choice on the author's part. It is at least symbolically appropriate for a study of modernism.[46] It also responds to the author's concern 'to respect the historical development of each constituent branch of modern culture (social thought, literature, architecture etc.), rather than to hide the pluralized reality behind homogenizing definitions'.[47] The rejection of facile assumptions about the *Zeitgeist* and the willingness to take internal development seriously is one of the many virtues of this study.

Schorske is also interested in the 'cohesion' of the different 'cultural elements' described in his various chapters, and their relation to a shared political experience, 'the crisis of a liberal

[44] Schama (1987); Boekhorst et al. (1992).
[45] Schorske (1981), xxvii, xix.
[46] Cf. Roth (1994a); Roth (1994b), 3–4.
[47] Schorske (1981), xix–xx.

polity'. Indeed, his book carries the subtitle, 'politics and culture'. In this way he tries to hold the balance between 'internalist' and 'externalist' explanations of cultural change. In practice, however, politics receives a chapter of its own, like painting and music. Connections are implied, but they are not always made explicit, at least not at any length. The final paragraphs discuss only Schoenberg and Kokoschka. The author has chosen not to write a concluding chapter which might have attempted to tie the threads together. Such a choice deserves to be respected whether it is dictated by modesty, honesty or the desire to leave readers free to draw their own conclusions. All the same, this renunciation is in a sense a flight from responsibility. The *raison d'être* of a cultural historian is surely to reveal connections between different activities. If this task is impossible, one might as well leave architecture to the historians of architecture, psychoanalysis to the historians of psychoanalysis, and so on.

The essential problem for cultural historians today, as I see it at any rate, is how to resist fragmentation without returning to the misleading assumption of the homogeneity of a given society or period. In other words, to reveal an underlying unity (or at least, underlying connections) without denying the diversity of the past. For this reason it may be useful to draw attention to a body of recent and distinguished work on the history of cultural encounters.

The Encounter Model

In the last few years, cultural historians have been taking increasing interest in encounters, and also in cultural 'clash', 'conflict', 'contest', or 'invasion', not to forget or minimize the destructive aspects of these contacts.[48] For their part, historians of discovery or colonialism have begun to look at the cultural as well as the economic social and political consequences of European expansion.

It would of course be unwise to treat these encounters as if they happened between two cultures, falling back into the language of cultural homogeneity and treating cultures as objectively bounded entities (individuals may have a strong sense of

[48] Axtell (1985); Bitterli (1986); Lewis (1995).

boundary, but in practice the frontiers are crossed again and again). The point to emphasize here is the relatively new interest in the way in which the parties involved perceived, understood, or indeed failed to understand one another. More than one recent monograph has emphasized mistranslation and the 'mistaken identity' between concepts in two cultural systems, a misunderstanding which may well have aided the process of coexistence. A dialogue of the deaf is still a kind of dialogue.[49] For example, in Africa and elsewhere Christian missionaries have often assumed that they 'converted' the local population, since in their view the acceptance of the jealous God of the Christians necessarily involved the rejection of other religions. On the other hand, as some Africanists have suggested, some of the converts may have been interested in appropriating certain spiritual techniques in order to incorporate them into the local religious system (above, p. 154). It is difficult to say who was manipulating whom, but it is at least clear that the different parties to the encounter were operating with different definitions of the situation.[50]

In some remarkable books, historical anthropologists have attempted to reconstruct the 'vision of the vanquished', the way in which the Caribs perceived Columbus, the Aztecs Cortés, or the Incas Pizarro.[51] The example which has given rise to most debate concerns the encounter between the Hawaiians and Captain Cook and his sailors. The art historian Bernard Smith studied European perceptions of the encounter along the lines of Aby Warburg's histories of schemata. The anthropologist Marshall Sahlins then tried to reconstruct the views of the Hawaiians. He noted that Cook arrived at the moment of the year when the Hawaiians expected their god Lono, and argued that his arrival was perceived as an epiphany of the god, thus assimilating the extraordinary new event, the arrival of strangers, into the cultural order. The argument has been challenged, and the debate continues.[52] In a similar fashion, Western sinologists, long concerned with the ways in which European missionaries and diplomats perceived the Chinese, have begun to think seriously about the manner in which the Chinese perceived the

[49] Lockhart (1994), 219; MacGaffey (1994), 259–60.
[50] Smith (1960); Prins (1980); McGaffey (1986), 191–216; cf. Hilton (1985).
[51] Portilla (1959); Wachtel (1971); Hulme (1987); Clendinnen (1992).
[52] Smith (1960); Sahlins (1985); Obeyesekere (1992); Sahlins (1995).

Westerners.[53] It has been argued, for instance, that in China the Virgin Mary was assimilated to the indigenous goddess of mercy, Kuan Yin, while in Mexico she was assimilated to the goddess Tonantzin, thus producing the hybrid Madonna of Guadalupe.[54]

Although I am a European historian of Europe, as earlier chapters will have made abundantly clear, I have cited these examples from Asia, Africa, America and Australia for two reasons. In the first place, some of the most exciting current research in cultural history has been taking place on the frontiers – on the frontiers of the subject, on the frontiers of Europe. In the second place, this work on frontiers may serve as an inspiration for the rest of us. If no culture is an island, not even Hawaii or Britain, it should be possible to make use of the encounter model to study the history of our own culture, or cultures, which we should view as various rather than homogeneous, multiple rather than singular. Encounters and interactions should therefore join the practices and representations which Chartier has described as the principal objects of the new cultural history. After all, as Edward Said recently remarked, 'The history of all cultures is the history of cultural borrowing.'[55]

The history of empires offers clear examples of cultural interaction. The historian Arnaldo Momigliano wrote a book on the limits of Hellenization, the interaction between Greeks, Romans, Celts, Jews and Persians inside and outside the Roman Empire.[56] When the so-called 'barbarians' invaded that empire, a process of cultural interaction took place which included not only the Romanization of the invaders but also the reverse, the 'Gothicization' of the Romans. In the late medieval or the early modern period, one might examine the frontier between the Ottoman Empire and Christendom in this way.

For example, a study has been made of religious interaction – or as the author put it, 'transferences' – at an unofficial level, such as the pilgrimages by Muslims to the shrines of Christian saints and vice versa. Art historians have studied the common material culture of the frontier, for example the use of the Turkish scimitar by Polish troops. Historians of literature have

[53] Gernet (1982); Spence (1990).
[54] Boxer (1975), ch. 4; Lafaye (1974).
[55] Said (1993), 261.
[56] Momigliano (1975).

compared the epic heroes on both sides of the border, the Greek Digenes Akritas, for example, and the Turkish Dede Korkut. In short, the frontier zone, whether Muslim or Christian, had much in common, in contrast to the rival centres of Istanbul and Vienna.[57]

A similar point might be made about medieval Spain. From the time of Américo Castro in the 1940s onwards, some historians have emphasized the symbiosis or *convivencia* of Spanish Jews, Christians, and Muslims, the cultural exchanges between them. For example, Jewish scholars were fluent in Arabic, and Hebrew poetry was inspired by the Arabic lyric. As on the eastern European border, the warriors on both sides used similar equipment and seem to have had similar values. The material culture of the 'Mozarabs' (Christians under Muslim rule) and the 'Mudejars' (Muslims under Christian rule) combined elements from both traditions. Some Catholic churches (like some synagogues) were built in the Muslim style, with horseshoe arches, tiles, and geometrical decoration on doors and ceilings. It is generally impossible to say whether pottery and other artefacts in the 'Hispano-Mauresque' style was made by or for Christians or Muslims, the repertoire of themes being a common one.[58]

Exchanges also took place in the domains of language and literature. Many people were bilingual. Some wrote Spanish in the Muslim script and others Arabic in the Roman alphabet. Some people used two names, one Spanish and one Arabic, which suggests that they had two identities. Romances of chivalry written in a similar style were popular on both sides of the religious frontier (above, chapter 9). Some lyrics switch from Spanish to Arabic within a single line. 'Que faray Mamma? Meu l'habib est' ad yana!' ('What shall I do, mother? My lover is at the door!'). The most spectacular examples of symbiosis come from the practices of popular religion. As was the case on the Ottoman–Habsburg border, there were shrines, such as that of San Ginés, which attracted devotion from Muslims and Christians alike.[59]

The cultural history of other nations might be written in terms

[57] Hasluck (1929); Angyal (1957); Mankowski (1959); Inalcik (1973), 186–202.
[58] Terrasse (1932, 1958).
[59] Castro (1948); Stern (1953); Galmés de Fuentes (1967); MacKay (1976); Mann et al. (1992).

of encounters between regions, such as north and south in Italy, France, or even England. In the case of colonial north America, David Fischer has identified four regional cultures or 'folkways' carried by four groups of immigrants, the East Anglians to Massachusetts, the Southerners to Virginia, the Midlanders to the Delaware and the Borderers to the 'Back Country'. Styles of language and building, as well as political and religious attitudes, remained distinct for centuries.[60]

This example suggests the possibility of a still more ambitious enterprise, that of studying cultural history as a process of interaction between different subcultures, between male and female, urban and rural, Catholic and Protestant, Muslim and Hindu, and so on. Each group defines itself in contrast to the others, but creates its own cultural style – as in the case of British youth groups in the 1970s, for example – by appropriating items from a common stock, and assembling them into a system with a new meaning.[61]

The sociological concept of 'subculture', which implies diversity within a common framework, and the concept of 'counterculture', which implies an attempt to invert the values of the dominant culture, deserve to be taken more seriously by cultural historians than they are at present.[62] Working with the concept of subculture has the advantage of making certain problems more explicit than before. Does the subculture include every aspect of the life of its members, or only certain domains? Is it possible to belong to more than one subculture at a time? Was there more in common between two Jews, one of whom was Italian, or two Italians, one of whom was Jewish?[63] Is the relation between the main culture and the subculture one of complementarity or conflict?

Social classes as well as religions might be analysed as subcultures. The late Edward Thompson was a severe critic of the view of culture as community which privileged shared meanings over conflicts of meaning. Ironically enough, he has himself been criticized for the communitarian model of workers' culture underlying his famous *Making of the English Working-Class*. We might attempt to go beyond this communitarian model with the help of

[60] Fischer (1989).
[61] Hebdige (1979).
[62] Yinger (1960); Clarke (1974); Clarke et al. (1975).
[63] Bonfil (1990).

Pierre Bourdieu, whose ethnography of contemporary France has stressed the extent to which the bourgeoisie and the working class have each defined themselves by contrast to the other.[64] In similar fashion, in a book which is or should be exemplary for historians, two Swedish ethnologists have placed the making of the Swedish middle class in the context of its members' struggle to differentiate themselves from both the nobility and the working class in cultural domains such as attitudes to time and space, dirt and cleanliness.[65] Solidarity within a group is usually strongest at the moment of sharpest conflict with outsiders. In this way cultural historians might contribute to the reintegration of history in an age of hyperspecialization when it has been broken into national, regional and disciplinary fragments.[66]

Consequences

In the case of cultural encounters the perception of the new in terms of the old, described in the last section, generally proves impossible to sustain over the long term. The new experiences first threaten and then undermine the old categories. The traditional 'cultural order' – as the American anthropologist Marshall Sahlins calls it – sometimes cracks under the strain of the attempt to assimilate them.[67] The next stage varies from culture to culture along a spectrum ranging from assimilation to rejection via adaptation and resistance, like the resistance to Protestantism in the Mediterranean world discussed by Fernand Braudel.[68] Why members of some cultures should be particularly interested in novelty or in the exotic is a question as fascinating as it is difficult to answer. The argument that more integrated cultures are relatively closed, while open and receptive cultures have less integration, runs the danger of circularity but has at least the virtue of presenting the problem from the receiver's point of view.[69] The paragraphs which follow will concentrate on receptivity at the expense of resistance.

The consequences of encounters between cultures were first

[64] Thompson (1963); Bourdieu (1979).
[65] Frykman and Löfgren (1979).
[66] Cf. Kammen (1984); Bender (1986).
[67] Sahlins (1981) 136–56.
[68] Braudel (1949), part 2, ch. 6, section 1.
[69] Ottenberg (1959); Schneider (1959).

studied systematically by scholars from New World societies where the encounters had been particularly dramatic. At the beginning of the century, North American anthropologists, including the German emigré Franz Boas, described the changes in American Indian cultures as a result of contact with white culture in terms of what they called 'acculturation', the adoption of elements from the dominant culture. A pupil of Boas, Melville Herskovits, defined acculturation as a more comprehensive phenomenon than diffusion and tried to explain why some traits rather than others were incorporated into the accepting culture.[70] This emphasis on the selection or screening of traits has proved illuminating. For example, in the case of the Spanish conquest of Mexico and Peru, it has been noted that the Indians adopted cultural elements from the 'donor culture' for which there were no local equivalents. It has also been argued that after a few years the adoption of new elements declines. A phase of appropriation is followed by cultural 'crystallization'.[71]

At this point, students of culture, beginning with specialists in the history of religion in the ancient Mediterranean world, have often spoken of 'syncretism'. Herskovits was particularly interested in religious syncretism, for instance the identification between traditional African gods and Catholic saints in Haiti, Cuba, Brazil and elsewhere. Another pupil of Boas, Gilberto Freyre, interpreted the history of colonial Brazil in terms of what he called the formation of 'a hybrid society', or the 'fusion' of different cultural traditions.[72] At least one historian of the Renaissance, Edgar Wind, employed the term 'hybridization' to describe the interaction of pagan and Christian cultures. His point was to reject a one-way analysis of the secularization of Renaissance culture, arguing that 'hybridization works both ways.' For example, 'a Madonna or a Magdalen could be made to resemble a Venus,' but on the other hand 'Renaissance art produced many images of Venus which resemble a Madonna or a Magdalen.'[73]

In similar fashion, the Cuban sociologist Fernando Ortiz argued that the term 'acculturation' should be replaced by 'transculturation' on the grounds that both cultures were changed as

[70] Herskovits (1938); cf. Dupront (1966).
[71] Foster (1960), 227–34; Glick (1979), 282–4.
[72] Freyre (1933); Herskovits (1937, 1938).
[73] Wind (1958), 29.

the result of their encounters, not just the so-called 'donor'. Ortiz was one of the first to suggest that we should speak of the American discovery of Columbus.[74] A good example of this kind of reverse acculturation in which the conquerors are conquered is that of the 'Creoles', the men and women who were of European origin but were born in the Americas and became, in the course of time, more and more American in their culture and consciousness.[75]

The assimilation of Christian saints to non-Christian gods and goddesses such as the West African Shango, the Chinese Kuan Yin, and the Nahuatl Tonantzin has its analogies in Europe. As Erasmus pointed out, a similar process had taken place in early Christian times, where saints like St George were assimilated to gods and heroes like Perseus. 'Accommodation' was the traditional term used to describe this process in the sixteenth century (as in the early church), when Jesuit missionaries to China and India, for instance, attempted to translate Christianity into the local cultural idioms by presenting it as compatible with many of the values of the mandarins and the brahmins.

Preoccupation with this problem is natural in a period like ours marked by increasingly frequent and intense cultural encounters of all kinds. A great variety of terms are used in different places and different disciplines to describe the processes of cultural borrowing, appropriation, exchange, reception, transfer, negotiation, resistance, syncretism, acculturation, enculturation, inculturation, interculturation, transculturation, hybridization (*mestizaje*), creolization, and the interaction and interpenetration of cultures. Following the revival of interest in the Mudejar art mentioned above (itself related to an increasing awareness of the Muslim world today), some Spaniards now speak of a process of 'mudejarism' in their cultural history.[76] Some of these new terms may sound exotic, and even barbarous. Their variety bears eloquent witness to the fragmentation of today's academic world. They also reveal a new conception of culture as *bricolage*, in which the process of appropriation and assimilation is not marginal but central.

Conceptual as well as empirical problems remain. The idea of

[74] Ortiz (1940), introduction.
[75] Brading (1991); Alberro (1992).
[76] Burns (1977); Goytisolo (1986).

'syncretism', for example, has been used to describe a range of situations, from cultural 'mixing' to synthesis. To use the term so loosely raises, or more exactly obscures, a number of problems.[77]

Among these problems is that of the intentions of the agents, of their interpretations of what they are doing, the emic point of view (above, p. 193). For example, in the case of the interaction between Christianity and African religions, we have to consider various scenarios. African rulers, as we have seen, may well have seen themselves as incorporating new elements into their traditional religion. In the case of the 'syncretism' of the African slaves in the Americas, their identification between St Barbara and Shango, for instance, they may well have been following the defensive tactics of conforming outwardly to Christianity while retaining their traditional beliefs. In the case of religion in contemporary Brazil, on the other hand, 'pluralism' might be a better term than syncretism, since the same people may participate in the practices of more than one cult, just as patients may seek cures from more than one system of medicine.

To return to 'traditional' language, individuals may have access to more than one tradition and choose one rather than another according to the situation, or appropriate elements from both to make something of their own. From the 'emic' point of view, what the historian needs to investigate is the logic underlying these appropriations and combinations, the local reasons for these choices. It is for this reason that some historians have been studying the responses of individuals to encounters between cultures, especially those who changed their behaviour – whether we call them 'converts', from the perspective of their new culture, or 'renegades', from the point of view of their old one. The point is to study these individuals – Christians who turned Muslim in the Ottoman Empire, or Englishmen who turned Indian in North America – as extreme and especially visible cases of response to the situation of encounter and to focus on the ways in which they reconstructed their identity.[78] The complexities of the situation are well illustrated by the study of a group of Brazilian blacks, descendants of slaves, who returned to West Africa because they considered it their home, only to find that the locals perceived them as Americans.[79]

[77] Apter (1991).
[78] Axtell (1985); Scaraffia (1993).
[79] Carneiro da Cunha (1985).

From outside, on the other hand, these people are examples of the general process of 'syncretism'. It has been suggested that we confine the use of this term to the 'temporary coexistence' of elements from different cultures, distinguishing it from a true 'synthesis'.[80] But how long is 'temporary'? Can we assume that synthesis or integration necessarily triumphs in the long term? In our time it is difficult not to be struck by movements of anti-syncretism or dis-integration, campaigns for the recovery of 'authentic' or 'pure' traditions.[81]

The concept of cultural 'hybridity' and the terms associated with it are equally problematic.[82] It is all too easy to slide (as Freyre, for instance, often did) between discussions of literal and metaphorical miscegenation, whether to sing the praises of cross-fertilization or to condemn the 'bastard' or 'mongrel' forms of culture which emerge from this process. Is the term 'hybridization' supposed to be descriptive or explanatory? Are new forms supposed to emerge by themselves in the course of a cultural encounter, or are they the work of creative individuals?

Linguistics offers another way of approaching the consequences of cultural encounters.[83] The meeting of cultures, as of languages, might be described in terms of the rise first of pidgin, a form of language reduced to essentials for the purpose of inter-cultural communication, and then of creole. 'Creolization' describes the situation when a pidgin develops a more complex structure as people begin to use it as their first language and for general purposes. Linguists argue that what was once perceived simply as error, as 'broken' English or 'kitchen' Latin, ought to be regarded as a variety of language with its own rules. A similar point might be made about (say) the language of architecture on the frontier between cultures.

In some contexts, the best linguistic analogy might be a 'mixed language' like the *media lengua* of Ecuador, in which Spanish vocabulary is combined with Quechua syntax, or the 'macaronic' Latin discussed in chapter 8 above. During the Renaissance, for example, the ornaments of one architectural style (the classical) were sometimes superimposed on the structures of another (the Gothic). In other contexts, a better analogy might be that of the

[80] Pye (1993).
[81] Stewart (1994).
[82] Young (1995).
[83] Glick (1979), 277–81; Hannerz (1992), 264–6.

bilinguals who 'switch' between one language and another according to the situation. As we have seen in the case of some nineteenth-century Japanese, it is possible for people to be bicultural, to live a double life, to switch from one cultural code to another.

To return to the situation today. Some observers are impressed by the homogenization of world culture, the 'Coca-Cola effect', though they often fail to take into account the creativity of reception and the renegotiation of meanings discussed earlier in the chapter. Others see mixing or hear pidgin everywhere. A few believe they can discern a new order, the 'creolization of the world'.[84] One of the great students of culture in our century, the Russian scholar Mikhail Bakhtin, used to emphasize what he called 'heteroglossia', in other words the variety and conflict of tongues and points of view out of which, so he suggested, new forms of language and new forms of literature (notably the novel) have developed.[85]

We have returned to the fundamental problem of unity and variety, not only in cultural history but in culture itself. It is necessary to avoid two opposite oversimplifications; the view of culture as homogeneous, which is blind to differences and conflicts, and the view of culture as essentially fragmented, which fails to take account of the ways in which all of us create our individual or group mixes, syncretisms or syntheses. The interaction of subcultures sometimes produces a unity of apparent opposites. Shut your eyes for a moment and listen to a South African speaking. It is not easy to tell whether the speaker is black or white. It is worth asking whether the black and white cultures of South Africa share other common features, despite their contrasts and conflicts, thanks to centuries of interaction.

For an outsider, whether historian or anthropologist, the answer to the question is surely 'Yes'. The similarities appear to outweigh the differences. To insiders, however, the differences probably outweigh the similarities. This point about differences in perspective is probably valid for many cultural encounters. It follows that a cultural history centred on encounters should not be written from one viewpoint alone. In the words of Mikhail

---

[84] Hannerz (1987); cf. Friedman (1994), 195–232.
[85] Bakhtin (1981).

212 Unity and Variety in Cultural History

Bakhtin, such a history has to be 'polyphonic'. In other words, it has to contain within itself a variety of tongues and points of view, including those of victors and vanquished, men and women, insiders and outsiders, contemporaries and historians.

Bibliography

Ackerman, Robert (1987) *J. G. Frazer*, Cambridge

Acton, William (1691) *A New Journal of Italy*, London

Addison, Joseph (1705) *Remarks on Several Parts of Italy*, rpr. in his *Works*, 4 vols, London 1890, vol. 1, 356–538

Alatas, Syed H. (1977) *The Myth of the Lazy Native: a Study of the Image of the Malays, Filipinos and Javanese from the Sixteenth to the Twentieth Century and its Function in the Ideology of Colonial Capitalism*, London

Alberro, Solange (1992) *Les Espagnols dans le Mexique colonial: histoire d'une acculturation*, Paris

Alencar, Edgar de (1965) *O Carnaval Carioca através da musica*, 2nd edn, Rio de Janeiro

Allport, Gordon W. and L. Postman (1945) 'The Basic Psychology of Rumour', rpr. in *The Process and Effect of Mass Communication*, ed. Wilbur Schramm, Urbana 1961, 141–55

Alsop, Joseph (1982) *The Rare Art Traditions*, London

Althusser, Louis (1971) *Lenin and Philosophy*, London

Amalvi, Christian (1984) 'Le 14–Juillet', in Nora, vol. 1, 421–72

Amuchástegui, A. J. Pérez (1988) *Mentalidades argentinas*, Buenos Aires

Amyraut, Moyse (1665) *Discours sur les songes divines dont il est parlé dans l'Écriture*, Saumur

Anderson, Benedict (1983) *Imagined Communities*, 2nd edn London 1991

Angyal, Andreas (1957) 'Die Welt der Grenzfestungen: Ein Kapitel aus der südosteuropäische Geistesgeschichte des 16. und 17. Jhts', *Südost Forschungen* 16, 311–42

Anselmo, A. J. (1926) *Bibliografia das obras impressas em Portugal no século xvi*, Lisbon

Antal, Frederick (1947) *Florentine Painting and its Social Background*, London

Apte, Michael (1985) *Humor and Laughter: an Anthropological Approach*, Ithaca

Apter, Andrew (1991) 'Herskovits's Heritage: Rethinking Syncretism in the African Diaspora', *Diaspora* 1, 235–60

Arantes, Antonio Augusto (1982) *O Trabalho e a Fala*, São Paulo

Archambault, Paul (1967) 'The Analogy of the Body in Renaissance Political Literature', *Bibliothèque d'Humanisme et Renaissance* 29, 21–53

Arens, W. (1979) *The Man-Eating Myth*, New York

Ariès, Philippe (1960) *Centuries of Childhood*, English trans. London 1962

Arnheim, Rudolf (1962) 'Review of Gombrich', *Art Bulletin* 44, 75–9

Arthos, John (1968) *Milton and the Italian Cities*, London

Ashmole, Elias (1966) *Diary*, ed. C. H. Josten, 5 vols, Oxford

Axtell, James (1985) *The Invasion Within: the Contest of Cultures in Colonial North America*, New York

Azpilcueta, Martín de (1582) *El silencio ser necessario en el choro*, Rome

Bachelard, Gaston (1947) *La formation de l'esprit scientifique*, Paris

Backman, E. Louis (1952) *Religious Dances in the Christian Church and in Popular Medicine*, London

Baczko, Bronislaw (1984) *Les imaginaires sociaux*, Paris

Bak, Hans, ed. (1993) *Multiculturalism and the Canon of American Culture*, Amsterdam

Bakhtin, Mikhail M. (1929) *Problems of Dostoyevsky's Poetics*, English trans. Manchester 1984

Bakhtin, Mikhail M. (1965) *Rabelais and his World*, English trans. Cambridge, Mass. 1968

Bakhtin, Mikhail M. (1981) 'From the Prehistory of Novelistic Discourse', in his *The Dialogic Imagination*, Austin, 41–83

Balandier, Georges (1965) *Daily Life in the Kingdom of the Kongo*, English trans. London 1968

Barasch, Moshe (1987) *Giotto and the Language of Gestures*, Cambridge, Mass.

Barnes, John (1947) 'The Collection of Genealogies', *Rhodes–Livingstone Journal* 5, 48–55

Baroja, Julio Caro (1965) *El Carnaval*, Madrid

Barolsky, Paul (1978) *Infinite Jest: Wit and Humor in Italian Renaissance Art*, New York

Baron, Hans (1955) *The Crisis of the Early Italian Renaissance*, Princeton

Bartlett, Frederick C. (1932) *Remembering: a Study in Experimental and Social Psychology*, Cambridge

Bartlett, Robert (1986) *Trial by Fire and Water: the Medieval Judicial Ordeal*, Oxford

Bastide, Roger (1958) *Le candomblé de Bahia*, Paris

Bastide, Roger (1966) 'The Sociology of the Dream', in *The Dream and Human Societies*, ed. Gustav E. von Grunebaum and Roger Caillois, Berkeley and Los Angeles, 199–212

Bastide, Roger (1970) 'Mémoire collective et sociologie du bricolage', *Année Sociologique*, 65–108

Battisti, Eugenio (1962) *L'antirinascimento*, Milan

Batts, Michael S. (1987) *A History of Histories of German Literature*, New York

Baumann, Gerd (1996) *Contesting Culture: Discourses of Identity in Multi-ethnic London*, London

Baxandall, Michael (1972) *Painting and Experience in Fifteenth-Century Italy*, Oxford

Beccaria, Gian Luigi (1968) *Spagnolo e spagnoli in Italia*, Turin

Beidelman, Thomas O., ed. (1971) *The Translation of Cultures*, London

Bell, Desmond (1986) 'The Traitor within the Gates', *New Society*, 3 Jan., 15–17

Bellori, Giovan Pietro (1672) *Le vite*, ed. Evelina Borea, Turin 1976

Bender, Thomas (1986) 'Wholes and Parts: the Need for Synthesis in American History', *Journal of American History* 73, 120–36

Bennassar, Bartolomé (1967) *Valladolid au siècle d'or*, The Hague

Bennassar, Bartolomé and Lucile Bennassar (1989) *Les chrétiens d'Allah*, Paris

Benz, Ernest (1969) *Die Vision*, Stuttgart

Beradt, Charlotte (1966) *Das Dritte Reich des Traums*, Munich

Berger, Philippe (1987) *Libro y lectura en la Valencia del Renacimiento*, 2 vols, Valencia

Bernardi, Claudio (1990) *La drammaturgia della settimana santa in Italia*, Milan

Besançon, Alain (1971) *Histoire et expérience du moi*, Paris

Birdwhistell, Ray L. (1970) *Kinesics and Context: Essays on Body-Motion Communication*, Philadelphia

Bishko, Charles J. (1963) 'The Castilian as Plainsman', in *The New World Looks at its History*, ed. Archibald R. Lewis and T. F. McGann, Austin, 47–65

Bitossi, Carlo (1976) 'Andrea Spinola. Elaborazione di un "manuale" per la classe dirigente', in Costantini et al. (1976), 115–75

Bitterli, Urs (1986) *Cultures in Conflict*, English trans. Cambridge 1989

Black, Jeremy (1985) *The British and the Grand Tour*, London

Blackbourn, David (1993) *Marpingen: Apparitions of the Virgin Mary in Bismarckian Germany*, Oxford

Bloch, Marc (1924) *The Royal Touch*, English trans. London 1973

Bloch, Marc (1925) 'Mémoire collective, tradition et coutume', *Revue de Synthèse Historique* 40, 73–83

Blumenberg, Hans (1960) *Paradigmen zu einer Metaphorologie*, Bonn

Blunt, John J. (1823) *Vestiges of Ancient Manners*, London

Boekhorst, Pieter, Peter Burke and Willem Frijhoff, eds (1992) *Cultuur en maatschappij in Nederland 1500–1850*, Meppel

Bogucka, Maria (1983) 'Le geste dans la vie de la noblesse polonaise aux 16e, 17e et 18e siècles', *Revue d'Histoire Moderne et Contemporaine* 30, 3–15

Bonfil, Robert (1990) *Rabbis and Jewish Communities in Renaissance Italy*, New York

Bonifacio, Giovanni (1616) *L'arte de' cenni*, Vicenza

Bonora, Ettore and Mario Chiesa, eds (1979) *Cultura letteraria e tradizione popolare in Teofilo Folengo*, Milan

Borromeo, Carlo (1758) *Instructiones Pastorum*, Augsburg

Borsellino, Nino (1973) *Gli anticlassicisti del '500*, Rome and Bari

Bourdieu, Pierre (1972) *Outlines of a Theory of Practice*, English trans. Cambridge 1977

Bourdieu, Pierre (1979) *Distinction*, English trans. London 1984

Bourdieu, Pierre and Jean-Claude Passeron (1970) *Reproduction in Education, Society and Culture*, English trans. Beverly Hills 1977

Boureau, Alain (1989) 'Propositions pour une histoire restreinte des mentalités', *Annales ESC* 44, 1491–1504

Bouwsma, William J. (1990) *A Usable Past*, Berkeley

Boxer, Charles R. (1975) *Mary and Misogyny*, London

Brading, David (1991) *The First America*, Cambridge

Brandes, Stanley (1980) *Metaphors of Masculinity*, New York

Braudel, Fernand (1949) *The Mediterranean and the Mediterranean World in the Age of Philip II*, English trans. London 1972–3

Braun, Lucien (1973) *Histoire de l'histoire de la philosophie*, Paris

Braun, Rudolf and David Gugerli (1993) *Macht des Tanzes – Tanz der Mächtigen: Hoffeste und Herrschaftszeremoniell, 1550–1914*, Munich

Bredekamp, Horst (1985) *Vicino Orsini und der heilige Wald von Bomarzo*, 2 vols, Worms

Bremmer, Jan and Herman Roodenburg, eds (1991) *A Cultural History of Gesture*, Cambridge

Brewer, John (1995) 'Culture as Commodity: 1660–1800', in *The Consumption of Culture 1600–1800*, ed. Ann Bermingham and John Brewer, London, 341–61

Brizzi, Gian Paolo (1976) *La formazione della classe dirigente nel '600–'700*, Bologna

[Bromley, William] (1692) *Remarks made in Travels through France and Italy*, rpr. London 1693

[Bromley, William] (1702) *Several Years' Travels*, London

Bronzini, Giovanni Battista (1966) *Tradizione di stile aedico dai cantari al Furioso*, Florence

Brown, Horatio ed., (1864) *Calendar of State Papers, Venetian*, 14 vols, London

Brown, Peter (1975) 'Society and the Supernatural', *Daedalus*, Spring, 133–47

Brown, Peter M. (1967) 'Aims and Methods of the Second *Rassettatura* of the Decameron', *Studi Secenteschi* 8, 3–40

Bruford, W. H. (1962) *Culture and Society in Classical Weimar*, Cambridge

Buarque de Holanda, Sergio (1959) *Visões de Paraíso*, Rio de Janeiro

Buckley, Anthony (1989) 'We're Trying to Find our Identity: Uses of History among Ulster Protestants', in *History and Ethnicity*, ed. Elizabeth Tonkin et al., New York, 183–97

Burckhardt, Jacob (1860) *Civilization of the Renaissance in Italy*, English trans. 1878, latest edn Harmondsworth 1990

Burke, Peter (1972) *Culture and Society in Renaissance Italy*, London

Burke, Peter (1978) *Popular Culture in Early Modern Europe*, 2nd edn Aldershot 1994

Burke, Peter (1982) 'Le roi comme héros populaire', *History of European Ideas* 3, 267–71

Burke, Peter (1984) 'How to be a Counter-Reformation Saint', in *Religion and Society in Early Modern Europe*, ed. Kaspar von Greyerz, London, 45–55, rpr. in Burke (1987), 48–62

Burke, Peter (1987) *Historical Anthropology of Early Modern Italy: Essays on Perception and Communication*, Cambridge

Burke, Peter (1991) 'Tacitism, Scepticism and Reason of State', in *The Cambridge History of Political Thought 1450–1700*, ed. James H. Burns, Cambridge

Burke, Peter (1992) *The Fabrication of Louis XIV*, New Haven

Burke, Peter (1993) 'The Rise of Literal-Mindedness', *Common Knowledge* 2, 108–21

Burke, Peter (1995) *The Fortunes of the Courtier*, Cambridge

Burke, Peter (1996) 'The Myth of 1453: Notes and Reflections', in *Querdenken: Dissens und Toleranz im Wandel der Geschichte: Festschrift Hans Guggisberg*, ed. Michael Erbe et al., Mannheim, 23–30

Burke, Peter (1997) 'The Demise of Royal Mythologies', in *Iconography, Propaganda and Legitimation*, ed. Allan Ellenius, Oxford

Burnet, Gilbert (1686) *Some Letters*, Amsterdam

Burns, Robert I. (1977) 'Mudejar History Today', *Viator* 8, 127–43

Butterfield, Herbert (1931) *The Whig Interpretation of History*, London

Butterfield, Herbert (1955) *Man on his Past*, Cambridge

Câmara Cascudo, Luis de (c.1974) *História dos nossos gestos*, São Paulo

Camporesi, Piero (1976) *La maschera di Bertoldo*, Turin

Canguilhem, Georges (1955) *La formation du concept de réflexe aux 17e et 18e siècles*, Paris

Caraffa, Ferrante (1880), 'Memorie', *Archivio Storico per le Provincie Napolesane* 5, 242–61

Cardano, Girolamo (1557) *De rerum varietate*, Basle

Carlton, Charles (1987) *Archbishop William Laud*, London
Carneiro da Cunha, Manuela (1985) *Negros, estrangeiros: os escravos libertos e sua volta à Africa*, São Paulo
Carstairs, G. Morris (1957) *The Twice-Born*, London
Carvajal, Gaspar de (1955) *Relación del nuevo descubrimento del famoso río Grande de las Amazonas*, ed. J. Hernández Millares, Mexico City and Buenos Aires
Castaneda, Carlos (1968) *The Teachings of Don Juan: a Yaqui Way of Knowledge*, rpr. Harmondsworth 1970
Castro, Américo (1948) *The Structure of Spanish History*, English trans. Princeton 1954
Cavalcanti, Maria Laura Viveiros de Castro (1994) *Carnaval Carioca*, Rio de Janeiro
Cebà, Ansaldo (1617) *Il cittadino di repubblica*, Genoa
Cebà, Ansaldo (1623) *Lettere*, Genoa
Certeau, Michel de (1980) *The Practice of Everyday Life*, English trans. Berkeley 1984
Chadwick, W. Owen (1957) *From Bossuet to Newman*, 2nd edn Cambridge 1987
Chambers, David and Brian Pullan, eds (1992) *A Documentary History of Venice*, Oxford
Chaney, Edward (1985) *The Grand Tour and the Great Rebellion*, Geneva
Chartier, Roger (1987) *The Cultural Uses of Print in Early Modern France*, Princeton
Chartier, Roger (1988) *Cultural History between Practices and Representations*, Cambridge
Chastel, André (1961) *Art et humanisme à Florence au temps de Laurent le Magnifique*, Paris
Chastel, André (1986) 'Gesture in Painting: Problems of Semiology', *Renaissance and Reformation* 10, 1–22
Chevalier, Maxime (1976) *Lectura y lectores en la España de los siglos xvi y xvii*, Madrid
Chiaramonti, Scipione (1625) *De conjectandis cuiusque moribus et latitantibus animi affectibus semiotike moralis, seu de signis*, Venice
Christian, William (1981) *Apparitions in Late Medieval Spain*, Princeton
Cian, Vittorio (1887) 'Un episodio della storia della censura in Italia nel secolo xvi: l'edizione spurgata del *Cortegiano*', *Archivio Storico Lombardo* 14, 661–727
Clanchy, Michael T. (1979) *From Memory to Written Record*, London
Clark, Alfred J. (1921) Appendix to Margaret Murray, *The Witch-Cult in Western Europe*, Oxford
Clark, Stuart (1983) 'French Historians and Early Modern Popular Culture', *Past and Present* 100, 62–99
Clark, Stuart (1997) *Thinking with Demons*, Oxford

Clarke, John et al. (1975) 'Subcultures, Culture and Class', in *Resistance Through Rituals*, ed. S. Hall and Tony Jefferson, rpr. London 1976, 9–74

Clarke, Michael (1974) 'On the Concept of Sub-culture', *British Journal of Sociology* 25, 428–41

Clendinnen, Inga (1992) *Aztecs*, Cambridge

Cohen, Tom V. (1988) 'The Case of the Mysterious Coil of Rope', *Sixteenth-Century Journal* 19, 209–21

Cohn, Norman (1975) *Europe's Inner Demons*, London

Cohn, Samuel K. (1988) *Death and Property in Siena*, Baltimore

Comparato, Vittorio I. (1979) 'Viaggatori inglesi in Italia', *Quaderni Storici* 42, 850–86

Connerton, Paul (1989) *How Societies Remember*, Cambridge

Copenhaver, Brian (1978) 'The Historiography of Discovery in the Renaissance: the Sources and Composition of Polydore Vergil's *De Inventoribus Rerum*', *Journal of the Warburg and Courtauld Institutes* 41, 192–214

Corbin, Alain (1982) *The Foul and the Fragrant*, English trans. Leamington 1986

Coryat, Thomas (1611) *Crudities*, rpr. London 1978

Costantini, Claudio (1978) *La Repubblica di Genova nell'età moderna*, Turin

Costantini, Claudio et al. (1976) *Dibattito politico e problemi di governo a Genova nella prima metà del seicento*, Florence

Cozzi, Gaetano (1958) *Il doge Niccolò Contarini*, Venice and Rome

Crick, Malcolm (1976) *Explorations in Language and Meaning*, London

Croce, Benedetto (1895) 'I Lazzari', rpr. in his *Aneddoti*, vol. 3, Bari 1954, 198–211

Crocker, Jon C. (1977) 'My Brother the Parrot', in *The Social Use of Metaphor*, ed. James D. Sapir and J. C. Crocker, Philadelphia

Croix, Alain (1981) *La Bretagne aux 16e et 17e siècles*, 2 vols, The Hague

Crombie, Alistair C. (1994) *Styles of Thinking in the European Tradition*, 3 vols, London

Crouzet, Michel (1982) *Stendhal et l'italianité: essai de mythologie romantique*, Paris

Crummey, Robert O. (1970) *The Old Believers and the World of Antichrist*, Madison

Cunha, Euclides da (1902) *Revolt in the Backlands*, English trans. Chicago 1944

Curtius, Ernst R. (1948) *European Literature and the Latin Middle Ages*, English trans. New York 1953

Da Matta, Roberto (1978) *Carnaval, malandros e herois*, Rio de Janeiro

D'Andrade, Roy (1961) 'Anthropological Studies of Dreams', in

Psychological Anthropology, ed. Francis L. K. Hsu, Homewood, Ill., 296–307

Darnton, Robert (1971) 'The Social History of Ideas', rpr. in his *The Kiss of Lamourette*, London 1990, 219–52

Darnton, Robert (1984) *The Great Cat Massacre*, New York

Darnton, Robert (1995) *The Forbidden Best-Sellers of Pre-revolutionary France*, New York

Davis, John (1973) *Land and Family in Pisticci*, London

Davis, Natalie Z. (1975) 'Women on Top', in her *Society and Culture in Early Modern France*, Cambridge 1987, 124–51

Davis, Natalie Z. (1987) *Fiction in the Archives*, Cambridge

Dear, Peter (1985) 'Totius in Verba: Rhetoric and Authority in the Early Royal Society', *Isis* 76, 145–61

Della Casa, Giovanni (1558) *Il Galateo*, Florence

Del Torre, Michelangelo (1976) *Le origini moderne della storiografia filosofica*, Florence

Demandt, Alexander (1978), *Metaphern für Geschichte*, Munich

De' Seta, Cesare (1981) 'L'Italia nello specchio del Grand Tour', in his *Architettura ambiente e società a Napoli nel '700*, Turin, 127–263

Diacon, Todd A. (1991) *Millenarian Vision, Capitalist Reality: Brazil's Contestado Rebellion, 1912–6*, Durham N.C.

Dickens, A. Geoffrey and John Tonkin (1985) *The Reformation in Historical Thought*, Cambridge, Mass.

Dijksterhuis, Eduard J. (1950) *The Mechanization of the World Picture*, English trans. Oxford 1961

Dinzelbacher, Peter (1981) *Vision und Visionslitteratur im Mittelalter*, Stuttgart

Dodds, Eric R. (1951) *The Greeks and the Irrational*, Berkeley and Los Angeles

Dodds, Eric R. (1965) *The Age of Anxiety*, Cambridge

Douglas, Mary (1970) *Natural Symbols*, London

Douglas, Mary (1980) 'Maurice Halbwachs', rpr. in her *In the Active Voice*, London 1982, 255–71

Dresden, Sem (1975) 'The Profile of the Reception of the Italian Renaissance in France', in *Itinerarium Italicum*, ed. Heiko Oberman and Thomas A. Brady, Leiden, 119–89

Drewal, Margaret Thompson (1989) 'Dancing for Ogun in Yorubaland and in Brazil', in *Africa's Ogun: Old World and New*, ed. Sandra T. Barnes, Bloomington, 199–234

Duby, Georges (1979) *The Three Orders*, English trans. Chicago 1980

Dürer, Albrecht (1956) *Schriftliche Nachlass*, vol. 1, ed. Hans Rupprich, Berlin

Dupront, Alphonse (1966) *L'acculturazione*, Turin

Durand, Gilbert (1948) *Les structures anthropologiques de l'imaginaire*, Paris

Durkheim, Émile (1912) *The Elementary Forms of the Religious Life*, English trans. 1915, rpr. New York 1961

Dutton, Paul (1994) *The Politics of Dreaming in Carolingian Europe*, Lincoln, Nebr.

Edelstein, Leon (1967) *The Idea of Progress in Classical Antiquity*, Baltimore

Edmondson, Munro S. (1955–6) 'Carnival in New Orleans', *Caribbean Quarterly* 4, 233–45

Eggan, Dorothy (1952) 'The Manifest Content of Dreams', *American Anthropologist* 54, 469–85

Eggan, Dorothy (1966) 'Hopi Dreams in Cultural Perspective', in *The Dream and Human Societies*, ed. Gustav E. von Grunebaum and Roger Caillois, Berkeley and Los Angeles, 237–66

Eisenstein, Elizabeth E. (1979) *The Printing Press as an Agent of Change*, Cambridge

Elias, Norbert (1939) *The Civilizing Process*, English trans. Oxford 1994

Elkanah, Yehuda (1981) 'A Programmatic Attempt at an Anthropology of Knowledge', in *Sciences and Cultures*, ed. Everett Mendelsohn and Y. Elkanah, Dordrecht, 1–76

Entwistle, William J. (1939) *European Balladry*, Oxford

Erikson, Erik H. (1968) 'In Search of Gandhi', *Daedalus* 695–729

Escarpit, Robert (1958) 'Histoire de l'histoire de la littérature', in *Histoire des littératures*, ed. Raymond Queneau, vol. 3, Paris, 1749–813

Evangelisti, Claudia (1992) 'Libelli famosi: processi per scritte infamanti nella Bologna di fine '500', *Annali della Fondazione Einaudi* 26, 181–237

Evans-Pritchard, Edward E. (1937) *Witchcraft, Oracles and Magic among the Azande*, Oxford

Evans-Pritchard, Edward E. (1940) *The Nuer*, Oxford

Evans-Pritchard, Edward E. (1956) *Nuer Religion*, Oxford

Evans-Pritchard, Edward E. (1965) *Theories of Primitive Religion*, Oxford

Evelyn, John (1955) *Diary*, ed. E. S. de Beer, 5 vols, Oxford

Febvre, Lucien (1938) 'History and Psychology', trans. in *A New Kind of History*, ed. Peter Burke, London 1973, ch. 1

Fentress, James and Chris Wickham (1992) *Social Memory*, Oxford

Fenzi, E. (1966) 'Una falsa lettera del Cebà e il Dizionario Politico-Filosofico di Andrea Spinola', *Miscellanea di Storia Ligura* 4, 111–65

Ferguson, Wallace K. (1948) *The Renaissance in Historical Thought*, Cambridge, Mass.

Fermor, Sharon (1993) 'Movement and Gender in Sixteenth-Century Italian Painting', in *The Body Imaged*, ed. Kathleen Adler and Marcia Pointon, Cambridge, 129–46

Ferreira, Jerusa Pires (1979) *Cavalaria em cordel*, Rio de Janeiro

Firth, Raymond (1934) 'The Meaning of Dreams', rpr. in his *Tikopia Ritual and Belief*, London 1967, 162–73

Fischer, David H. (1989) *Albion's Seed: Four British Folkways in America*, New York

Fleck, Ludwik (1935) *Genesis and Development of a Scientific Fact*, English trans. Chicago 1979

Foglietta, Uberto (1559) *Della repubblica di Genova*, Rome

Foisil, Madeleine (1970) *La révolte des nu-pieds*, Paris

Fontes, Anna (1987) 'Pouvoir (du) rire. Théorie et pratique des facéties aux 15e et 16e siècles: des facéties humanistes aux trois recueils de L. Domenichi', *Réécritures* 3, Paris, 9–100

Fortes, Meyer (1987) *Religion, Morality and the Person*, Cambridge

Foster, George (1960) *Culture and Conquest: America's Spanish Heritage*, Chicago

Foucault, Michel (1961) *Madness and Civilization*, English trans. New York 1965

Foucault, Michel (1966) *The Order of Things*, English trans. London 1970

Foucault, Michel (1971) *L'ordre du discours*, Paris

Frankl, Paul (1960) *The Gothic: Literary Sources and Interpretations through Eight Centuries*, Princeton

Frank-van Westrienen, Anna (1983) *De Groote Tour*, Amsterdam

Freud, Sigmund (1899) *The Interpretation of Dreams*, English trans. London 1960

Freud, Sigmund (1905) *Jokes and their Relation to the Unconscious*, English trans. 1913, rev. edn New York 1965

Freud, Sigmund (1929) 'Some Dreams of Descartes: Letter to M. Leroy', in *Works*, vol. 21, London 1961, 203–4

Freyre, Gilberto (1933) *The Masters and the Slaves*, English trans. New York 1940

Friedlaender, Walter (1955) *Caravaggio Studies*, Princeton

Friedman, John B. (1981) *The Monstrous Races in Medieval Art and Thought*, Cambridge, Mass.

Friedman, Jonathan (1994) *Cultural Identity and Global Process*, London

Fry, Peter, Sérgio Carrara and Ana Luiza Martins-Costa (1988) 'Negros e brancos no carnaval da Velha República', in *Escravidão e invenção da liberdade*, ed. João José Reis, São Paulo, 232–63

Frye, Northrop (1959) *Anatomy of Criticism*, New York

Frykman, Jonas and Orvar Löfgren (1979) *Culture Builders*, English trans. New Brunswick 1987

Frykman, Jonas and Orvar Löfgren, eds (1996) *Force of Habit: Exploring Everyday Culture*, Lund

Fumaroli, Marc (1980) *L'âge de l'éloquence: rhétorique et res literaria de la Renaissance au seuil de l'époque classique*, Geneva

Furet, François (1984) 'La Révolution dans l'imaginaire politique français', *Le Débat* 30, 173–81

Fussell, Paul (1975) *The Great War and Modern Memory*, Oxford
Gaeta, Franco (1961) 'Alcuni considerazioni sul mito di Venezia', *Bibliothèque d'Humanisme et Renaissance* 23, 58–75
Galbraith, John K. (1958) *The Affluent Society*, 2nd edn Harmondsworth 1962
Galmés de Fuentes, Alvaro (1967) *El libro de las batallas*, Oviedo
Garber, Jörn (1983) 'Von der Menschheitsgeschichte zur Kulturgeschichte', in *Kultur zwischen Bürgertum und Volk*, ed. Jutta Held, Berlin, 76–97
García, Carlos (1617) *La oposición y conjunción de los dos grandes luminares de la tierra, o la antipatia de franceses y españoles*, ed. M. Bareau, Edmonton 1979
Garlan, Yvon and Claude Nières, eds (1975) *Les révoltes bretonnes de 1675*, Paris
Gay, Peter (1959) *The Party of Humanity*, New York
Geertz, Clifford (1973) *The Interpretation of Cultures*, New York
Gellner, Ernest (1974) *Legitimation of Belief*, Cambridge
Gernet, Jacques (1982) *China and the Christian Impact*, English trans. Cambridge 1985
Gilbert, Felix (1990) *History: Politics or Culture?* Princeton
Gilman, Stephen (1960–3) 'Bernal Díaz del Castillo and *Amadís de Gaula*', in *Studia Philologica, Homenaje a Damas Alonso*, 3 vols, Madrid, vol. 2, 99–114
Ginzburg, Carlo (1966) *The Night Battles*, English trans. London 1983
Ginzburg, Carlo (1976) *Cheese and Worms*, English trans. London 1981
Ginzburg, Carlo (1978) 'Titian, Ovid and Sixteenth-Century Codes for Erotic Illustration', rpr. in his *Myths, Emblems, Clues*, London 1990, 77–95
Ginzburg, Carlo (1990) 'Deciphering the Sabbath', in *Early Modern European Witchcraft*, ed. Bengt Ankarloo and Gustav Henningsen, Oxford, 121–38
Gismondi, Michael A. (1985) 'The Gift of Theory', *Social History* 10, 211–30
Glick, Thomas F. (1979) *Islamic and Christian Spain in the Early Middle Ages*, Princeton
Góes, Fred de (1982), *O país do Carnaval Elétrico*, São Paulo
Goethe, Johan Wolfgang von (1951) *Italienische Reise*, ed. H. von Einem, Hamburg
Goldwasser, Maria Júlia (1975), *O Palácio do Samba*, Rio de Janeiro
Gombrich, Ernst H. (1960a) 'Vasari's *Lives* and Cicero's *Brutus*', *Journal of the Warburg and Courtauld Institutes* 23, 309–21
Gombrich, Ernst H. (1960b) *Art and Illusion*, London
Gombrich, Ernst H. (1969) 'In Search of Cultural History', rpr. in his *Ideals and Idols*, London 1979, 25–59
Gombrich, Ernst H. (1984) 'Architecture and Rhetoric in Giulio

Romano's Palazzo del Te', in his *New Light on Old Masters*, Oxford 1986, 161–70

Goody, Jack (1977) *The Domestication of the Savage Mind*, Cambridge

Gorak, Jan (1991) *The Making of the Modern Canon: Genesis and Crisis of a Literary Idea*, London

Gossman, Lionel (1968) *Medievalism and the Ideologies of the Enlightenment*, Baltimore

Gothein, Eberhard (1889) *Die Aufgaben der Kulturgeschichte*, Leipzig

Goubert, Pierre (1982) *The French Peasantry in the Seventeenth Century*, English trans. Cambridge 1986

Goulemot, Jean-Marie (1986) 'Histoire littéraire et mémoire nationale', *History and Anthropology* 2, part 2, 225–35

Goytisolo, Juan (1986) 'Mudejarism Today', English trans. in his *Saracen Chronicles*, London 1992, ch. 1

Graf, Arturo (1916) 'Un buffone di Leone X', in his *Attraverso il '500*, Turin, 365–90

Graham, Loren, Wolf Lepenies and Peter Weingart (1983) *Functions and Uses of Disciplinary Histories*, Dordrecht

Graham, Sandra L. (1988) *House and Street: the Domestic World of Servants and Masters in Nineteenth-Century Rio de Janeiro*, Cambridge

Granet, Marcel (1934) *La pensée chinoise*, Paris

Gray, Richard (1991) *Black Christians and White Missionaries*, New Haven

Grayson, Cecil (1959) *A Renaissance Controversy, Latin or Italian?* Oxford

Greenblatt, Stephen (1988a) *Shakespearean Negotiations: the Circulation of Social Energy in Renaissance England*, Oxford

Greenblatt, Stephen, ed. (1988b) *Representing the English Renaissance*, Berkeley and LA

Grendi, Edoardo (1987) *La repubblica dei genovesi*, Bologna

Grendler, Paul (1969) *Critics of the Italian World*, Madison

Grendler, Paul (1977) *The Roman Inquisition and the Venetian Press, 1540–1605*, Princeton

Grendler, Paul (1988) *Schooling in Renaissance Italy: Literacy and Learning 1300–1600*, Baltimore

Griffith, Richard, Otoya Miyagi and Akira Tago (1958) 'Typical Dreams', *American Anthropologist* 60, 1173–9

Grinten, Evert van der (1952) *Enquiries into the History of Art-Historical Writing*, Delft

Grove's Dictionary of Music and Musicians (1980) ed. S. Sadie, 20 vols, London

Grudin, Robert (1974) 'The Jests in Castiglione's *Il Cortegiano*', *Neophilologus* 58, 199–204

Gruzinski, Serge (1988) *The Conquest of Mexico*, English trans. Cambridge 1993

Guazzo, Stefano (1574) *La civil conversazione*, ed. Amedeo Quondam, 2 vols, Modena 1993

Guénée, Bernard (1976–7) 'Temps de l'histoire et temps de la mémoire au Moyen Age', rpr. in his *Politique et histoire au Moyen Age*, Paris 1981, 253–63

Guerri, Domenico (1931) *La corrente popolare nel Rinascimento*, Florence

Gundersheimer, Werner (1966) *Louis Le Roy*, Geneva

Gurevich, Aaron Y. (1984) 'Two Peasant Visions', rpr. in his *Historical Anthropology of the Middle Ages*, Cambridge 1992, 50–64

Haase, Roland (1933) *Das Problem des Chiliasmus und der Dreissig-Jährigen Krieg*, Leipzig

Habermas, Jürgen (1962) *The Structural Transformation of the Public Sphere*, English trans. Cambridge 1989

Haitsma Mulier, Eco O. G. (1980) *The Myth of Venice*, Assen

Halbwachs, Maurice (1925) *Les cadres sociaux de la mémoire*, Paris

Halbwachs, Maurice (1941) *La topographie légendaire des évangiles en terre sainte: étude de mémoire collective*, Paris

Halbwachs, Maurice (1950) *The Collective Memory*, English trans. New York 1980

Hale, John R. (1954) *England and the Italian Renaissance*, 2nd edn London 1963

Hall, Calvin S. (1951) 'What People Dream About', *Scientific American*, May, 60–9

Hall, Stuart (1980) 'Cultural Studies: Two Paradigms', rpr. in Storey (1996), 31–48

Hallowell, A. Irving (1966) 'The Role of Dreams in Ojibwa Culture', in *The Dream and Human Societies*, ed. Gustav E. von Grunebaum and Roger Caillois, Berkeley and Los Angeles,

Hallpike, Christopher R. (1979) *The Foundations of Primitive Thought*, Oxford

Hanlon, Gregory (1993) *Confession and Community in Seventeenth-Century France*, Philadelphia

Hannerz, Ulf (1987) 'The World in Creolization', *Africa* 57, 546–59

Hannerz, Ulf (1992) *Cultural Complexity*, New York

Harbsmeier, Michael (1982) 'Reisebeschreibungen als mentalitäts-geschichtliche Quellen', in *Reiseberichte als Quellen europäischer Kulturgeschichte*, ed. Antoni Mączak and Hans Jürgen Teuteberg, Wolfenbüttel, 1–32

Harley, George W. (1950) *Masks as Agents of Social Control in North-East Liberia*, Cambridge, Mass.

Harris, Victor (1966) 'Allegory to Analogy in the Interpretation of Scriptures', *Philological Quarterly* 45, 1–23

Haskell, Francis (1993) *History and its Images*, New Haven

Hasluck, Frederick W. (1929) *Christianity and Islam under the Sultans*, 2 vols, Oxford

Hauser, Arnold (1951) *The Social History of Art*, 2 vols, London

226 *Bibliography*

Hay, Denys (1952) *Polydore Vergil*, Oxford
Headley, John M. (1963) *Luther's View of Church History*, New Haven
Hebdige, Dick (1979) *Subculture: the Meaning of Style*, London
Heers, Jacques (1961) *Gênes au xve siècle: activité économique et problèmes sociaux*, Paris
Heesterman, Johannes C. (1985) *The Inner Conflict of Traditions*, Chicago
Heger, E. (1932) *Die Anfänge der neueren Musikgeschichtschreibung um 1770 bei Gerbert, Burney und Hawkins*, rpr. Baden-Baden 1974
Heikamp, Detlev (1969) 'Les merveilles de Pratolino', *L'Oeuil* 171, 16–27
Heinz, Günther (1972) 'Realismus und Rhetorik im Werk des Bartolomeo Passarotti', *Jahrbuch Kunsthistorisches Sammlung in Wien* 68, 153–69
Herskovits, Melville J. (1937) 'African Gods and Catholic Saints in New World Negro Belief', *American Anthropologist* 39, 635–43
Herskovits, M. J. (1938) *Acculturation: a Study of Culture Contact*, New York
Hervey, Mary (1921) *The Life, Correspondence and Collections of Thomas Howard, Earl of Arundel*, Cambridge
Herzfeld, Michael (1985) *The Poetics of Manhood: Contest and Identity in a Cretan Mountain Village*, Princeton
Hill, Errol (1972) *The Trinidad Carnival*, Austin
Hilton, Anne (1985) *The Kingdom of Kongo*, Oxford
Hobsbawm, Eric J. (1959) *Primitive Rebels*, Manchester
Hobsbawm, Eric J. and Terence O. Ranger, eds (1983) *The Invention of Tradition*, Cambridge
Hofmann, Christine (1985) *Das Spanische Hofzeremoniell von 1500–1700*, Frankfurt
Hollander, John (1961) *The Untuning of the Sky*, Princeton
Hollinger, David A. (1980) 'T. S. Kuhn's Theory of Science and its Implications for History', in *Paradigms and Revolutions*, ed. Gary Gutting, Notre Dame, 195–222
Horton, Robin (1967) 'African Traditional Thought and Western Science', *Africa*, 155–86
Horton, Robin (1982) 'Tradition and Modernity Revisited', in *Rationality and Relativism*, ed. Martin Hollis and Steven Lukes, Oxford, 201–60
Howard, Deborah (1975) *Jacopo Sansovino: Architecture and Patronage in Renaissance Venice*, New Haven
Huizinga, Johan (1919) *Autumn of the Middle Ages*, English trans. Chicago 1995
Huizinga, Johan (1929) 'The Task of Cultural History', English trans. in *Men and Ideas*, New York 1960, 17–76
Huizinga, Johan (1938) *Homo Ludens*, English trans. London 1970

Hulme, Peter (1987) *Colonial Encounters*, London
Hulme, Peter (1994) 'Tales of Distinction', in *Implicit Understandings*, ed. Stuart B. Schwartz, Cambridge, 157–97
Hunt, Lynn, ed (1989) *The New Cultural History*, Berkeley
Huntington, Archer M, ed. (1905) *Catalogue of the Library of F. Columbus*, New York
Huppert, George (1970) *The Idea of Perfect History*, Urbana
Hutton, Patrick H. (1993) *History as an Art of Memory*, Hanover and London
Ife, Barry W. (1985) *Reading and Fiction in Golden Age Spain*, Cambridge
Iggers, Georg G. (1982) 'The University of Göttingen 1760–1800 and the Transformation of Historical Scholarship', *Storia della Storiografia* 2, 11–36
Impey, Oliver and Arthur Macgregor, eds (1985) *The Origins of Museums: the Cabinet of Curiosities in Sixteenth- and Seventeenth-Century Europe*, Oxford
Inalcik, Halil (1973) *The Ottoman Empire: the Classical Age, 1300–1600*, London
Irving, Washington (1824) *Tales of a Traveller*, 2 vols, Paris
Jaeger, Werner (1933) *Paideia*, vol. 1, English trans. Oxford 1939
Jameson, Fredric (1972) *The Prison-House of Language*, Princeton
Jardine, Nicholas (1984) *The Birth of History and Philosophy of Science*, Cambridge
Jauss, Hans-Robert (1974) *Toward an Aesthetic of Reception*, English trans. Minneapolis 1982
Javitch, Daniel (1991) *Proclaiming a Classic: the Canonization of the Orlando Furioso*, Princeton
Jorio, Andrea di (1832) *La mimica degli antichi investigata nel gestire napoletano*, rpr. Naples 1964
Josselin, Ralph (1976) *Diary*, ed. Alan D. Macfarlane, London
Joutard, Philippe (1976) *La Sainte-Barthélemy: ou les résonances d'un massacre*, Neuchâtel
Jung, Carl Gustav (1928) 'General Aspects of Dream Psychology', in his *Collected Works*, vol. 8, London 1960, 237–80
Jung, Carl Gustav (1930) 'Dream-Analysis in its Practical Application', in his *Modern Man in Search of a Soul*, London 1933, 1–31
Jung, Carl Gustav (1945) 'On the Nature of Dreams', in his *Collected Works*, vol. 8, London 1960, 281–300
Kagan, Richard L. (1990) *Lucrecia's Dreams: Politics and Prophecy in Sixteenth-Century Spain*, Berkeley
Kammen, Michael (1984) 'Extending the Reach of American Cultural History', rpr. in his *Selvages and Biases*, Ithaca 1987, 118–53
Kantorowicz, Ernst H. (1957) *The King's Two Bodies*, Princeton
Kaplan, Steven L., ed. (1984) *Understanding Popular Culture*, Berlin
Kelley, Donald R. (1970) *Foundations of Modern Historical*

Scholarship: Language, Law and History in the French Renaissance, New York

Kelley, Donald R. and Richard H. Popkin, eds (1991) *The Shapes of Knowledge from the Renaissance to the Enlightenment*, Dordrecht

Kessler, Johan (1540) *Sabbata*, ed. T. Schiess, Leipzig 1911

Kidder, Daniel (1845) *Sketches of Residence and Travels in Brazil*, 2 vols, New York

Kinser, Samuel (1990) *Carnival American Style: Mardi Gras at New Orleans and Mobile*, Chicago

Klaniczay, Gábor (1984) 'Shamanistic Elements in Central European Witchcraft', rpr. in his *The Uses of Supernatural Power*, Cambridge 1990, 151–67

Klingender, Francis (1947) *Art and the Industrial Revolution*, London

Knowlson, James R. (1965) 'The Idea of Gesture as a Universal Language', *Journal of the History of Ideas* 26, 495–508

Knox, Dilwyn (1989) 'On Immobility', in *Begetting Images*, ed. Mary B. Campbell and Mark Rollins, New York, 71–87

Knox, Dilwyn (1990) 'Ideas on Gesture and Universal Languages c.1550–1650', in *New Perspectives on Renaissance Thought*, ed. John Henry and Sarah Hutton, London, 101–36

Knox, Dilwyn (1995) 'Erasmus' *De Civilitate* and the Religious Origins of Civility in Protestant Europe', *Archiv für Reformationsgeschichte* 86, 7–47

Knox, Ronald (1950) *Enthusiasm*, Oxford

Kohl, Benjamin G. and Ronald G. Witt, eds (1978) *The Earthly Republic: Italian Humanists on Government and Society*, Philadelphia

Koselleck, Reinhart (1972) '*Begriffsgeschichte* and Social History', rpr. in his *Futures Past*, 1979, English trans. Cambridge, Mass. 1985, 73–91

Koselleck, Reinhart (1979) 'Terror and Dream', in his *Futures Past*, English trans. Cambridge, Mass. 1985, 213–30

Kris, Ernst (1953) *Psychoanalytic Explorations in Art*, London

Kroeber, Alfred L. and Clyde Kluckhohn (1952) *Culture: a Critical Review of Concepts and Definitions*, rpr. New York 1963

Kuhn, Thomas S. (1962) *The Structure of Scientific Revolutions*, Chicago

Kula, Witold (1962) *Economic Theory of the Feudal System*, English trans. London 1976

Lafaye, Jacques (1974) *Quetzlcóatl and Guadalupe: the Formation of Mexican National Consciousness, 1531–1813*, English trans. Chicago 1976

Lakatos, Imre and A. Musgrave, eds (1970) *Criticism and the Growth of Knowledge*, London

Lakoff, George and Mark Johnson (1980) *Metaphors We Live By*, Chicago

Landes, Ruth (1947) *The City of Women*, rpr. New York 1996

Lanza, Maria (1931) 'Un rifacitore popolare di leggende cavalleresche', *Il Folklore Italiano* 6, 134–45

Larivaille, Paul (1980) *Pietro Aretino fra Rinascimento e Manierismo*, Rome

Larsen, Sidsel S. (1982) 'The Glorious Twelfth: the Politics of Legitimation in Kilbroney', in *Belonging*, ed. Anthony P. Cohen, London, 278–91

Lassels, Richard (1654) 'Description of Italy', in Chaney (1985), 147–231

Lassels, Richard (1670) *A Voyage of Italy*, rpr. London 1698

Laud, William (1847–60) *Works*, 7 vols, Oxford

Lavin, Irving (1983) 'Bernini and the Art of Social Satire', *History of European Ideas* 4, 365–78

Lazard, Sylvie (1993) 'Code de comportement de la jeune femme en Italie au 14e siècle', in *Traités de savoir-vivre italien*, ed. Alain Montandon, Clermont, 7–23

Lazzaro, Claudia (1990) *The Italian Renaissance Garden*, New Haven

Le Braz, Anatole (1922) *La légende de la mort*, 4th edn, Paris

Lefebvre, Georges (1932) *The Great Fear*, English trans. London 1973

Le Goff, Jacques (1971) 'Dreams in the Culture and Collective Psychology of the Medieval West', English trans. in his *Time, Work and Culture in the Middle Ages*, Chicago 1980, 201–4

Le Goff, Jacques (1974) 'Mentalities', English trans. in *Constructing the Past*, ed. Jacques Le Goff and Pierre Nora, Cambridge 1985, 166–80

Le Goff, Jacques (1982) 'Les gestes de St Louis', in *Mélanges Jacques Stiennon*, Paris, 445–59

Le Goff, Jacques (1983) 'Christianity and Dreams', English trans. in his *The Medieval Imagination*, Chicago 1988, 193–231

Le Goff, Jacques (1984) 'The Dreams of Helmbrecht the Elder', in his *The Medieval Imagination*, Chicago 1988, 232–42

Le Goff, Jacques (1985) 'Gestures in Purgatory', English trans. in his *The Medieval Imagination*, Chicago 1988, 86–92

Le Goff, Jacques (1988) *Histoire et mémoire*, Paris

Leiris, Michel (1958) *La possession et ses aspects théatraux chez les Éthiopiens de Gondar*, Paris

Leonard, Irving A. (1933) *Romances of Chivalry in the Spanish Indies*, Berkeley

Leonard, Irving A. (1949) *Books of the Brave*, Cambridge, Mass.

Leopoldi, José Savio (1978) *Escola da Samba, ritual e sociedade*, Rio de Janeiro

Lercari, Giovanni Battista (1579) *Le discordie e guerre civili dei genovesi nell'anno 1575*, Genoa 1857

Le Roy Ladurie, Emmanuel (1979) *Carnival*, English trans. London 1980

Levine, Joseph M. (1977) *Dr Woodward's Shield*, Berkeley

Levine, Robert M. (1992) *Vale of Tears: Revisiting the Canudos Massacre in North-East Brazil, 1893–7*, Berkeley and Los Angeles

Levinson, Leonard L. (1972) *Bartlett's Unfamiliar Quotations*, London

Lévi-Strauss, Claude (1955) *Tristes tropiques*, English trans. London 1973

Lévy-Bruhl, Lucien (1927) *La mentalité primitive*, Paris

Lévy-Bruhl, Lucien (1949) *Notebooks*, English trans. Oxford 1975

Lewis, Bernard (1995) *Cultures in Conflict: Christians, Muslims and Jews in the Age of Discovery*, New York

Lincoln, Jackson S. (1935) *The Dream in Primitive Cultures*, London

Linger, Daniel Touro (1992) *Dangerous Encounters: Meanings of Violence in a Brazilian City*, Stanford

Lipking, Lawrence (1970) *The Ordering of the Arts*, Princeton

Lippe, Rudolf zu (1974) *Naturbeherrschung am Menschen*, Frankfurt

Llosa, Mário Vargas (1969) 'Carta de batalla por *Tirant lo Blanc*', rpr. as introduction to *Tirant lo Blanc*, Madrid 1970, 9–41

Lloyd, Geoffrey (1990) *Demystifying Mentalities*, Cambridge

Lockhart, James (1994) 'Sightings: Initial Nahua Reactions to Spanish Culture', in *Implicit Understandings*, ed. Stuart Schwartz, Cambridge, 218–48

Lopez, Roberto (1952) 'Économie et architecture médiévales', *Annales: Économies, Sociétés, Civilisations* 7, 433–8

Lord, Albert B. (1960) *The Singer of Tales*, Cambridge, Mass.

Lotman, Jurij M. (1984) 'The Poetics of Everyday Behaviour in Eighteenth-Century Russia', in *The Semiotics of Russian Culture*, ed. Ann Shukman, Ann Arbor, 231–56

Lovejoy, Arthur O. (1936) *The Great Chain of Being*, Cambridge, Mass.

Lowenthal, David (1985) *The Past is a Foreign Country*, Cambridge

Lucchi, Piero (1982) 'Leggere scrivere e abbaco', in *Scienze, credenze occulte, livelli di cultura*, ed. Paola Zambelli, Florence, 101–20

Luck, Georg (1958) '*Vir Facetus*: a Renaissance Ideal', *Studies in Philology* 55, 107–21

Luzio, Alessandro and Rodolfo Renier (1891) 'Buffoni, nani e schiavi dei Gonzaga ai tempi d'Isabella d'Este', *Nuova Antologia* 118, 618–50; 119, 112–46

Lyons, Francis S. L. (1979) *Culture and Anarchy in Ireland, 1890–1939*, Oxford

Lyotard, Jean-François (1979) *The Post-Modern Condition*, English trans. Manchester 1984

Macdonagh, Oliver (1983) *States of Mind*, London

Macfarlane, Alan D. (1970) *The Family Life of Ralph Josselin*, Cambridge

MacGaffey, Wyatt (1986) *Religion and Society in Central Africa*, Chicago

MacGaffey, Wyatt (1994) 'Dialogues of the Deaf: Europeans on the

Atlantic Coast of Africa', in *Implicit Understandings*, ed. Stuart B. Schwartz, Cambridge, 249–67

MacKay, Angus (1976) 'The Ballad and the Frontier in Late Medieval Spain', *Bulletin of Hispanic Studies* 52, 15–33

MacKay, Angus (1977) *Spain in the Middle Ages: From Frontier to Empire*, London

MacKenney, Richard (1987) *Tradesman and Traders: the World of the Guilds in Venice and Europe, c.1250–c.1650*, London

McLaughlin, Martin (1988) 'Histories of Literature in the Quattrocento', in *The Languages of Literature in Renaissance Italy*, ed. Peter Hainsworth et al., Oxford, 63–80

Mączak, Antoni (1978) *Travel in Early Modern Europe*, English trans. Cambridge 1995

Mączak, Antoni and Hans Teuteberg, eds (1982) *Reiseberichte als Quellen europäischer Kulturgeschichte*, Wolfenbüttel

Malaguzzi Valeri, Francesco (1913–23) *La corte di Lodovico il Moro*, 4 vols, Milan

Malinowski, Bronislaw (1931) 'Culture', in *Encyclopaedia of the Social Sciences*, vol. 4, rpr. New York 1948, 621–45

Mandelbaum, JonnaLynn K. (1989) *The Missionary as a Cultural Interpreter*, New York

Mankowski, Tadeusz (1959) *Orient w Polskiej Kulturze Artystycznej*, Wroclaw

Mann, Vivian et al., eds (1992) *Convivencia: Jews, Muslims and Christians in Medieval Spain*, New York

Mannheim, Karl (1927) *Conservatism: a Contribution to the Sociology of Knowledge*, English trans. London 1986

Marín, Francisco Rodríguez (1911) *Franciso Pacheco Maestro de Velázquez*, Madrid

Marquand, Allan (1922) *Andrea della Robbia and his Atelier*, 2 vols, Princeton

Mars, Louis (1946) *La crise de possession dans le Vaudou*, Port-au-Prince

Martin, Jean-Clément (1987) *La Vendée et la France*, Paris

Martin, John (1987) 'Popular Culture and the Shaping of Popular Heresy in Renaissance Venice', in *Inquisition and Society in Early Modern Europe*, ed. Stephen Haliczer, London, 115–28

[Martyn, Thomas] (1787) *The Gentleman's Guide in his Tour through Italy*, London

Marwick, Max (1964) 'Witchcraft as a Social Strain-Gauge', *Australian Journal of Science* 26, 263–8

Masini, Eliseo (1621) *Il Sacro Arsenale*, rpr. Rome 1665

Mauss, Marcel (1935) 'The Techniques of the Body', English trans. in *Economy and Society* 2 (1973), 70–88

Maxwell, Gavin (1956) *God Protect Me from My Friends*, London

Mazzotti, Giuseppe (1986) *The World at Play in Boccaccio's 'Decameron'*, Princeton

232   *Bibliography*

Meinhold, Peter (1967) *Geschichte der kirchlichen Historiographie*, Freiburg and Munich

Melisch, Stephan (1659) *Visiones Nocturnae*, English trans. *Twelve Visions*, London 1663

Meyer, Marlyse (1993) *Caminhos do Imaginário no Brasil*, São Paulo

Michalek, Boleslaw (1973) *The Modern Cinema of Poland*, Bloomington

Michéa, René (1939) 'Goethe au pays des *lazaroni*', in *Mélanges Jules Legras*, Paris, 47–62

Miller, Patricia Cox (1994) *Dreams in Late Antiquity*, Princeton

Molmenti, Pompeo (1879) *Storia della Venezia nella vita privata*, 3 vols, new edn Bergamo 1927–9

Momigliano, Arnaldo D. (1963) 'Pagan and Christian Historiography in the Fourth Century', rpr. in his *Essays in Ancient and Modern Historiography*, Oxford 1977, 107–26

Momigliano, Arnaldo D. (1975) *Alien Wisdom: the Limits of Hellenism*, Cambridge

Montaigne, Michel de (1992) *Journal*, ed. François Rigolot, Paris

Montandon, Alain, ed. (1995) *Les espaces de la civilité*, Mont-de-Marsan

Monteiro, Duglas Teixeira (1974) *Os errantes do novo século*, São Paulo

Monter, E. William (1969) *Calvin's Geneva*, New York

Moore, John (1781) *A View of Society and Manners in Italy*, Dublin

Morgan, Edmund S. (1988) *Inventing the People*, New York

Morris, Colin (1975) '*Judicium Dei*', in *Church, Society and Politics*, ed. Derek Baker, Oxford, 95–111

Morris, Desmond (1977) *Manwatching: a Field Guide to Human Behaviour*, London

Morris, Desmond et al. (1979) *Gestures: Their Origins and Distribution*, London

Moryson, Fynes (1617) *An Itinerary*, rpr. Amsterdam 1971

Muchembled, Robert (1990) 'Satanic Myths and Cultural Reality', in *Early Modern European Witchcraft*, ed. Bengt Ankarloo and Gustav Henningsen, Oxford, 139–60

Muir, Edward (1981) *Civic Ritual in Renaissance Venice*, Princeton

Muir, Edward and Guido Ruggiero, eds (1990) *Sex and Gender*, Baltimore

Mulkay, Michael (1988) *On Humour*, Cambridge

Murray, Alexander (1978) *Reason and Society in the Middle Ages*, Oxford

Niedermann, Joseph (1941) *Kultur: Werden und Wandlungen des Begriffs von Cicero bis Herder*, Florence

Nipperdey, Thomas (1981) 'Der Kölner Dom als Nationaldenkmal', rpr. in his *Nachdenken über die deutsche Geschichte*, Munich 1986, 156–71

Nora, Pierre, ed. (1984–92), *Les lieux de mémoire*, 7 vols, Paris

Norton, Frederick J. and Edward Wilson (1969) *Two Spanish Chapbooks*, Cambridge

Obeyesekere, Gananath (1992) *The Apotheosis of Captain Cook*, Princeton

Österberg, Eva (1991) *Mentalities and Other Realities*, Lund

Omari, Mikelle Smith (1994) 'Candomblé', in *Religion in Africa*, ed. Thomas D. Blakeley et al., London, 135–59

Ortalli, Gherardo (1993) 'Il giudice e la taverna', in *Gioco e giustizia nell'Italia di Comune*, ed. Gherardo Ortalli, Treviso and Rome, 49–70

Ortiz, Fernando (1940) *Cuban Counterpoint: Tobacco and Sugar*, English trans. New York 1947

Ortiz, Fernando (1952) 'La transculturación blanca de los tambores de los negros', rpr. in his *Estudios etnosociológicos*, Havana 1991, 176–201

Ortiz, Fernando (1954) 'Los viejos carnavales habaneros', rpr. in his *Estudios etnosociológicos*, Havana 1991, 202–11

Ottenberg, Simon (1959) 'Ibo Receptivity to Change', in *Continuity and Change in African Cultures*, ed. William Bascom and Melville J. Herskovits, Chicago, 130–43

Owen, Stephen (1986) *Remembrances*, Cambridge, Mass.

Ozouf, Mona (1984) 'Le Panthéon', in Nora, vol. 1, 139–66

Pallares-Burke, Maria Lúcia (1996) *Nísia Floresta, O Carapuceiro e Outras Ensaios de Tradução Cultural*, São Paulo

Pallavicino, Giulio (1975) *Inventione di scriver tutte le cose accadute alli tempi suoi (1583–1589)*, ed. Edoardo Grendi, Genoa

Pálsson, Gísli (1993) *Beyond Boundaries: Understanding, Translation and Anthropological Discourse*, Oxford

Panofsky, Erwin (1939) *Studies in Iconology*, New York

Paoli, Ugo E. (1959) *Il latino maccheronico*, Padua

Parker, Richard G. (1991) *Bodies, Pleasures and Passions*, Boston

Paschetti, Bartolommeo (1583) *Le bellezze di Genova*, Genoa

Pearse, Andrew (1955–6) 'Carnival in Nineteenth-Century Trinidad', *Caribbean Quarterly* 4, 175–93

Peloso, Silvano (1984) *Medioevo nel sertão*, Rome

Pereira, Leonardo Affonso de Miranda (1994) *O Carnaval das Letras*, Rio de Janeiro

Phillips, Henry (1980) *The Theatre and its Critics in Seventeenth-Century France*, Oxford

Piccolomini, Alessandro (1539) *La Rafaella*, rpr. Milan 1969

Pike, Kenneth L. (1954) *Language in Relation to a Unified Theory of the Structure of Human Behaviour*, rev. edn The Hague and Paris 1967

Pittock, Joan H. (1973) *The Ascendancy of Taste*, London

Pittock, Murray (1991) *The Invention of Scotland*, London

Plaisance, Michel (1972) 'La structure de la beffa dans le Cene d'A. F.

Grazzini', in Rochon, 45–98

Pocock, John G. A. (1972) *Politics, Language and Time*, London

Pocock, John G. A. (1975) *The Machiavellian Moment*, Princeton

Poleggi, Ennio (1968) *Strada Nuova*, Genoa

Poleggi, Ennio (1969) 'Genova e l'architettura di villa nel secolo xvi', *Bollettino Centro Andrea Palladio* 11, 231–40

Popper, Karl (1934) *The Logic of Scientific Discovery*, English trans. London 1959

Portilla, Miguel León- (1959) *Visión de los vencidos*, Mexico City

Prandi, Stefano (1990) *Il cortegiano ferrarese*, Florence

Pratt, Mary Louise (1992) *Imperial Eyes: Travel Writing and Transculturation*, London

Pred, Alan (1986) *Place, Practice and Structure*, Cambridge

Price, Simon R. F. (1986) 'The Future of Dreams: From Freud to Artemidorus', *Past and Present* 113, 3–37

Prins, Gwyn (1980) *The Hidden Hippopotamus*, Cambridge

Propp, Vladimir (1976) 'Ritual Laughter in Folklore', in his *Theory and History of Folklore*, Manchester 1984

Pye, Michael (1993) *Syncretism v Synthesis*, Cardiff

Queiroz, Maria Isaura Pereira de (1978), 'Évolution du Carnaval Latino-Américain', *Diogène* 104, 53–69

Queiroz, Maria Isaura Pereira de (1992) *Carnaval brasileiro*, São Paulo

Quondam, Amedeo (1982) 'L'accademia', in *Letteratura Italiana*, ed. Alberto Asor Rosa, Turin, vol. 1, 823–98

Rackham, Bernard (1952) *Italian Maiolica*, 2nd edn London 1963

Radding, Charles M. (1978) 'The Evolution of Medieval Mentalities', *American Historical Review* 83, 577–97

Radding, Charles M. (1979) 'Superstition to Science', *American Historical Review* 84, 945–69

Radin, Paul (1936) 'Ojibwa and Ottawa Puberty Dreams', in *Essays in Anthropology Presented to Alfred L. Kroeber*, ed. Robert H. Lowie, Berkeley, 233–64

Rajna, Pio (1872) *Ricerche intorno ai Reali di Francia*, Bologna

Rak, Michele (1971) *La parte istorica: storia della filosofia e libertinismo erudito*, Naples

Ranger, Terence O. (1975) *Dance and Society in Eastern Africa 1890–1970: the Beni Ngoma*, London

Rassem, Mohammed and Justin Stagl, eds (1980) *Statistik und Staatsbeschreibung in der Neuzeit*, Paderborn

Ray, John (1673) *Observations Topographical, Moral and Physiological*, London

Raymond, John (1648) *An Itinerary*, London

Real, Katarina (1967) *O Folclore no Carnaval de Recife*, 2nd edn Recife 1990

Rebora, Piero (1936) 'Milano in Shakespeare e negli scrittori inglesi del suo tempo', in *Civiltà italiana e civiltà inglese*, Florence, 209–27

Reik, Theodor (1920) 'Uber kollektives Vergessen', *International Zeitschrift für Psychanalyse* 6, 202–15

Reusch, Franz H., ed. (1886) *Die 'indices librorum prohibitorum' des sechszehnten Jahrhunderts*, Tübingen

Rey, Abel (1930) *La science orientale avant les grecs*, Paris

Richardson, Brian (1994) *Print Culture in Renaissance Italy*, Cambridge

Ricoeur, Paul (1981) *Hermeneutics and the Human Sciences*, Cambridge, 182–93

Risério, António (1981), *Carnaval Ijexá*, Salvador

Robertson, Clare (1992) *'Il Gran Cardinale': Alessandro Farnese, Patron of the Arts*, New Haven and London

Rochon, André, ed. (1972) *Formes et significations de la beffa*, Paris

Rochon, André, ed. (1975) *Formes et significations de la beffa*, vol. 2, Paris

Rodini, Robert J. (1970) *A. F. Grazzini*, Madison

Rogers, Samuel (1956) *Italian Journal*, ed. John R. Hale, London

Rosa, João Guimarães (1956) *Grande Sertão: Veredas*, São Paulo

Roth, Michael S., ed. (1994a) 'Performing History: Modernist Contextualism in Carl Schorske's Fin-de-Siècle Vienna', *American Historical Review* 99, 729–45

Roth, Michael S., ed. (1994b) *Rediscovering History*, Stanford

Rotunda, Dominic P. (1942) *Motif-Index of the Italian Novella in Prose*, Bloomington

Rousso, Henry (1987) *The Vichy Syndrome*, English trans. Cambridge, Mass. 1991

Rubiès, Joan Pau (1995) 'Instructions for Travellers', *History and Anthropology*, 1–51

Rubin, Patricia L. (1995) *Giorgio Vasari: Art and History*, New Haven

Ruggiero, Guido (1993) *Binding Passions: Tales of Magic, Marriage and Power at the End of the Renaissance*, New York

Sahlins, Marshall (1981) *Historical Metaphors and Mythical Realities*, Ann Arbor

Sahlins, Marshall (1985) *Islands of History*, Chicago

Sahlins, Marshall (1995) *How 'Natives' Think*, Chicago

Said, Edward (1978) *Orientalism*, London

Said, Edward (1993) *Culture and Imperialism*, 2nd edn New York 1994

Sallmann, Jean-Michel, ed. (1992) *Visions indiennes, visions baroques: les métissages de l'inconscient*, Paris

Samuel, Raphael (1994) *Theatres of Memory*, London

San Carlo e il suo tempo (1986), Rome

Sánchez, Alberto (1958) 'Los libros de caballerías en la conquista de América', *Anales Cervantinos* 7, 237–60

Sapegno, Maria Serena (1993) *'Storia della letteratura italiana* di

Girolamo Tiraboschi', in *Letteratura Italiana: Le Opere*, ed. Alberto Asor Rosa, vol. 2, Turin, 1161–95

Sapir, James D. and Jon C. Crocker, eds (1977) *The Social Use of Metaphor*, Philadelphia

Savelli, Rodolfo (1981) *La repubblica oligarchica: legislazione, istituzioni e ceti a Genova nel '500*, Milan

Scaraffia, Lucetta (1993) *Rinnegati: per una storia dell'identità occidentale*, Rome and Bari

Schäfer, Dietrich (1891) *Geschichte und Kulturgeschichte*, Jena

Schama, Simon (1987) *The Embarrassment of Riches*, London

Schmitt, Jean-Claude (1981) 'Gestus/Gesticulatio', in *La lexicographie du latin médiéval*, Paris, 377–90

Schmitt, Jean-Claude (1990) *La raison des gestes dans l'occident médiéval*, Paris

Schneider, Harold K. (1959) 'Pakot Resistance to Change', in *Continuity and Change in African Cultures*, ed. William Bascom and Melville J. Herskovits, Chicago, 144–67

Schorske, Carl E. (1980) *Fin-de-Siècle Vienna: Politics and Culture*, Cambridge

Schudson, Michael (1992) *Watergate: How We Remember, Forget and Reconstruct the Past*, paperback edn New York 1993

Schwartz, Benjamin (1959) 'Some Polarities in Confucian Thought', in *Confucianism in Action*, ed. David S. Nivison and Arthur F. Wright, Stanford, 50–62

Scott, James C. (1976) *The Moral Economy of the Peasant: Rebellion and Subsistence in South East Asia*, New Haven

Screech, Michael M. (1979) *Rabelais*, London

Seeberg, Erich (1923) *Gottfried Arnold*, Meerane

Seidensticker, Edward (1983) *Low City, High City: Tokyo from Edo to the Earthquake, 1867–1923*, Harmondsworth

Seigel, Jerrold E. (1968) *Rhetoric and Philosophy in Renaissance Humanism*, Princeton

Sells, A. Lytton (1964) *The Paradise of Travellers*, London

Sennett, Richard (1977) *The Fall of Public Man*, Cambridge

Sewall, Samuel (1878), *Diary*, Boston

Seznec, Jean (1940) *The Survival of the Pagan Gods*, English trans. New York 1953

Sharp, Cecil (1907) *English Folksong*, London

Sharp, Samuel (1766) *Travels*, London

Shumway, Nicolas (1991) *The Invention of Argentina*, Berkeley

Sieber, Roy (1962) 'Masks as Agents of Social Control', rpr. in *The Many Faces of Primitive Art,* ed. Douglas Fraser, Englewood Cliffs 1966, 257–62

Simson, Olga Rodrigues de Moraes von (1991–2) 'Mulher e Carnaval: mito e realidade', *Revista de História* 125–6, 7–32

Singer, Milton (1968) 'The Concept of Culture', in *International*

Encyclopaedia of the Social Sciences, ed. D. L. Sills, New York, vol. 3, 527–43

Skippon, Philip (1732) 'An Account of a Journey', in *A Collection of Voyages*, ed. A. and J. Churchill, 6 vols, London, vol. 6, 485–694

Slater, Candace (1982) *Stories on a String: the Brazilian Literatura de Cordel*, Berkeley

Smith, Bernard (1960) *European Vision and the South Pacific*, 2nd edn New Haven 1985

Smith, Henry N. (1950) *Virgin Land*, Cambridge, Mass.

Snyders, Georges (1964) *La pédagogie en France aux 17e et 18e siècles*, Paris

Sodré, Nelson Werneck (1966) *Historia da imprensa no Brasil*, São Paulo

Soihet, Raquel (1993) 'Subversão pelo Riso: Reflexões sobre Resistência e Circularidade Cultural no Carnaval Carioca (1890–1945)', Tese de Prof. Titular, UFF, Rio de Janeiro

Sorrentino, Andrea (1935) *La letteratura italiana e il Sant'Ufficio*, Naples

Spence, Jonathan (1990) *The Question of Hu*, London

Spicer, Joaneath (1991) 'The Renaissance Elbow', in Bremmer and Roodenburg, 84–128

Spinola, Andrea (1981) *Scritti scelti*, ed. Carlo Bitossi, Genoa

Stagl, Justin (1980) 'Die Apodemik oder "Reisekunst" als Methodik der Sozialforschung vom Humanismus bis zur Aufklärung', in Rassem and Stagl, 131–202

Stagl, Justin (1990) 'The Methodizing of Travel in the Sixteenth Century: a Tale of Three Cities', *History and Anthropology* 4, 303–38

Starkey, David (1977) 'Representation through Intimacy', in *Symbols and Sentiments*, ed. Ioan M. Lewis, London and New York, ch. 10

Stern, Samuel M., ed. (1953) *Les chansons mozarabes*, Palermo

Stewart, Charles, ed. (1994) *Syncretism/anti-Syncretism*, London

Storey, John, ed. (1996) *What is Cultural Studies?* London

Stoye, John W. (1952) *English Travellers Abroad 1604–67*, rev. edn New Haven 1989

Swedenborg, Emmanuel (1744) *Journal of Dreams*, English trans. Bryn Athyn 1918

Tacchella, Lorenzo (1966) *La riforma tridentina nella diocesi di Tortona*, Genoa

Tafuri, Manfredo (1969) *Jacopo Sansovino e l'architettura del '500 a Venezia*, Padua

Tanturli, Giuliano (1976) 'Le biografie d'artisti prima del Vasari', in *Il Vasari storiografo e artista*, Florence

Taviani, Francesco (1969) *La commedia dell'arte e la società barocca*, Rome

Terrasse, Henri (1932) *L'art hispano-mauresque des origines au 13e siècle*, Paris

Terrasse, Henri (1958) *Islam d'Espagne: une rencontre de l'Orient et de l'Occident*, Paris

Tesauro, Emmanuele (1654) *Il cannocchiale aristotelico*, rpr. Turin 1670

Theweleit, Klaus (1977) *Male Fantasies*, English trans., 2 vols, Cambridge 1987–9

Thomas, Henry (1920) *Spanish and Portuguese Romances of Chivalry*, Cambridge

Thomas, Keith V. (1977) 'The Place of Laughter in Tudor and Stuart England', *Times Literary Supplement*, 21 Jan.

Thompson, Edward P. (1963) *The Making of the English Working Class*, London

Thompson, Edward P. (1971) 'The Moral Economy of the English Crowd', rpr. in Thompson (1991), 185–258

Thompson, Edward P. (1991) *Customs in Common*, 2nd edn Harmondsworth 1993

Thompson, Paul (1978) *The Voice of the Past*, 2nd edn Oxford 1988

Thompson, Stith (1955–8) *Motif-Index of Folk Literature*, 6 vols, Copenhagen

Thornton, John K. (1983) *The Kingdom of the Kongo*, Madison

Tillyard, Eustace M. W. (1943) *The Elizabethan World Picture*, London

Tindall, William Y. (1934) *John Bunyan, Mechanick Preacher*, New York

Tomalin, Margaret (1982) *The Fortunes of the Warrior Maiden in Italian Literature*, Ravenna

Trexler, Richard (1980) *Public Life in Renaissance Florence*, New York

Trompf, Garry W. (1979) *The Idea of Historical Recurrence in Western Thought from Antiquity to the Reformation*, Berkeley

Turler, Hieronymus (1574) *De arte peregrinandi*, rpr. Nuremberg 1591; English trans. *The Traveller*, 1575, rpr. Gainesville 1951

Turner, Graeme (1990) *British Cultural Studies*, 2nd edn London 1996

Turner, Victor (1983), 'Carnaval in Rio', in *The Celebration of Society*, ed. F. E. Manning, Bowling Green, 103–24

Vansina, Jan (1961) *Oral Tradition*, English trans. London 1965; rev. version, *Oral Tradition as History*, Madison 1985

Varese, Claudio, ed. (1955) *Prosatori volgari del Quattrocento*, Milan and Naples

Verger, Pierre (1969) 'Trance and Convention in Nago-Yoruba Spirit Mediumship', in *Spirit Mediumship and Society in Africa*, ed. John Beattie and John Middleton, London, 50–66

Veryard, Ellis (1701) *An Account of a Journey*, London

Vickers, Brian (1984) 'Analogy v Identity', in *Occult and Scientific Mentalities in the Renaissance*, ed. Brian Vickers, Cambridge, 95–163

Vovelle, Michel (1982) *Ideologies and Mentalities*, English trans. Cambridge 1990

Wachtel, Nathan (1971) *The Vision of the Vanquished*, English trans. Hassocks 1977

Wafer, Jim (1991) *The Taste of Blood: Spirit Possession in Brazilian Candomblé*, Philadelphia

Wagner, Roy (1975) *The Invention of Culture*, 2nd edn Chicago 1981

Walzer, Michael (1965) *The Revolution of the Saints*, Cambridge, Mass.

Warburg, Aby (1932) *Gesammelte Schriften*, 2 vols, Leipzig and Berlin

Warner, W. Lloyd (1959) *The Living and the Dead*, New Haven

Watt, Ian and Jack Goody (1962–3) 'The Consequences of Literacy', *Comparative Studies in Society and History* 5, 304–45

Weber, Eugen (1976) *Peasants into Frenchmen*, London

Wellek, René (1941) *The Rise of English Literary History*, Chapel Hill

Welsford, Enid (1935) *The Fool*, London

White, Christopher (1995) *Thomas Howard, Earl of Arundel*, Malibu

White, Hayden V. (1973) *Metahistory*, Baltimore

White, Lynn (1962) *Medieval Technology and Social Change*, Oxford

Whorf, Benjamin L. (1956) *Language, Thought and Reality*, Cambridge, Mass.

Wickham, Chris J. (1985) 'Lawyer's Time: History and Memory in Tenth- and Eleventh-Century Italy', in *Studies in Medieval History Presented to R. H. C. Davis*, ed. Henry Mayr-Harting and Robert I. Moore, London, 53–71

Wiener, Martin J. (1981) *English Culture and the Decline of the Industrial Spirit, 1850–1980*, Cambridge

Williams, Raymond (1958) *Culture and Society*, London

Williams, Raymond (1961) *The Long Revolution*, London

Williams, Raymond (1977) *Marxism and Literature*, Oxford

Williams, Raymond (1981) *Culture*, London

Wilson, Monica Hunter (1951) 'Witch-Beliefs and Social Structure', rpr. in *Witchcraft and Sorcery*, ed. Max Marwick, Harmondsworth 1970, 252–63

Wind, Edgar (1958) *Pagan Mysteries in the Renaissance*, Oxford

Witte, Johannes (1928) *Japan zwischen zwei Kulturen*, Leipzig

Wittkower, Rudolf (1942) 'Marvels of the East: a Study in the History of Monsters', rpr. in *Allegory and the Migration of Symbols*, London 1977, 45–74

Wittkower, Rudolf (1967) 'Francesco Borromini, his Character and Life', rpr. in *Studies in the Italian Baroque*, London 1975, 153–66

Wolf, Eric (1956) 'Aspects of Group Relations in a Complex Society: Mexico', *American Anthropologist* 58, 1065–78

Woodhouse, John, ed. (1982) 'Avvertimenti necessari per i cortegiani', *Studi Secenteschi* 23, 141–61

Wotton, Henry (1907) *Letters and Papers*, ed. Logan P. Smith, Oxford

Yates, Frances (1966) *The Art of Memory*, London

Yinger, John M. (1960) 'Contraculture and Subculture', *American Sociological Review*, 25, 625–35

Young, Robert J. C. (1995) *Colonial Desire: Hybridity in Theory, Culture and Race*, London

Zaluar, Alba (1978) 'O Clóvis ou a Criatividade Popular num Carnaval Massificado', *Cadernos do CERU*, Rio de Janeiro, 50–63

Index